Antonov's Heavy Transports

The An-22, An-124/225 and An-70

Yefim Gordon, Sergey Komissarov and Dmitriy Komissarov

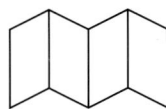

MIDLAND

An imprint of
Ian Allan Publishing

Antonov's Heavy Transports
© 2004 Yefim Gordon, Sergey Komissarov
and Dmitriy Komissarov

ISBN 1 85780 182 2

Published by Midland Publishing
4 Watling Drive, Hinckley, LE10 3EY, England
Tel: 01455 254 490   Fax: 01455 254 495
E-mail: midlandbooks@compuserve.com

Midland Publishing is an imprint of
Ian Allan Publishing Ltd

Worldwide distribution (except North America):
Midland Counties Publications
4 Watling Drive, Hinckley, LE10 3EY, England
Telephone: 01455 254 450   Fax: 01455 233 737
E-mail: midlandbooks@compuserve.com
www.midlandcountiessuperstore.com

North American trade distribution:
Specialty Press Publishers & Wholesalers Inc.
39966 Grand Avenue, North Branch, MN 55056, USA
Tel: 651 277 1400   Fax: 651 277 1203
Toll free telephone: 800 895 4585
www.specialtypress.com

© 2004 Midland Publishing
Design concept and layout by
Polygon Press Ltd. (Moscow,Russia)
Line drawings by Antonov ANTK

This book is illustrated with photographs by
Antonov ANTK, Yefim Gordon, Dmitriy
Komissarov, Sergey Komissarov, Yuriy Kirsanov,
Leonid Yakutin, Vyacheslav Martyniuk, Boris
Vdovenko, Peter Davison, Volga-Dnepr Airlines,
ITAR-TASS, as well as from the archives of
Yefim Gordon, Sergey and Dmitriy Komissarov,
Jane's All the World's Aircraft and the Russian
Aviation Research Trust.

Printed in England by
Ian Allan Printing Ltd
Riverdene Business Park, Molesey Road,
Hersham, Surrey, KT12 4RG

Contents

Front cover: An-22 RA-09343 tucks up its undercarriage on take-off. Too bad that the picture does not convey the very impressive sound emitted by the Antheus.
Rear cover, top: Another view of the stunning Mriya/Buran combination; bottom: Russian Air Force An-22A RA-08832 awaits the next mission.

Title page: Wearing the original registration CCCP-480182 and sporting an instrumented air data boom, the An-225 performs an early test flight with the Buran space shuttle on top. Note the deployed leading-edge slats and the Aero L-39C chase aircraft on the left.

Below: Led by a GAZ-69 jeep, three theatre ballistic missile launchers on a PT-76 amphibious tank chassis have just left the hold of an An-22 at Moscow-Domodedovo during the 9th July 1967 airshow. Note the Airborne Forces badge on the vehicles and the row of smaller An-12 transports in the background.

Introduction

Oleg Konstantinovich Antonov was one of the first aircraft designers to become aware of the necessity of creating dedicated transport aircraft for the carriage of cargoes and materiel. This was demonstrated by the emergence in 1956 of the twin-turboprop An-8 military transport, the first of its kind in the USSR, dubbed *Letayushchiy kit* ('Flying whale') by those who operated it. It was followed by a whole family of 'cargo carriers'. In the 1960s-1980s the four-turboprop An-12 and the smaller twin-turboprop An-26 gained especially wide renown in the world, both on the military scene and on the commercial market; the An-32 (a powered-up, 'hot-and-high' derivative of the An-26) and the twin-turbofan An-72/An-74 short take-off and landing (STOL) military/commercial transports also became well known. However, it was the An-22 *Antey* (Antheus), the An-124 Ruslan and the An-225 Mriya heavy airlifters that became the object of particular pride and joy for the Design Bureau. A rightful place in this family also belongs to the An-70, a new-generation medium transport aircraft; this is a promising new 'air truck' with excellent characteristics, although its development was plagued by various vicissitudes.

The Soviet Air Force had barely coped with the service introduction of the An-12 transport when the first sketches of the *izdeliye* (product) 100, the future An-22, appeared on the drawing boards of the GSOKB-473 (*Gosoodarstvennoye soyooznoye opytno-konstrooktorskoye byuro* – State Union Experimental Design Bureau) led by Oleg K. Antonov. (Note: *Izdeliye* such-and-such was a common term for designating various Soviet/Russian military hardware items so as not to reveal the true service designations. The 'Union' bit in the official designation of the Antonov OKB meant that it had 'all-Union' (national) importance.) Not only the Armed Forces felt a need for a machine capable of airlifting bulky hardware items with dimensions similar to those of a railway carriage. Special requirements were posed by the speedy development of the areas of the High North, Siberia and the Far East where settlements were not infrequently several hundred kilometres apart and the main transport routes were provided by rivers and roads suitable for use only in winter time. There was

an urgent need for a transport system adapted to these harsh conditions.

The story of the aircraft that came subsequently to bear the name of the legendary athlete from Greek mythology began in the late 1950s, when the projects of the An-20 and An-20A transport aircraft were offered. Powered respectively by two and four NK-12 turboprops designed by OKB-276 led by Nikolay Dmitriyevich Kuznetsov, they were intended for carrying cargoes and combat hardware weighing up to several dozen tonnes over distances of up to 5,000 km (3,107 miles).

The An-20A was followed up by a project provisionally designated VT-22. Powered by four NK-12MV engines, the aircraft was intended to carry cargoes weighing up to 50 tonnes (110,250 lb); with a load of 40 tonnes (88,200 lb) it would have a range of 3,500 km (2,175 miles).

Approximately at the same time OKB-156 headed by Andrey Nikolayevich Tupolev, the doyen of Soviet aircraft design, offered a project of the Tu-114VTA heavy transport aircraft (VTA stands for *Voyenno-trahnsportnaya aviahtsiya* – Military Transport Aviation, the Soviet Air Force's airlift branch). Based on the Tu-114 *Rossiya* (Russia) four-turboprop long-haul airliner, it was intended to carry up to 300 troops or up to 40 tonnes of cargo over a distance of 5,000 km; it differed from the commercial version in having a ventral cargo hatch closed by a loading ramp, a suitably reinforced cabin floor, fewer windows, cargo handling devices and a rear cannon barbette for self-defence. A more interesting project designated Be-16 was submitted by the Taganrog-based OKB-49 led by Gheorgiy Mikhaïlovich Beriyev. Both of these aircraft, as well as the An-20A, were to be powered by NK-12MV turboprops, but it was the VT-22 that eventually materialised as the An-22; this project incorporated all the best features that had been included into the design of its predecessors.

In accordance with the concept evolved by the customer, the An-22 was to carry the cargoes to an airfield or an unpaved airstrip that was closest to the destination point; thereupon the cargoes were to be transported to the launch site by the V-12 twin-rotor heavy-lift helicopter which was under development in OKB-329 led by Mikhail Leont'ye-

General Designer Oleg Konstantinovich Antonov (1906-1984), head of GSOKB-473.

vich Mil'. The fuselage of the mighty V-12 was designed to accommodate cargoes of similar dimensions. But the exigencies of the times settled things their own way. The V-12 programme lagged three years behind schedule and eventually was discontinued altogether at the State acceptance trials stage when the missile system which the helicopter was to carry – its main *raison d'être* – was axed. This cancellation also had a negative effect on the An-22 programme; however, there were other tasks demanding the existence of the Antheus and the programme survived.

Creating the An-22 was indisputably a great achievement for the Soviet aircraft industry. This machine was an embodiment of the utmost potential of the 1950s aviation technology; it became a step on the way to new aircraft with still greater load-carrying capability. The novel features incorporated in the An-22 consisted primarily in the methods of manufacturing large one-piece panels and airframe assemblies that had been mastered by the production plant. Of course, the Antheus also made use of the most up-to-date electronic equipment, but it did not exert any influence on the development of heavier machines, including the An-124. Possibly, the only feature inherited by the new cargo

Above: Pyotr V. Balabuyev succeeded Antonov as General Designer of the Antonov OKB.

machine was the landing gear featuring independent multiple main units provided with individual retraction mechanisms.

In the early 1970s the OKB led by Oleg K. Antonov offered to the customer three heavy aircraft projects – the An-122, the An-124 and the An-126. The latter was a six-engined giant with a T-tail. The military opted for the '124', the future Ruslan, which ensured the carriage of nearly the entire list of items of the Soviet military hardware. The future giant was to be based on engines delivering a thrust in excess of 20 tonnes (44,000 lb) and possessing high fuel efficiency; the Zaporozhye-based OKB-478 aero engine design bureau was tasked with developing these engines. A peak of heavy transport aircraft design was reached in the An-225 which incorporated many components of the An-124 airframe and was intended for the transportation of outsize ultra-heavy cargoes not only internally but also atop the fuselage.

The most difficult job that fell to the lot of the staff of the Antonov ANTK during the recent decade was the marketing of the An-70 new-generation transport aircraft which was being developed as a joint venture by numerous Ukrainian and Russian enterprises. At the design stage and the initial flight test stage the machine seemed to have a bright future in store for it. It enterprises attracted interest in the West. However, big politics and persistent teething troubles with the engines became an obstacle on its way to the world market. Nevertheless, the An-70 remains one of the most promising transport aircraft of our time.

In the course of the last ten years the Antonov ANTK has won the reputation of a leader in the transportation of super-heavy, outsize and non-standard cargoes. Charter flights to any point of the globe are performed primarily by the An-124-100 Ruslan. The Antonov Design Bureau's airline operates five An-124-100s, two An-22s, four An-12s and seven more specialised Antonov aircraft.

Acknowledgements

In creating this book the authors have used official materials of the Antonov ANTK, as well as articles published in the Ukrainian magazine *Aviatsiya i Vremya* (Aviation and Time) and several Russian magazines. As usual, the authors would like to thank the Russian Aviation Research Trust and Nigel Eastaway, as well as the editorial group of Soviet Transports (Peter Hillman, Stuart Jessup, Tony Morris and Guus Ottenhof) for the assistance rendered during the writing on this book.

Left: The An-8, illustrated here by CCCP-79166, was the Antonov OKB's first dedicated military transport.

Below: The An-8 evolved into the highly successful An-12. These Soviet Air Force An-12BPs in a rather non-standard colour scheme took part in the 9th July 1967 airshow at Moscow-Domodedovo.

Chapter 1

The Early Studies

An-20 transport and assault aircraft (*izdeliye* Yu) project

On 31st July 1958 the Central Committee of the Communist Party of the Soviet Union and the Soviet Council of Ministers jointly issued directive No.854-404 tasking the GSOKB-473 design bureau led by Chief Designer Oleg K. Antonov with designing a transport and assault aircraft with a lifting capacity of 25 to 40 tonnes (55,125-88,200 lb), intended for the Soviet Army's Airborne Troops. This was followed on 8th August by order No.313 to the same effect issued by the State Committee for Aviation Hardware (GKAT – *Gosoodarstvennyy komitet po aviatsionnoy tekhnike*).

(Note: In 1947-57 GKAT had been known as the Ministry of Aircraft Industry (MAP – *Ministerstvo aviatsionnoy promyshlennosti*); it was 'demoted' to State Committee status because the Soviet leader Nikita S. Khrushchov's favoured missile systems over manned aircraft. In 1965, however, GKAT regained its original name and ministerial status when Khrushchov was deposed.)

According to the general operational requirement (GOR), the aircraft was intended for carrying ground troops and their largest hardware items, such as, for example, the T-54 main battle tank weighing 36 tonnes (79,380 lb) and various military cargoes, as well as for delivering airborne troops with their combat vehicles, engineering and other materiel to landing sites or by paradropping, for carrying of airfield equipment and other cargoes for the Air Force, for transporting wounded personnel on stretchers or seats and for the carriage of fuel or other liquids in easily removable tanks.

Work on the advanced development project (ADP) of an aircraft coded *izdeliye* Yu (the last-but-one letter of the Cyrillic alphabet) and subsequently allocated the service designation An-20 was already initiated before the issuance of the official CofM/CPSU Central Committee directive and the GKAT order; it was completed in June 1958. To meet the requirements based on the aircraft's main mission (delivery of heavy combat and engineering materiel with their crews either to landing sites or by paradropping) the flight-deck and the vehicle crew cabin were pressurised, while the cargo hold (equipped with a large rear loading hatch) housing the materiel to be transported or paradropped was left unpressurised. According to calcula-

tions, the optimum flight altitude was 10,000 m (32,800 ft), and the maximum range reached 5,000 km (3,108 miles).

The aircraft was capable of accommodating a large number of assault troopers (up to 171). Since part of the personnel in this mission type were accommodated in the unpressurised cargo hold, the carriage of troops was effected at lower altitudes of 4,000-6,000 m (13,120-19,680 ft) and implied the use of oxygen masks. According to the views prevalent at that time, the transportation of assault troops at high altitudes under combat conditions could best be effected by special transport aircraft of smaller size or by turboprop- and turbojet-powered airliners with pressurised cabins featuring a reduced pressure differential, with provisions for fighter escort.

The dimensions of the cargo hold made it possible to transport virtually the whole range of the Soviet Army's combat and engineering hardware items for delivery to landing sites. In the event of paradropping the aircraft's design made it possible to drop combat or engineering hardware items and other military cargoes in containers weighing up to 16 tonnes (35,280 lb) through the rear cargo hatch, followed by the paradropping of the vehicle crews or paratroopers.

The powerplant of the An-20 (*izdeliye* Yu) comprised two NK-12M turboprops, each delivering 15,000 ehp at take-off and driving eight-blade reversible-pitch contra-rotating propellers of 6.4 m (21 ft) diameter. These engines designed by Nikolay D. Kuznetsov's OKB-276 had already found use on the Tupolev Tu-95 strategic bomber and its transcontinental/intercontinental airliner derivative, the Tu-114, which would considerably

simplify the mastering and operation of the new military transport by the Soviet Air Force. With one dead engine the aircraft could continue its climb with a rate of about 2 m/sec (394 ft/min).

The structural and aerodynamic layout of the An-20 was similar to that of the An-8 and An-12 transport and assault aircraft designed by the OKB-473 earlier – that is, it had shoulder-mounted wings with the engines mounted in tractor configuration in nacelles adhering directly to the wing underside, a conventional tail unit and a tricycle landing gear with main gear fairings flanking the fuselage. A distinctive feature of the An-20 was a relatively low height of the cargo floor above the airfield surface (the height of the cargo floor sill was 1,460 mm/4 ft 9⅜ in), which permitted straight-in loading from a truck bed. The high-wing layout enabled the ground transport vehicles to move freely under the aircraft's wings (the propeller blade tip clearance was 2.2 m/7 ft 2⅝ in).

At a normal take-off weight of 108.3 tonnes (238,801 lb) the aircraft could attain a maximum speed of 690 km/h (429 mph) at an altitude of 8,000 m (26,240 ft). With the maximum paradroppable cargo of 40 tonnes (88,200 lb) the aircraft had a design range of 2,700 km (1,678 miles); with a cargo of 25 tonnes (55,125 lb) the range was increased to 5,000 km (3,108 miles). The service ceiling was 12,000 m (39,370 ft), the take-off run being 1,000 m (3,280 ft) and the landing run 1,200 m (3,940 ft).

In August 1960 the development work on the An-20 was discontinued at the order of GKAT in connection with a change in the GOR issued by the Air Force.

An 'in-flight' shot of a display model depicting the projected An-20 airlifter.

Structural description of the An-20

Type: Twin-turboprop heavy military transport. The airframe is of all-metal construction.

Fuselage: The fuselage had a rectangular cross-section with rounded-off angles. To make disembarkation and paradropping possible, the rear fuselage was upswept and its flattened undersurface incorporated a large loading hatch 3.8 m (12 ft $5\frac{39}{64}$ in) wide and 10.1 m (33 ft 1⅝ in) long. The hatch was closed by a loading ramp and an aft-hinged rear door; the latter incorporated an additional hatch closed by double doors. For para-dropping the ramp was lowered to horizontal position, forming an extension of the cargo floor, and the rear door opened upwards.

The unpressurised cargo hold measuring 21 m (68 ft 10¾ in) in length (including the loading ramp), 3.6 m (11 ft 9½ in) in width and 3.5 m (11 ft 5¾ in) in height could accommodate 143 paratroopers or, in the event of airfield disembarkation, 170 troops. Provision was made for the paratroopers to leave the aircraft in four flows, two of them through air-drop hatches in the floor at the front of the cargo hold and two through the rear loading hatch. The cargo floor was equipped with tie-down fittings for cargoes and vehicles; tip-up seats for paratroopers were installed along the cargo hold walls. The cargo hold was designed as unpressurised, therefore the transportation of personnel, even with oxygen masks, was permitted at altitudes not exceeding 6,000 m (19,680 ft).

The forward fuselage incorporated two pressurised compartments: the flightdeck for five crew and a cabin for cargo attendants/vehicle crews (27 persons). In the medevac version the cargo hold was fitted with standard army-type stretchers for the transportation of 144 wounded persons.

Wings: Cantilever shoulder-mounted monoplane wings of trapezoidal planform with a torsion-box structure; no sweepback, span 58 m (190 ft 3½ in) and an area of 278.8 m^2 (3,001.27 sq ft). The wings were fitted with two-section double-slotted extension flaps powered by electrically remote-controlled hydraulic actuators.

Tail unit: Conventional cantilever tail surfaces; the vertical and horizontal tail had a trapezoidal planform.

Landing gear: Hydraulically retractable tricycle type; all three units retracted forward. The nose unit was fitted with twin wheels measuring 1,100 x 400 mm (43.3 x 15.75 in); the main units had four-wheel bogies with 1,450 x 520 mm (57 x 20.5 in) wheels which stowed in large fairings flanking the centre fuselage when retracted. The tyre pressure of 5.0

Basic dimensions of the An-20

Length overall (less cannon barrels)	45,25 m (148 ft 5½ in)
Wing span	58.00 m (190 ft 3½ in)
Height on ground	14.65 m (48 ft 0¾ in)
Distance from the aircraft's centreline to the engine's axis	6.20 m (20 ft 4 in)
Ground clearance with the oleo legs compressed	0.96 m (3 ft 1¾ in)
Propeller blade tip clearance	2.20 m (7 ft 2⅝ in)
Height of cargo floor sill above the ground	1.46 m (4 ft 9½ in)
Horizontal tail arm (from CG at 25% MAC to 25% of horizontal tail MAC)	21.75 m (71 ft $4\frac{19}{64}$ in)
Vertical tail arm (from CG at 25% MAC to 25% of vertical tail MAC)	22.0 m (72 ft 2 in)
Fuselage	
Length (less cannon barrels), m (ft)	45.25 m (148 ft 5½ in)
Width (less landing gear fairings), m (ft)	4.80 m (15 ft 9 in)
Width (including landing gear fairings), m (ft)	8.00 m (26 ft 3 in)
Height, m (ft)	4.80 m (15 ft 9 in)
Fuselage maximum cross-section area, m^2 (sq ft)	21.22 m (228.4)
Internal dimensions of the cargo hold	
(except the area under the wing torsion box):	
width	4.50 m (14 ft 9 in)
height forward of the torsion box	3.70 m (12 ft 1⅝ in)
height aft of the torsion box	3.90 m (12 ft 9½ in)
length	18.20 m (58 ft 8½ in)
(in the area under the wing torsion box):	
width	3.6 m (11 ft 9¾ in)
height	3.5 m (11 ft 5¾ in)
Dimensions of the rear cargo hatch):	
width	3.8 m (12 ft $5\frac{39}{64}$ in)
length	10.10 m (33 ft 1⅝ in)
Volume of the pressurised cabin (measured over the external surface), m^3 (cu ft)	106.0 (3,744)
Volume of flightdeck, m^3 (cu ft)	33.5 (1,183.2)
Volume of cabin for cargo attendants, m^3 (cu ft)	72.5 (2,560.7)
Wings and tail unit	
Wing centre section span	16.00 m (52 ft 6 in)
Inner wing section span	10.10 m (33 ft 1⅝ in)
Outer wing section span	10.90 m (35 ft 9 in)
Wing centre section chord and inner wing section root chord	6.40 m (20 ft $11\frac{31}{32}$ in)
Wingtip chord	2.00 m (6 ft 6¾ in)
Wing area (including the part over the fuselage), m^2 (sq ft)	278.80 (3,001.3)
Wing aspect ratio	12.05
Outer wing panel taper	3.2
Mean aerodynamic chord (MAC)	5.25 m (17 ft $2\frac{11}{16}$ in)
Position of MAC relative to the wing centre section chord on the aircraft's centreline:	
along the wing span	12.03 m (39 ft 5⅝ in)
along the aircraft's length	0.575 m (1 ft $10\frac{11}{16}$ in)
Outer wing panel sweepback at quarter-chord	3°
Wing airfoil and thickness/chord ratio:	
wing centre section/inner wings	TsAGI S-5 – 17.7%
at joint between inner/outer wings	TsAGI S-3 – 16.0%
at wingtips	TsAGI S-3 – 14%
Ailerons:	
Length, m (ft)	10.6 (34 ft 9⅜in)
Chord (percentage of wing chord)	33.0
Aileron total area, m^2 (sq ft)	21.70 (233.6)
Same, as percentage of wing area	7.8
Aileron aerodynamic balance, %	29.0
Flaps:	
Wing centre section flap length	5.30 (17 ft $4\frac{11}{16}$in)
Wing outer panel flap length	10.10 (33 ft 1⅝ in)
Chord as percentage of wing chord	35.0
Total flap area, m^2 (sq ft)	61.15 (658.3)
Same as percentage of wing area	21.9

Horizontal tail:	
Span, m (ft)	17.50 (57 ft 5 in)
Chord at aircraft's centreline	5.75 (18 ft 10⅝ in)
Chord at tailplane tips	2.30 (7 ft 6½ in)
Area (incl. part overlapping with fuselage), m² (sq ft)	70.50 (759)
Same as percentage of wing area	25.3
Aspect ratio	4.35
Taper	2.5
Sweepback at quarterchord	10°30'
Elevator chord as percentage of tailplane chord	35.0
Elevator area, m² (sq ft)	21.60 (232.5)
Same as percentage of tailplane area	30.60

Weights of the An-20

Weight objects	Weight, kg (lb)
Normal take-off weight (at maximum range of 5,000 km/3,100 miles)	108,300 (238,500)
Empty weight	57,145 (126,000)
Load	51,150 (112,785)
Crew, five persons with parachutes	450 (920)
Fuel * (tanks fully filled)	24,100 (53,140)
Oil	360 (790)
Ammunition load	463 (1,021)
Oxygen	128 (282)
Food rations	30.0 (66)
Toilet chemicals	27.0 (60)
Water	16.0 (35)
Flares	380.0 (838)
Additional load	200.0 (441)
Assault materiel or troops to be delivered †	25,000 (55,125)

* Fuel weight includes 5% fuel reserves
† Weight of assault materiel includes the weight of struts, belts and fittings for the installation of stretchers in the medevac version – 550 kg (1,210 lb)

Basic specifications of the An-20

	Operational requirement	Design characteristics
Crew, persons	6	5
Max. speed at 8,000m (26,250 ft), km/h (mph)	650-700 (404-435)	690 (429)
Transportable assault load, tonnes (lb):		
normal	25.0 (55,125)	25.0 (55,125)
maximum	40.0 (88,200)	40.0 (88,200)
Take-off run at normal take-off weight, m (ft) †	800-1,000 (2,624-3,280)	890 (2,920)
Landing run, m (ft)	1,000-1,200 (3,280-3,936)	950 (3,116)
Practical range at an altitude of 8,000-10,000 m (26,250-32,810 ft) with 1-hour fuel reserves (fuel specific gravity 0.755), km (miles):		
with a normal assault load of 25.0 tonnes	5,000 (3,108)	5,000 (3,108) *
with a maximum assault load of 40.0 tonnes	3,000 (1,865)	2,700 (1,678)
Number of assault troopers, armed and equipped, carried for airfield disembarkation	200	171
Number of stretcher cases carried	160	144 (96 stretchers, 48 seated)

* 5% fuel reserves on landing
† Normal take-off weight of 108.3 tonnes (238,800 lb)

kg/cm² (71 psi) enabled the aircraft to operate from grass strips and perform landing disembarkation of troops in field conditions.

Powerplant: Two Kuznetsov NK-12M turbo-props with a 15,000-ehp take-off rating and a 8,080-ehp cruise rating driving eight-blade contra-rotating reversible-pitch propellers of 6.4 m (21 ft) diameter. A detailed description of the engine is found in Chapter 2.

Armament: Defensive armament consisted of a DB-35-AO-9 powered turret at the aft extremity of the fuselage mounting two 23-mm (.90 calibre) AO-9 cannons which were aimed automatically by a gun-laying radar. In the event of a radar failure they were remote-controlled by the flight engineer from the flightdeck.

An-20A heavy transport and assault aircraft (project)

The An-20 design served as a basis for the development of its heavier version, the An-20A. Despite the similar designation, the An-20A was a very different aircraft; it was a scaled-up An-20 powered by four 15,000-ehp NK-12MVs instead of two, driving eight-blade reversible-pitch contra-rotating propellers. The An-20A was intended for carrying heavy and bulky military and civil cargoes with a total weight of up to 70-90 tonnes (154,350-198,450 lb) over long distances and for delivering assault troops and materiel to landing sites or by paradropping.

The aircraft could swallow virtually the whole range of transportable combat and engineering hardware used by the Soviet Army in the late 1950s: big strategic and tactical missiles, their launchers, heavy tanks and the like. The aircraft could also find wide use in the national economy of the USSR and other Socialist countries for the purpose of transporting a wide range of technical equipment and bulk loads to construction sites in far-off areas and for carrying out other kinds of work which required a speedy airlifting of heavy cargoes over big distances, as well as for catering for the needs of scientific expeditions and rescue services. The An-20A could prove eminently suitable for commercial transportation of bulk loads; calculations showed that cargo transportation costs per tonne-kilometre would be lower as compared to any other Soviet aircraft, thanks to the high payload and high cruising speed.

Depending on the weight of the cargoes to be transported, the design range of the An-20 varied from 1,000 to 10,500 km (6,526 miles) at an altitude of 10,000 m (32,800 ft) and a cruising speed of 590-630 km/h (367-392 mph).

The work on this aircraft did not proceed beyond the ADP stage. Experience gained in the course of projecting the An-20 and An-20A was used in the work on subsequent heavy transport aircraft designed by GSOKB-473.

Above: Another 'in-flight' view of the An-20 model. The main landing gear design was similar to that of the An-8, the bogies somersaulting as they retracted, except that the main units retracted forward, not aft.

These views illustrate well the An-20's distinctive nose profile reminiscent of the Douglas C-133 Cargomaster, the double-deck crew section and the anhedral and sweepback on the detachable outer wings only. Note the forward location of the oil coolers and the remote-controlled tail barbette with gun-laying radar.

Chapter 2

Antonov's First Giant

VT-22 heavy assault transport (project)

In the course of the work conducted by GSOKB-473 on the An-20 heavy twin-engined assault transport aircraft and its super-heavy four-engined version, the An-20A, the military changed their requirements, reducing the upper limit of the maximum load from 70-90 tonnes (154,350-196,450 lb) to 50 tonnes (110,250 lb). Therefore, pursuant to instructions issued by GKAT, the design team led by Oleg K. Antonov commenced a new round of calculations with a view to adapting the aircraft to the required load. In August 1960 the OKB completed a technical proposal on the new version of a military transport aircraft which was allocated the provisional designation VT-22 (*voyenno-trahnsportnyy* [*samolyot*] – military airlifter). The aircraft was intended for carrying cargoes weighing up to 50 tonnes (110,250 lb) over distances of 3,500-4,000 km (2,175-2,486 miles) and for paradropping cargoes weighing up to 15 tonnes (33,075 lb). Like the An-20A, the VT-22 was powered by four NK-12MV turboprops with a maximum rating of 15,000 ehp driving eight-bladed contraprops. The landing gear comprised a twin-wheel nose unit and four main units with four-wheel bogies; two of the main gear units retracted into the inboard engine nacelles, the other two into fairings flanking the fuselage. The 'inverted gull' wings had a crank near the inboard engines. Provision was made for fitting the wings with a boundary layer control system. The dimensions of the cargo hold (30.0 x 4.4 x 4.4 m/98 ft 5⅛ in x 14 ft 5¼ in x 14 ft 5¼ in) enabled this aircraft, as distinct from the previous project, to tackle the task of transporting virtually the whole range of Soviet combat and engineering materiel types.

At an all-up weight of 170 tonnes (374,850 lb) the design cruising speed was 650 km/h (404 mph), and the practical range with an assault (paradrop) load of 50 tonnes (110,250 lb) was 3,500 km (2,175 miles).

The project of the VT-22 served as the basis for the production An-22 heavy assault transport aircraft.

An-22 Antheus heavy assault transport prototype (*izdeliye* 100)

In the early 1960s the Soviet Ministry of Defence tasked the aircraft industry with creating an integrated system intended for airlifting intercontinental ballistic missiles (ICBMs) which were the backbone of the Soviet Union's offensive nuclear potential. According to the concept, the *special cargoes* (this quaint term denoted the missile, the associated launch equipment and the like) were to be airlifted to the airfield lying nearest to the launch site and then carried by helicopter directly to the launch silo. Since the basic features of the VT-22 largely met the task thus posed, GSOKB-473 led by Oleg K. Antonov was entrusted with the development of such an aircraft. At the same time the army wished to obtain a fully-fledged strategic military transport aircraft capable of carrying not only missiles but also all items of combat and engineering materiel that could be transported by rail. The national economy was also in need of an aircraft for delivering bulky cargoes – in particular, to the development areas of Siberia, the High North and the Far East where they could not be delivered by surface transport without dismantling.

The work on the new aircraft was sanctioned by joint directive No.1117-465 issued by the Central Committee of the Communist Party and the Council of Ministers on 13th October 1960, followed up by a GKAT order dated 9th November 1960. The work on the new aircraft, which received the in-house designation *izdeliye* 100, was directed by Deputy Chief Designer A. Ya. Belolipetskiy; V. I. Kabayev was appointed project designer, while V. S. Rosanov became project engineer on behalf of GKAT.

Despite its considerable experience in developing military transport aircraft, design work on a machine of such huge dimensions featuring such a big payload confronted GSOKB-473 with numerous new problems associated with the layout, aerodynamics, structural strength, production methods and the like. For example, when selecting the dimensions of the cargo hold, the OKB together with TsNII-30 (the main research institute involved in the project on behalf of the customer) conducted a thorough analysis of all the outsize military and civil hardware items weighing up to 50 tonnes (110,250 lb) that were in existence in the country, taking into account the average distances and frequency of transportation of every cargo item. This painstaking work resulted in determining the optimum dimensions of the cargo hold to suit the envisaged transportation tasks.

In its technical requirements for the new aircraft the customer specified an increase in the size of a single (unit) cargo suitable for paradropping to 20 tonnes (44,100 lb). It proved fairly difficult to tackle this task because the movement of such a heavy item along an unusually long cargo hold (nearly 30 m/100 ft, including the cargo ramp) involved a considerable change of the CG position, which could not be easily counteracted by control inputs. An attempt was made to solve the task by eliminating the need for moving the cargoes; the air-dropping of the cargoes was to be effected through large hatches in the cargo hold floor. However, this option had to be given up because it entailed an inevitable complication of the structure and an increase in its weight. A large volume of research work, including experiments with air-dropping of simulated heavy-weight cargoes from the An-8 and An-12, eventually corroborated that it was possible in principle to utilise the traditional method of paradropping on the '*izdeliye* 100' aircraft. To ensure free passage of cargoes through the rear hatch at the moment of paradropping, the rear fuselage was made upswept. Later, when the machine was already under construction, it became clear that the rearmost part of the fuselage ought to be angled downward slightly to reduce drag. Thus, the '100' acquired its characteristic 'beaver tail'.

The designers rejected the conventional tail unit used hitherto on Antonov's transport machines; they surmised that the fuselage weakened by a huge rear cargo hatch aperture would be unable to sustain the considerable torsion forces arising during rudder deflection, side-slipping or a sudden gust of side wind. It was important to reduce these loads also for the purpose of reducing the deformations of the cargo hatch area, because the cargo hatch was to be tightly sealed: for the transportation of troops the fuselage had to be pressurised to a differential of 0.25 kg/cm² (3.57 psi). It was decided to make use of twin fins and rudders, but this decision posed an unexpected problem: mounting the vertical tails at the tips of horizontal tail brought about a drastic reduction of its flutter onset speed. For a long time the

Above: A large-scale model of the An-22 in the definitive project configuration in TsAGI's T-101 wind tunnel. The model features contra-rotating propellers and a functioning landing gear (the closed mainwheel well doors are discernible in this view).

The model accurately replicated the functioning rear cargo hatch and the entry doors which doubled as slipstream deflectors for paradropping. Note the slipstream shields on the sides of the cargo ramp protecting the troopers coming out that way.

Three more views of the same wind tunnel model; the people in the upper and middle photos lend scale, indicating the sheer size of the thing. Note the movable control surfaces.

Above: The first prototype An-22, CCCP-46191 (c/n 01-01), seen during taxying trials. All An-22s wore this colour scheme when they left the factory – that is, except for the Antonov OKB badge on the nose which was applied only to the prototypes.

issue of the tail unit's layout remained unresolved. 'Once I woke up at night – Antonov recalled – and, out of habit, began thinking about the things that weighed on my mind and were the source of the greatest concern. If the vertical tail surfaces mounted on the horizontal tail become a source of flutter due to their mass, they should be located in such a way that their mass becomes a positive factor instead of a negative one. This means that the

vertical tails need to be moved forward and placed ahead of the tailplane's rigidity axis… As simple as that!' That was the birth of the twin fin-and-rudder layout characteristic for the '100' in which the vertical tails are moved forward relative to the stabiliser and are mounted at 70% of its span.

For the first time in the Antonov OKB's practice, irreversible hydraulic actuators were used in all three channels of the manual con-

trol system. To simplify the design and cut weight, cables were used for linkages to the slide valves of the actuators. In an emergency the crew could switch over to servo-tab actuated manual control. After thorough development conducted on an An-12 flying testbed the servo-tab actuated control system was perfected to such a degree that an actuator failure did not produce any change in the handling of the aircraft.

Another view of the first prototype with the flaps deployed. The original An-12 style glazed nose and the position of the radome ahead of the starboard main gear unit are clearly visible.

A requirement stipulating the ability of such a heavy aircraft to operate from different types of airfields, including unpaved airfields with a surface strength as low as 6 kg/cm² (88.35 lb/sq in), dictated the use of a multi-wheel undercarriage with fat low-pressure tyres featuring relatively high sides. After studying various options, the designers adopted a layout with main gear units consisting of three twin-wheel struts mounted in tandem on each side of the fuselage; the struts retracted upwards. Despite certain drawbacks (an inevitable increase in structural weight and the like), this arrangement offered considerable advantages. In particular, this type of landing gear ensures smooth negotiation of uneven places on runways and taxiways, and it can be stowed more easily in the retracted position. The use of levered suspension with shock absorbers located outside the struts made it possible to obtain a long stroke of the shock absorbers while keeping the struts short; this, in its turn, facilitated lowering the floor of the cargo hold to a minimum height over the surface of the airfield. Provision was made on the *izdeliye* 100 for retracting and extending the main landing gear struts not only all at once but also in succession, which afforded considerably enhanced safety in operation (subsequently this was fully borne out when, after an abnormal (incomplete) extension of the main landing gear, production An-22s made safe landings on four struts instead of six). Provision was made for adjusting the pressure in the mainwheel tyres between 2.5 and 5 kg/cm² (35.56 and 71.13 psi) depending on the airfield surface and weather conditions, weight and CG position of the aircraft, but operational experience did not confirm the need for such a system, and it was subsequently deleted.

The new military transport was to be powered by four NK-12MV turboprops designed by Nikolay D. Kuznetsov's OKB-276 which were manufactured in series by the Kuibyshev engine plant No.24 and powered the Tupolev Tu-95 strategic bomber. The engines were located on the '100' aircraft in such a way that some 4% of the wing surface was affected by the powerful propeller wash which increased the wing lift by nearly 30%. To obtain the necessary take-off performance, the maximum power output of the NK-12MV engines was quite sufficient, but the AV-60 eight-bladed contra-rotating propellers of 5.6 m (18 ft 4½ in) diameter used on the Tu-95s were optimised for cruise flight and had a take-off thrust of only 8,800 kgp (19,404 lbst). The '100' aircraft required a new propeller with a take-off thrust of no less than 13,000 kgp (28,665 lbst). However, the technical proposal for the VT-22 and, consequently, the Government directive on the development of

Top and above: CCCP-46191 seen during manufacturer's flight tests. The bottom portions of the fins have been repainted white, 'Antey' (Antheus) nose titles have been applied and the An badge has been revised.

Close-up of the first prototype's Nos 1 and 2 engines, showing the downward-angled jetpipes and the port side exhaust ports of the engines' jet fuel starters closed by circular covers.

Above: An air-to-air shot of the first prototype An-22 during trials.

the new military transport aircraft did not envisage a modernisation of the powerplant. Therefore it cost Antonov much nerve-racking to persuade GKAT that this work was necessary; the ministry was afraid that series production of the engines and propellers would be disrupted. Support rendered by the military, the Central Aero- & Hydrodynamics Institute (TsAGI – *Tsentrahl'nyy aero- i ghidrodinamicheskiy institoot*), the Central Aero Engine Institute (TsIAM – *Tsentrahl'nyy institoot aviatsionnovo motorostroyeniya*) and OKB-276 helped overcome the reluctance of officials. The Stoopino-based OKB-120 design bureau (later known as SKBM – **Stoo**pinskoye konstrooktorskoye byuro mashinostroyeniya, Stoopino Machinery Design Bureau), after conducting a large volume of calculations and experimental research together with TsAGI, developed the AV-90 eight-bladed contra-rotating propeller

An-22 CCCP-46191 sits parked at Moscow-Sheremet'yevo on the taxiway leading to runway 25L. The north apron and the departure building of what is now Sheremet'yevo-1 are visible beyond, with the characteristic 'mushroom' satellite (a late addition) nearing completion; the old control tower is on the right.

measuring 6.2 m (20 ft 4 in) in diameter, and Kuznetsov's design bureau adapted the engine to this propeller. The modified engine received the designation NK-12MA, the A meaning 'adapted for the Antonov aircraft'. The result was a unique powerplant delivering a maximum thrust of 14,600 kgp (32,190 lbst) and possessing a specific fuel consumption of 224 g (0.49 lb)/kW·h; this powerplant remained unrivalled for more than 30 years.

The design of the *izdeliye* 100 incorporated for the first time a wide use of large-size one-piece parts: stamped panels measuring 15 m (49 ft 2½ in) in length and large-size stamped parts measuring up to 5 m (16 ft 4⅞ in) in length and weighing up to 1 tonne (2,205 lb), which made it possible to reduce the structure weight by 5 tonnes (11,025 lb) and the consumption of metal by more than 17 tonnes (37,485 lb). Thereby the number of parts was reduced by 550, and the number of holders and fasteners by 114,000. Several of the biggest stampings ever used in aircraft construction were joined by bolts to form this structure. These parts were stamped at the Kuibyshev Metallurgic Plant by a hydraulic press, the most powerful in the world (it produced a pressure of 75,000 tonnes/165,375,000 lb), from the new V93 high-strength aluminium alloy developed by the All-Union Institute for Aircraft Materials (VIAM – *Vsesoyooznyy institoot aviatsionnykh materiahlov*) together with the Verkhnyaya Salda Metal Foundry. Subsequently operational experience revealed an important drawback of the V93: this alloy proved to be

Above: One Ukrainian transporter carries another. To give a demonstration of the An-22's ability to swallow large vehicles, a LAZ-695B bus is backed into the hold of CCCP-46191. Only two of the three vehicle loading ramps are attached to the cargo ramp's trailing edge in this case.

vulnerable to corrosion and tended to produce cracks under high stresses, which affected the aircraft's service life.

The mock-up review commission for the *izdeliye* 100 convened in August 1961; it was chaired by Air Marshal Nikolay S. Skripko, Commander-in-Chief of the Military Transport Aviation. The commission had an opportunity to get acquainted with the transport capabilities of the projected aircraft: 112 different items of military hardware were loaded in turn

into the mock-up. This produced a tremendous impression on the commission members, including Skripko, who, after having inspected the mock-up crammed with hardware, asked in disbelief: 'Will the aircraft really be able to take-off with this load?'

The *izdeliye* 100 was being created at a high tempo. Detail design was initiated in December 1961, and on 20 April 1963 the fuselage of the first prototype (c/n 01-01 – ie, Batch 1, first aircraft in the batch), was taken

The An-22 made its international debut at the 1965 Paris Air Show. The first prototype is seen here at Le Bourget in company with other Soviet exhibits: An-12B CCCP-11359, An-24B CCCP-46791, the second prototype IL-62 (CCCP-06176), Tu-124V CCCP-45072... and a LAZ-695B. A curious aspect of the Paris shows is that the aircraft were lumped together in this fashion.

Above: An-22 CCCP-46191 arrives in style at Le Bourget on 15th June 1965, taxying in past the Bréguet 341 experimental short take-off and landing tactical transport.

Above: The Antheus dwarfed the other exhibits and drew huge crowds of spectators at the show.

The An-22 is a fairly elegant aircraft for a heavy transport, especially of this size – a fact that was admitted by the Western observers who had expected to see an uncouth monster of an aircraft.

out of the jig. Assembly of the static test airframe (c/n 01-02) was completed in January of the following year. Both of them were built in Kiev at the prototype construction facility of GSOKB-473 in broad co-operation with other aircraft industry enterprises. Structural members of the wings, fuselage and landing gear came from the Tashkent aircraft plant No.84. The huge wheels of the *izdeliye* 100 aircraft were manufactured at the Rubin (Ruby, pronounced *roobin*) plant in the town of Balashikha, Moscow region, and at the Yaroslavl' Tyre Factory. A special chamber was constructed at the Bol'shevik plant in Kiev for vulcanising the tyres of these wheels. Things did not always run smoothly. The process of simultaneous design work and prototype construction necessitated in some cases a revision of the work already done. For example, a set of manufactured panels of the wing middle section had to be rejected after tests conducted in TsAGI's strength laboratory. Nevertheless, the first flying prototype was completed in the summer of 1964.

On 18th August the first prototype carrying the registration CCCP-46191 (a bit unusual, it should be noted, since the 46xxx registration block was reserved for the An-24 regional airliner) was officially turned over for flight testing; the festive ceremony coincided with the Aviation Day celebrations which take place on the third Sunday of August. The machine was rolled out from the assembly shop without the detachable outer wing panels because the wing span exceeded the width of the gates by nearly 20 m (65 ft 7⁷⁄₁₆ in), and wooden blocks had to be placed under the nosewheel leg in order to lower the tail because the vertical tails, too, were too high to pass through the gates. From that moment onwards the new military transport aircraft became officially known as the An-22 and received the popular name Antey (Antheus; in Greek mythology, the giant son of Gaea, the earth goddess). As the AV-90 propellers had not yet been tested thoroughly enough, the first prototype was initially fitted with NK-12MV engines driving AV-60 propellers.

For several days the machine remained parked on a section of the factory apron near the assembly workshop fenced off by plywood sheets. Here the outer wing panels were installed, the aircraft systems were checked and adjusted and the powerplant underwent trial runs. The very first start-up of an engine created such a powerful blast that Deputy Chief Designer A. Ya. Belolipetskiy who happened to be passing by was swept off his feet, and a sentry-box with a guard was turned over and thrown aside.

Meanwhile, the static test airframe was placed in the OKB's laboratory and used for structural testing of the main units and assemblies which lasted until December 1966.

At the beginning of 1964 a special team was formed for the purpose of preparing the An-22's first flight; it was relieved of any other duties. The team comprised nearly 100 persons selected from the most experienced engineering staff and flight personnel. Pilots were selected by a commission presided by A. N. Gratsianskiy, Hero of the Soviet Union, Deputy Chief Designer for flight testing. Mark L. Gallai, a well-known test pilot, took part in its work on behalf of the Flight Research Institute named after Mikhail M. Gromov (LII – **Lyotno-issled**ovatel'skiy insti**toot**). Four candidates were selected for the first flight. These were Yuriy V. Koorlin, I. Ye. Davydov, V. I. Terskiy and D. F. Mitronin. They were sent to LII where they made several flights in a Tu-95 under the guidance of Ivan M. Sukhomlin, chief test pilot of OKB-156 led by Andrey Nikolayevich Tupolev. After this, Koorlin was appointed captain of the first crew of the *izdeliye* 100, with Terskiy as co-pilot; by that time they had logged 7,500 and 2,500 hours respectively.

The first taxi runs and high-speed runs of the An-22 took place as early as August, but on the whole the ground tests proceeded at a slow pace. The aircraft was rolled back into the workshop several times for modifications: stainless steel was substituted for titanium in the structures of the pressurisation system, hydraulic system units were modified and so on. Many problems stemmed from the multistrut landing gear. By the way, at a later stage, too, most of the troubles experienced during the testing of the An-22 were associated with the landing gear. Not before 9th February 1965 was a mission document for the first flight signed, and on 11th February the testing procedures council fixed the date of the first flight as 20th February; however, due to Koorlin's illness the flight had to be postponed for yet another week.

The airfield of aircraft plant No.473 at Kiev-Svyatoshino used by the Antonov OKB was located within the city limits (in fact, it is now in the middle of a heavily built-up area) and had a fairly short runway; according to documents, it had a length of 1,800 m (5,904 ft), while Koorlin who personally made the measurements claimed that it was 1,750 m (5,740 ft) long. Hence to ensure safety in the event of an aborted take-off, an area adjoining the end of the runway was covered with sand. However, on 27th February the sand froze and the stopway turned into a potential source of danger (ironically, the Russian term for 'stopway' – *polosa bezopahsnosti* – translates literally as 'safety strip'). Nevertheless, a decision was taken not to postpone the flight any more. This decision was due not least to the crew's confidence in the success of the mission. On its maiden flight the An-22 was piloted by a crew comprising captain Yuriy V.

Koorlin, co-pilot V. I. Terskiy, navigator P. V. Koshkin, flight engineer V. M. Vorotnikov, radio operator N. F. Drobyshev, flight electrics engineer M. P. Rachenko and project engineer for flight testing V. N. Shatalov. With a take-off weight of 165 tonnes (363,825 lb), the aircraft easily lifted off the runway after a run of 1,200 m (3,936 ft). The landing was scheduled to take place at the OKB's flight test facility at Kiev-Gostomel'; however, this airfield, which had no paved runway in those days and had become soggy after a recent thaw, froze on that day, resulting in an uneven surface, and a decision was taken to perform the landing at Uzin AB (Kiev Region). The first flight lasted 1 hour 10 minutes and, according to the crew reports, went normally. The second flight of the Antheus took place a month later. In Uzin the aircraft performed three flights for the purpose of determining its airfield performance, and on 10 May the aircraft flew over to Gostomel were the testing was resumed.

In June the testing was suspended due to a decision to unveil the aircraft to the outside world at the 25th Paris Air Show. As soon as An-22 CCCP-46191 landed in Le Bourget, it unquestionably became a 'show-stealer'. On 15th June 1965, the fifth day of the show, a radio announcer interrupted a morning programme to inform the listeners: 'The biggest aircraft in the world is arriving at our capital from the Soviet Union; this aerial giant – went on the announcer, his voice betraying some doubt – can accommodate 720 passengers or lift an 80-tonne cargo'.

The press lavished its attention on the aircraft. 'The aircraft was expected to produce the impression of a shapeless, big-bellied monster, but what one saw at the end of the runway was an elegant and 'thoroughbred' machine which touched down very softly, with no trace of shaking…', wrote the French daily *L'Humanité* the following day. 'The Soviet Union shows to us that it is far ahead of other countries in the creation of potent cargo transport aircraft,' noted another French newspaper, *Le Figaro*, on the same day.

The An-22 did not take part in the demonstration flights because it had made only six test flights before Paris and the top ministry officials considered it too risky to grant an approval to demonstrate the machine in the air. For the first time a large delegation from the Kiev-based OKB visited such a representative air show. It included Oleg K. Antonov, Pyotr V. Balabuyev, A. Ya. Belolipetskiy, N. P. Smirnov, V. G. Anisenko, R. S. Korol', Yu. F. Krasontovich, V. N. Ghel'prin, N. A. Pogorelov, I. Ye. Davydov, A. Kroots, Z. Solovey *et al*. The spacious cargo hold of the An-22 became a place for meetings and press conferences. After this demonstration the An-22 was allocated the NATO reporting name *Cock* (most

The second prototype An-22, CCCP-56391, begins its landing gear retraction sequence. Note the Le Bourget '67 exhibit code 235 and the heat-resistant plates on the undersurface of the flaps in line with the engine jetpipes.

probably in the unprintable meaning of the word, since all these reporting names were supposed to be more or less derogatory). As regards its payload, which was stated as 60 tonnes (132,300 lb) during the air show, and the dimensions of the cargo hold (33.4 x 4.4 x 4.4 m/109 ft 7 in x 14 ft 5½ in x 14 ft 5½ in), the An-22 had no equals among the world's aircraft at that time (in actual fact a 60-tonne payload could be only carried in special cases and on condition of limitations imposed on the vertical g-force). Before its emergence it was the Lockheed C-141 StarLifter with a payload of 32.6 tonnes (71,880 lb) that was considered to be the leader among aerial cargo lifters. Subsequently Antonov accentuated the fact that creation of the Antheus gave birth to a new generation of aircraft which were termed 'wide-body aircraft'.

Upon returning from France the An-22 resumed its test programme. Shortly thereafter the aircraft underwent an engine change, one of its NK-12MV engines being replaced with an NK-12MA driving an AV-90 propeller; after a few test flights the aircraft was completely re-engined with the new powerplants.

Testing of the first Antheus was an arduous affair. Once, when the aircraft was ferried from Borispol to Gostomel, a situation arose which was fraught with an accident. Immedi-

ately after the take-off two loud bangs were heard in the underfloor section of the fuselage. After an inspection, flight engineer Vorotnikov reported to captain Koorlin that the starboard forward main undercarriage strut had suffered a structural failure: its shock absorber attachment fittings had disintegrated. As the landing gear was extended, only the rear main strut on the starboard side deployed normally; as it turned out after the landing, the No.2 starboard main gear strut was also damaged. Although the cause was traced to a manufacturing defect, subsequently the KT-109 wheels weighing 530 kg (1,170 lb) were replaced by the more lightweight KT-133s (450 kg/990 lb).

In the autumn, in connection with unstable weather conditions in Kiev, the An-22 was ferried to Tashkent where the flight testing went on.

An-22 Antheus heavy assault transport of the first (pre-production) batch

The Tashkent aircraft plant No.84, which had taken part in the construction of the An-22 prototype, embarked on the series manufacture of these machines pursuant to Ministry of Aircraft Industry order No.119 dated 10th June 1965.

Launching production of a transport aircraft of unique size posed quite a few prob-

lems for the engineers and workers of the Tashkent Aircraft Plant, known the Tashkent Aircraft Production Association named after Valeriy P. Chkalov (TAPO – *Tashkentskoye aviatsionnoye proizvodstvennoye obyedineniye*) from 1973 onwards. Many of these problems were to be tackled for the first time in Soviet and Russian aircraft construction practice. The production facilities of the plant were substantially expanded, all production technologies were updated. Thanks to the presence of a branch office of the Antonov OKB at the Tashkent Plant, many novel features that had been developed and tested in Kiev earlier were successfully incorporated in series production. The branch comprising 150 specialists was headed by Pyotr V. Balabuyev between 1961 and 1965; in subsequent years it was headed successively by Kh. G. Sarymsakov, N. A. Pogorelov, Ya. N. Prikhod'ko, and I. G. Yermokhin.

A wide use of large-size panels in the An-22's structure made it possible to put into effect a very advanced method of airframe assembly based on the use of holes locating and fixing the different parts in place. This method was developed by S. M. Ioffe, a leading specialist of the Plant. This made it possible to decrease the required man-hours by 15%, shorten the assembly period, reduce the list of jigs and tools and their cost. Automatic argon-arc welding devices were introduced for the welding of parts made of aluminium and magnesium alloys. In 1971 the plant started using *Atmosfera-4T* (Atmosphere-4T) inhabited chambers for welding titanium parts; these chambers were hermetically sealed compartments filled with pure argon in which the welders worked in pressure suits, like cosmonauts. The plant was quick in mastering the new production technique involving the combined use of bonding and welding in the joints between structural panels of the fuselage and tail unit. The length of welded seams on the aircraft totalled nearly 12 km (39,360 ft). As a result of using these and other novel features and methods in the course of series production the man-hours required for the manufacture of the An-22 were reduced by a factor of seven.

On 16th November 1965 the first Tashkent-built An-22 (CCCP-56391, c/n 6340103 – ie, year of manufacture 1967, plant No.84, Batch 1, third aircraft in the batch of ten) left the jigs of the assembly line. This aircraft took to the air on 27th January 1966 with a crew captained by Yuriy V. Koorlin. In the course of 1966-1967 the plant built seven more aircraft of the first (pre-production) batch. Manufacturer's tests of these aircraft were conducted mainly at the OKB's flight test facility at Kiev-Gostomel'. (Note: The digits 34 in the c/n were chosen as a code for the Tashkent plant back in 1952 because plant No.84, which was originally located in Khimki (a northern suburb of Moscow), was evacuated to Tashkent in late 1941 in the face of the German offensive, taking up residence at the site of the unfinished Tashkent aircraft factory No.34 (which, as such, never built a single aircraft). Someone got the idea of using the number of the (for all practical purposes) non-existent plant No.34 as a code, obviously in order to confuse would-be spies.)

The first four production machines were initially flown by aircrews from Kiev, while all subsequent machines were flown by aircrews from Tashkent. For example, the fifth An-22 built (originally CCCP-76591, later reregistered CCCP-08822; c/n 6340105) took to the air in December 1966 with factory test pilot K. V. Beletskiy as crew captain. An important contribution to the testing and flight development of production machines was also made by test pilot V. I. Sviridov (he was later awarded the Order of Lenin for the testing of the Antheus), navigators B. Ya. Tver'ye and V. V. Demagin, flight engineer V. M. Vasil'yev.

On 27th October 1966 An-22 CCCP-56391 put the beginning to a series of world records set by the Antheus. A crew captained by I. Ye. Davydov, an OKB test pilot, lifted a cargo of 88.103 tonnes (194,267 lb) to an altitude of 6,600 m (21,650 ft), establishing thereby 12 records in one flight. The world record set in 1958 by US pilot G. M. Thompson on the Douglas C-133 Cargomaster – a load of 53.5 tonnes (117,967 lb) taken to an altitude of 2,000 m (6,560 ft) – was bettered by as much as 34.6 tonnes (76,293 lb).

In the course of the following year a big volume of flight testing was devoted to studying the behaviour of the An-22 during paradropping of troops and cargoes. Three machines took part in these tests: CCCP-56391 (c/n 6340103) and CCCP-76591 No.1 (c/n 6340105) conducted the paradropping at Gostomel', while CCCP-67691 No.1 (c/n 7340106) operated at the test range of Kedainiai (the then Soviet Lithuania). Interestingly, the third digit in the registrations of the first An-22s taking part in the trials matched their sequential number, while the last two digits were always 91: CCCP-46191 was the first airframe built, CCCP-56391 was third, CCCP-76591 No.1 and CCCP-67691 No.1 were the fifth and sixth examples (the registrations later passed to an Il'yushin IL-76MD transport and a Let L-410UVP feederliner respectively). C/n 01-04 was the fatigue test airframe.

Initially the tests conducted from altitudes of 1,500 to 2,000 m (4,920 to 6,560 ft) involved the air-dropping of dummies, hardware mock-ups on parachute platforms with primitive cardboard and foam-plastic shock-absorbing devices (the RPS retro-rocket parachute system used at present for the landing of air-droppable platforms was still under test then), and ingots weighing up to 20 tonnes (44,100 lb). This was followed by the airdropping of light tanks weighing 15-18 tonnes (33,075-39,690 lb) from altitudes of 800-1,000 m (2,624-3,280 ft). As a result, the basic issues associated with paradropping heavy cargoes from the An-22 were resolved. In particular, the tests helped determine the range of permissible speeds for paradropping which proved to be between 310 and 400 km/h (193-249 mph). It was established that in an emergency, when the cargo to be dropped became stuck after having been displaced, continued flight followed by a safe landing could be conducted only with a CG no further aft than 36% MAC. Stable operation of extractor parachutes having an area of 5-14 m² (53.8-150.7 sq ft) was achieved with a withdrawal line some 60 m (200 ft) long.

Stage by stage the methods of airdropping single cargoes weighing up to 20 tonnes (44,100 lb) were developed, tested and introduced into operational service. Incidentally, this weight remains a limiting size for cargoes dropped even from the heavier An-124 Ruslan military transport aircraft.

In June 1967 the Antheus was presented again at the Paris Air Show. Again the aircraft (this time it was CCCP-56391) did not take part in the demonstration flight programme, but it made several flights to Paris before the

Again Moscow-Sheremet'yevo, same taxiway on the north side, but the aircraft is different. This picture was probably taken when CCCP-56391 was due to depart to Paris. The ZiS-150 lorry in the foreground is a ground power unit.

Above: CCCP-56391 in flight. Note that the NK-12 was a fairly smoky engine, and the efflux soot was deposited *on top* of the An-22's slotted flaps when these were deployed. Exhaust staining is also apparent on the lower portions of the fins.

The third flying example of the An-22, CCCP-76591 No.1, was in the static park of the 9th July 1967 airshow at Moscow-Domodedovo. Like the two preceding examples, it carried the legend 'Antey' on the nose. This aircraft was later reregistered CCCP-08822.

Above: CCCP-67691 No.1, the sixth An-22 built and the fourth to fly, is seen here on final approach. Two blades on the No.2 propeller's front row are NOT missing, as implied by the photo; contraprops are wont to create such optical illusions. The aircraft later received Soviet Air Force insignia (tactical code unknown) but ultimately reverted to the civil register as CCCP-08837.

Right: CCCP-67691 No.1 was used for paradropping trials, hence the black photo calibration markings on the main landing gear fairings and around the cargo hatch. Note the rails on the underside of the cargo door; these mated with the rails on the cargo hold roof when the door was opened, allowing the electric hoists to move all the way aft to pick up a cargo.

Below: Seen at Le Bourget in 1971, the same aircraft dwarfs the surrounding machines (two French Rockwell Commanders, a Swiss Gates Learjet 24 and an RAF Westland Wessex C.2; note the Aeroflot IL-18 in the background. Understandably enough, people queued to come aboard the Soviet giant.

Above: CCCP-76591 No.1 was also used for paradropping tests and wore appropriate markings. Note the entry door opened for paradropping personnel.

show to deliver virtually the all of the Soviet non-flying exhibits, including the Vostok spaceship. Shortly thereafter the An-22 was publicly shown also in the Soviet Union. On 9th July 1967 a grand air fest – the first such event in six years – was staged at Moscow-Domodedovo airport; the flying display included the first three production An-22s demonstrating the delivery of heavy combat materiel to a landing site. The demonstration was a part of the air display arranged to commemorate the 50th anniversary of the October Revolution.

On 17th October a crew captained by Davydov amazed the world again: flying An-22 CCCP-56391, they lifted a cargo of 100,400.6 kg (221,383.3 lb) to an altitude of 7,848 m (25,749 ft). The aircraft's load consisted of specially manufactured concrete slabs weighing 6 to 12 tonnes (13,230-24,460 lb) apiece. By now the absolute payload-to-altitude records set by the An-22 have been bettered by the Lockheed C-5A Galaxy and

the An-124, yet to this day 41 world records set by the Antheus still remain valid.

State acceptance trials of the An-22 commenced in October 1967. Among their participants were leading specialists of the Soviet Air Force State Research Institute named after Valeriy P. Chkalov (GK NII VVS – *Gosoodarstvennyy krasnoznamyonnyy naoochno-issledovatel'skiy institoot Voyenno-vozdooshnykh seel*) at Chkalovskaya airbase about 30 km (18.5 miles) east of Moscow: test pilot A. Timofeyev, test navigator M. Kotlyuba, engineer N. Zhukovskiy and others. In the course of the trials 40 flights were performed for the purpose of determining the An-22's stalling characteristics. For safety reasons the aircraft was fitted with a spin recovery parachute; its attachment line, 100 m (330 ft) long, could sustain a force of 50 tonnes (110,250 lb). The flights were conducted over a desert area in the vicinity of Tashkent, the aircraft being piloted by a reduced crew which comprised captain

Koorlin, co-pilot Ketov and flight engineer Vorotnikov, who doubled as navigator and radio operator. The tests resulted in a conclusion that, given the correct and timely actions of the pilot, the An-22 recovered from a stall without delay, which rendered spin entry rather unlikely. All one had to do to recover from a stall was to push the control column forwards beyond the neutral position with the ailerons and rudders held neutral. However, pushing the control column forwards to the limit of its travel provokes a steep dive, and subsequent recovery from this becomes a difficult task. During the tests the need for making use of the spin recovery parachute never arose, although the installation was tested in one of the flights: when the aircraft was in level flight, the parachute was deployed and then jettisoned eight seconds later. The parameters of a steady spin in a broad range of CG positions (16.6-39.5% MAC) were studied on a scaled-strength model in TsAGI's vertical wind tunnel.

In June 1969 An-22 CCCP-56391 was again on display at the Paris Air Show; this time it treated the spectators to several demonstration flights. These included a dramatic low-altitude flight; piloted by Yuriy V. Koorlin, the machine passed at a height of no more than 20 m (65 ft) with the two starboard engines shut down and the propellers feathered (on the side visible to the spectators).

In 1973 the Air Force Research Institute for Operation and Repair of Aviation Hardware (NIIERAT VVS – *Naoochno-issledovatel'skiy institoot ekspluatahtsiï i remonta aviatsionnoy tekhniki Voyenno-vozdooshnykh seel*) teamed up with GSOKB-473 to evolve a programme for testing the An-22 'fleet leader' aircraft. It envisaged special

Parachutists leave an An-22 via the cargo hatch and the entry doors; note the screens flanking the cargo ramp to keep harmful vortices out. All insignia have been retouched away by a zealous censor.

monitoring of machines operated in an accelerated tempo in terms of flight hours logged and landings accomplished. This work made it possible to raise the aircraft's designated service life by the present time to 8,000 flight hours or 3,000 cycles.

After the completion of the flight test programme the machines with the tactical codes '10 Red' (ex-CCCP-46191, c/n 01-01) and '03 Red' (ex-CCCP-56391, c/n 6340103), as well as an example registered CCCP-09301 (c/n 9340203), remained at the disposal of the Antonov OKB. An-22s CCCP-08822 (c/n 6340105), CCCP-08837 (ex-CCCP-76691, c/n 7340106) and CCCP-08838 (c/n 7340107) were delivered to the 81st VTAP (*voyenno-trahnsportnyy aviapolk* – Military Airlift Regi-

ment) at Ivanovo-Severnyy AB in 1973, 1975 and 1977 respectively.

In recognition of their outstanding contribution to the testing of the An-22, test pilots Yu. V. Koorlin and I. Ye. Davydov were awarded the title of Hero of the Soviet Union in 1966 and 1971 respectively. In 1973 Pyotr V. Balabuyev and a group of TAPO employees were awarded a State Prize for the creation of a highly efficient production facility for manufacturing heavy aircraft; the TAPO employees included V. N. Sivets, S. I. Kadyshev, A. S. Systsov, G. V. Mel'nikov, I. A. Stasenko, S. M. Ioffe, Ye. S. Khalapov, M. K. Mirzafakhin, B. B. Viktorov and I. M. Mirsaïdov. In April 1974 the KMZ (*Kiyevskiy mashinos-troitel'nyy zavod* – Kiev Mechanical Plant; that

was the new unclassified name of the Antonov Design Bureau) received the Order of Labour Red Banner, and leading designers V. G. Anisenko, V. I. Kabayev, V. P. Rychik and V. N. Shatalov were awarded the Lenin Prize. A year later a big group of KMZ specialists was decorated with orders and medals of the USSR. Deputy Chief Designers P. V. Balabuyev, A. Ya. Belolipetskiy and turner V. V. Naumenko were awarded the title of Hero of Socialist Labour.

An-22 Antheus production heavy assault transport aircraft

Production of the An-22 gathered momentum. The number of machines built per year rose from five in 1969 to eleven in 1975. In the

Rough-field capability was designed into the An-22 from the outset, and the initial production aircraft were tested on unpaved airstrips both in the summer (top) and in the winter.

An-22 *sans suffixe* production

C/n	Registration/tactical code	Notes
01-01	CCCP-46191	First prototype. Repainted in Soviet Air Force insignia as, see next line
	'10 Red'	Converted to An-22PZ wing transporter and registered as, see next line
	CCCP-180151, CCCP-64459, UR-64459	Operated by Antonov Design Bureau; later deconverted
01-02	No registration (static test airframe)	
6340103	CCCP-56391	Second prototype. Repainted in Soviet Air Force insignia as, see next line
	'03 Blue'	Converted to An-22PZ wing transporter and registered as, see next line
	CCCP-64460	Deconverted and leased to SiGi Air Cargo, Bulgaria, as, see next line
	LZ-SGB	Returned and leased to Air Sofia, Bulgaria, as, see next line
	LZ-SFD	Returned and operated by Antonov Design Bureau as, see next line
	UR-64460	Sold to Technikmuseum Speyer, Germany; last flight to Speyer 29-12-99
01-04	No registration (fatigue test airframe)	
6340105	CCCP-76591 No.1, CCCP-08822	
7340106	CCCP-67691 No.1	Repainted in Soviet Air Force insignia, tactical code unknown; became, see next line
	CCCP-08837	Shot down in Kabul 28-10-1984
7340107	CCCP-08838	
8340108	CCCP-09317	
8340109	CCCP-08840	
8340110	CCCP-09310	
8340201	'39 Red'	First aircraft with twin nose radomes. Became, see next line
	CCCP-08839	
8340202	CCCP-09302, RA-09302	
9340203	CCCP-09301	
9340204	CCCP-09304, RA-09304	
9340205	CCCP-09305 No.1	
9340206	CCCP-09306, RA-09306	
00340207	CCCP-09303	Crashed in the Bermuda Triangle en route from Keflavik to Halifax 18-7-70
00340208	CCCP-09325, RA-09325	
00340209	CCCP-09334	WFU after hard landing; preserved Soviet/Russian Air Force Museum, Monino
00340210	CCCP-09346, RA-09346	
00340301	CCCP-09308, RA-09308	
00340302	CCCP-09315, RA-09315	
01340303	CCCP-09321, RA-09321	
01340304	CCCP-09323, RA-09323	
01340305	CCCP-09330	
01340306	CCCP-09336, RA-09336	
01340307	CCCP-09313, RA-09313	
01340308	CCCP-09316, RA-09316	
01340309	CCCP-09322, RA-09322	
01340310	CCCP-09326, RA-09326	
02340401	CCCP-09332, RA-09332	
02340402	CCCP-09333, RA-09333	
02340403	CCCP-09335, RA-09335	
02340404	CCCP-09345, RA-09345	
02340405	'49 Red'	Became, see next line
	CCCP-09349	Crashed Seshcha AB, Bryansk, ?-6-77
02340406	CCCP-09319	
02340407	CCCP-09324, RA-09324	
02340408	CCCP-09331, RA-09331	Crashed Migalovo AB, Tver', 18-1-94
02340409	CCCP-09339	
03340410	CCCP-09347	

following year series production of the An-22 was terminated – a premature decision, as it turned out. Between November 1965 and January 1976 the Tashkent aircraft factory delivered 66 An-22s, including 28 An-22As (see opposite page). Later the demand for this aircraft in the national economy proved so great that consideration was given to the possibility of resuming series production. However, TAPO was not in a position to do so,

having no spare capacity (it was fully occupied with producing the IL-76 transport).

Beginning with the second production batch, the *Polyot-1* (Flight-1) integrated flight/navigation system based on the *Initsiativa-4* (Initiative-4) ground mapping radar was replaced by the more advanced **Koopol-22** (Cupola-22; or rather, in this context, **koo**pol **para**shoo**ta** – parachute canopy) flight/navigation system. Hence the extensively glazed

navigator's station in the extreme nose and the large teardrop radome under the front end of the starboard main gear fairing gave way to a ground mapping radar in a chin radome and a weather radar in a nose radome ahead of the restyled nose glazing, giving the aircraft its distinctive nose profile. The forward radome could not be blended smoothly into the nose contour (probably due to the need to avoid internal radar echoes), resulting in a characteristic 'dog nose' shape. The airworthy Batch 1 aircraft were upgraded in due course by relocating the radome to the chin position, retaining the original navigator's station glazing.

Up to the end of 1969, production An-22s had seven-digit construction numbers, the year of manufacture being designated by a single digit. From 1970 onwards the year was designated by two digits (00 = 1970, 01 = 1971 and so on); for instance, the final An-22 *sans suffixe* (CCCP-09347) built in 1973 is c/n 03340410. Most An-22s were quasi-civilian, wearing Aeroflot titles and registrations in the CCCP-088xx and CCCP-093xx blocks; only a few aircraft briefly wore overt military markings with large tactical codes on the forward fuselage.

Production An-22s saw fairly intensive operational use. For example, during the period between January 1969 and May 1993 720 NK-12MA engines and 2,700 AV-90 propellers were replaced on the military An-22s. During some years the An-22 fleet logged as many as 14,000 flight hours. In the course of service practically the entire fleet underwent scheduled comprehensive modifications aimed at introducing new equipment items and units, eradicating faults that had come to light, increasing the reliability and extending the service life. The modifications were carried out either directly at TAPO or *in situ* by the plant's specialists in accordance with schedules approved by the Ministry of Aircraft Industry and the Air Force.

In the early 1980s, when the high-time aircraft (c/ns 6340105, 7340106 and 7340107) had logged the specified number of flight hours before the first scheduled overhaul, this posed the problem of selecting a repair facility for it. A decision was taken to organise An-22 refurbishment work at the military aircraft overhaul plant located at Ivanovo-Severnyy AB (known since 1997 as ARZ No.308; ARZ = *aviaremontnyy zavod* – aircraft repair plant) which had previously refurbished military An-2s, An-24s, An-26s and An-30s. The enterprise was supplied without delay with the repair documentation; its production facilities were expanded. On 18th January 1983 the first refurbished An-22 left the workshops of this enterprise. One by one, on a scheduled basis, the aircraft of this type were sent for repairs; in the subsequent years, as the enterprise accumulated experience, the duration of the repair work was reduced to 7-8 months.

An-22A heavy assault transport aircraft (project)

In 1966 design studies were undertaken on the An-22A (first use of the designation) – a version of the aircraft possessing a take-off weight of 250 tonnes (551,250 lb) and a payload of 80 tonnes (176,400 lb). The plans in hand envisaged reinforcing the structure and

An-22A production

C/n	L/n	Registration/tactical code	Notes
03340501		CCCP-09318	Crashed Sechsha AB 22-12-77
033480209	05-02	CCCP-09320, RA-09320	
033480212	05-03	CCCP-09327, RA-09327	
033480219	05-04	CCCP-09328, RA-09328	
033480225	05-05	CCCP-09337, RA-09337	
033480228	05-06	CCCP-09338, RA-09338	
033481234	05-07	CCCP-09340	
043481240	05-08	CCCP-09305 No.2, RA-09305	
043481244	05-09	CCCP-09307 No.2, UR-09307	
043481250	05-10	CCCP-09309, **no code**	**Camouflage c/s, callsign '309'**
043481251	06-01	CCCP-09311	Crashed Moscow-Vnukovo 2-6-80
043481256	06-02	CCCP-09312, RA-09312	
043482263	06-03	CCCP-09314	
043482266	06-04	CCCP-09341, RA-09341	
043482272	06-05	CCCP-09343, RA-09343	
043482276	06-06	CCCP-09329, RA-09329	
043482282	06-07	'42 Blue', CCCP-09342, RA-09342	
053482288	06-08	CCCP-09344, RA-09344	
053483292	06-09	'48 Red', CCCP-09348, RA-09348	
053483299	06-10	CCCP-09303	Crashed Migalovo AB 11-11-92
053483302	07-01	CCCP-08829, RA-08829	
053483308	07-02	CCCP-08830, RA-08830	
053483311	07-03	CCCP-08831, RA-08831	
053484317	07-04	CCCP-08832, RA-08832	
053484321	07-05	'33 Red', CCCP-08833, RA-08833	
053484327	07-06	'34 Red', CCCP-08834	
053484331	07-07?	CCCP-08835	
053485336	07-08?	CCCP-08836, RA-08836	

boosting the engine power to 18,000 ehp. In response to military requirements the designers intended to protect the flightdeck with armour plating and fit the aircraft with a rear fuselage cannon turret.

An-22A Antheus production heavy assault transport aircraft

Improvements were continuously introduced into An-22s in the course of its production. Among the changes effected was a modification of the electric power supply system. Instead of direct current, most of the consumers now were powered by three-phase alternating current. A more powerful APU was installed in the starboard landing gear fairing; it comprised twin TA-6A1 turbine generators and a TG-60/2S turbine generator, the external identification feature being the twin APU exhausts located above one another ahead of the starboard entry door. Improved NK-12MA Srs 3 engines with the same power rating of 15,000 ehp replaced the initial model; they were started pneumatically instead of by self-contained turbine starters. The control system was provided with servos combining the functions of a hydraulic actuator and a device for switching from powered to manual control mode. These and other improvements made it possible to reduce structural weight, enhance operational reliability and reduce the amount of maintenance man-hours.

To start with, these modifications were effected to An-22 *sans suffixe* CCCP-09301 (c/n 9340203) which the OKB had at its disposal; on the basis of the results of manufacturer's tests and State acceptance trials conducted in 1972 a decision was taken to manufacture this version from batch 5 onwards under the designation An-22A. Thus, CCCP-09301 effectively became the An-22A prototype. However, this designation failed to catch on in the Air Force, and the aircraft was still referred to in service simply as the An-22.

As distinct from the An-22 *sans suffixe*, production An-22As (except the first production example, CCCP-09318, c/n 03340501, which first flew on 30th June 1973) received nine-digit construction numbers under a new system designed to confuse foreign intelligence services. The first four digits of the An-22A c/ns retained their meanings (a two-digit year-of-manufacture designator and the code 34 for the Tashkent plant No.84). The remaining digits (commonly referred to in the West as 'the famous last five') were devoid of any particular meaning so as not to reveal the batch number and the number of the aircraft in the batch (and hence how many had been built); the first two and last three of these digits accrued independently. However, in order to keep track of production under the customary

Above and below: Oleg K. Antonov shows the project of a 724-seat airliner derivative of the An-22 to MAP officials. The pictures on the wall show the upper cabin with eight-abreast seating and the lower cabin.

system a parallel system of four-digit fuselage numbers or line numbers (consisting of the batch number and then the number of the aircraft in the batch) was introduced. Thus, for example, the second production An-22A (CCCP-09320, c/n 033480209) is l/n 0502 and the last aircraft off the line (CCCP-08836, c/n 053485336) is presumably l/n 0708.

Between 1961 and 1970 the OKB worked on a series of An-22 versions which did not proceed further than a technical proposal or the advanced development project stage. In addition, An-22s *sans suffixe* c/ns 0101 and 6340103, and later also 7340203 and An-22A l/n 05-09, became an integral part of the Antonov OKB, its 'workhorses'. They were 'dogships' used for developing and testing the necessary improvements, for conducting additional tests and carrying out transportation jobs required by the enterprise.

Amphibious military transport aircraft based on the An-22 (project)

In 1961-62, in parallel with the work on the 'izdeliye 100' aircraft, the Antonov OKB conducted design studies on its amphibious derivative pursuant to a decision taken by the Soviet Ministry of Defence; the aircraft was intended for long-range airlifting of military hardware and cargoes weighing up to 30 tonnes (66,140 lb), including missiles and their fuel. The amphibian was expected to ensure delivery of cargoes both by airdropping and to landing sites or by alighting on water. The aircraft was also intended for delivering supplies to submarines at sea, for search-and-rescue operations, mine-laying and anti-submarine warfare.

The fuselage of the *izdeliye* 100 was suitably modified to feature boat-hull contours with the necessary Vee planing bottom and planing steps. In the first version the aircraft

was fitted with fuselage-mounted sponsons for lateral stability on the water; the second version featured underwing stabilising floats and a retractable hydro-ski undercarriage featuring a hydro-ski as the nose unit and two hydrofoils as the main units. A model of the first version of the amphibian to 1/20th scale was tested in the TsAGI towing basin for the purpose of determining its hydrodynamic characteristics.

An-22 double-deck airliner (project)

In parallel with the design work on the baseline cargo version of the Antheus studies were made of a passenger version of the aircraft. The fuselage was to be stretched by 15 m (49 ft 2½ in), accommodating a double-deck passenger cabin seating 724 passengers; the cabin was to be provided with a cinema hall, a bar, a special compartment for mothers with babies and with sleeping compartments. Although this version did not proceed further than the drawing board, one of the An-22s of the 81st VTAP *did* perform a passenger transportation flight in the autumn of 1972. The flight was carried out for the purpose of evacuating Soviet military personnel from Egypt; the aircraft took on board 700 persons (precisely the number promised by Oleg K. Antonov during the 1965 Paris Air Show).

An-22PLO ultra-long-range ASW aircraft with a nuclear powerplant (project)

In accordance with a directive adopted by the Central Committee of the Communist Party and the Council of Ministers of the USSR on 26th October 1965 GSOKB-473 led by Oleg K. Antonov conducted design work on super long-range low altitude ASW aircraft with a nuclear powerplant, designated An-22PLO (*protivolodochnaya oborona* – anti-submarine warfare). Its powerplant comprised a small-size nuclear reactor developed under the guidance of Academician Aleksandr Petrovich Aleksandrov, together with its system of radiation shielding, a distributing unit, a system of piping and special turboprop engines developed under the direction of Nikolay D. Kuznetsov. The engines used conventional jet fuel during take-off and landing, and in cruise the propulsive power was provided by the reactor. The engine was to deliver a maximum power output of 13,000 and 8,900 ehp respectively.

According to calculations, the aircraft would be able to remain on station for 50 hours and would have a range of 27,500 km (17,090 miles). Within the framework of this programme research was conducted with a view to developing methods of protecting the crew from the radiation emitted by the onboard reactor. In 1970 An-22 *sans suffixe* CCCP-08837 (c/n 6340106) was fitted with a point source of neutron radiation possessing a capacity of 3 kW and provided with a multi-layer protective bulkhead. Yuriy V. Koorlin performed ten flights on this machine with the radiation source operating. Later, in August 1972, a small nuclear reactor in a protective lead capsule was installed on An-22 *sans suffixe* CCCP-08838 (c/n 7340107). Piloted by Samovarov and Gorbik, this aircraft performed 23 flights in Semipalatinsk, Kazakhstan; these flights furnished the necessary information on the effectiveness of the radiation shielding.

An-122 heavy military transport (project)

Further development of the Antheus proceeded under the designation An-122. This machine was intended for the transportation of cargoes weighing up to 120 tonnes (244,600 lb) over a distance of 2,500 km (1,554 miles).

An-22PS marine search and rescue system (project)

In accordance with a decision adopted by the CofM Presidium's Commission on Defence Industry Matters (VPK – *Voyenno-promyshlennaya komissiya*) on 15th March 1967, design work was started on the An-22PS search and rescue system involving the use of aircraft and marine vessels (PS = *poiskovo-spasahtel'nyy* – SAR, used attributively). The Antheus was fitted with equipment for conducting a search for the crews of ships and aircraft in distress, with one or two rescue boats with their crews and with the means for paradropping the boats. The work did not proceed further than the ADP stage.

An-22P intercontinental airborne missile system (project)

In 1969-70 GSOKB-473 led by Oleg K. Antonov together with TsAGI, the State Scientific Research Institute for Aircraft Systems (GosNII AS – *Gosoodarstvennyy naoochno-*

Top: While still wearing Soviet Air Force insignia and the tactical code '10 Red' stemming from an Air Force lease after the end of the trials programme, the first prototype was modified to become the first of two An-22PZ aircraft optimised for carrying An-124 wing subassemblies externally. Here it is prepared for towing by a Kirovets K-710 heavy-duty tractor; an An-124 port wing panel is installed upside-down on the fuselage.

Centre right and above right: '10 Red' takes off with an An-124 starboard wing panel. An extra fin taken in stock form from an An-26 had to be fitted to ensure adequate directional stability with this load. Besides showing clearly the fairing and supporting struts between the load and the fuselage, these photos show that the aircraft has not yet been updated (the radar is still under the starboard main gear fairing).

Right: The An-124 wing centre section assembly was carried almost like an external baggage box on a car!

27

Above: The second An-22PZ, CCCP-64460, a few seconds before landing. Note the relocated radar and the sooty streak on the starboard main gear fairing aft of the APU exhaust.

issledovatel'skiy institoot aviatsionnykh sistem) and other R&D institutions conducted research work with a view to creating the An-22P airborne intercontinental ballistic missile (ICBM) system based on the An-22. The aircraft was a flying launch pad; it was equipped with three ICBM launch tubes installed vertically in the fuselage.

An-22PZ special cargo transporter ('Carrier')

An important chapter in the Antheus' biography revealing new aspects of its transport capabilities was opened when the An-22 prototypes began to be used for carrying externally mounted wing centre sections and wing outer panels of the An-124 Ruslan and the An-225 Mriya from Tashkent to Kiev, and later also to Ul'yanovsk. Practical implementation of this project (dubbed 'Transport') was preceded by a large volume of calculations and research work on comparative analysis of transportation of the mentioned cargoes by surface transport, by ship and by air. Air transportation proved to be the optimum solution which ensured a high degree of production completeness in the assembly of the wing

Top left: A gantry crane lowers an An-124 wing panel onto the fuselage of An-22PZ CCCP-64460 in a hangar at the Tashkent plant which manufactured these assemblies. This photo gives a view of the dorsal fairing's interior.

Above left: A BelAZ-7420 airport tug tows a heavily laden An-22PZ during an intermediate stop. Judging by the tug's licence plate (35 76 VZT, in Cyrillic characters), the scene is Volgograd-Goomrak airport.

Left: CCCP-64459 eventually underwent a similar upgrade with a chin radome. The An-22PZs were the only An-22s to wear Aeroflot's 1973-standard livery; note that CCCP-64459 also carried the Soviet flag on the centre fin, unlike the other machine.

sections to be transported, their safety under transportation and regularity of deliveries. Various versions of the 'aerial cargo hauler' were considered.

A big volume of aerodynamic and structural strength research showed that the so-called 'special cargo No.1' (An-124 wing centre section) and 'special cargo No.2' (An-124 wing panel assembly) could be carried externally, obviating the need for a substantial modification of the aircraft. (In passing, it may be noted that usually in Soviet aerospace industry/military parlance the term *spetsgrooz* (special cargo) referred to nuclear munitions.) Priority in the deliveries was given to the wing centre section; therefore the prototype Antheus (c/n 0101), then on lease to the Soviet Air Force as '10 Red', was initially modified for the carriage of the 'special cargo No.1'. To this end two faired forward cargo attachment points were mounted on the aircraft's wing centre section, supplemented by two rear attachment fittings which were mounted just aft of the wings and connected with the cargo floor structure by internal bracing struts. The aircraft thus modified received the designation An-22PZ (*Perevozchik* – carrier) and the non-standard registration CCCP-180151.

(Note: The highly unusual six-digit registrations encountered on some Antonov development aircraft since 1980 are explained as follows. The first and the last digits sometimes correspond to the aircraft type: for instance, the first new-build An-32 was originally registered CCCP-380122 (3+2 = An-32); the An-74 prototype was CCCP-780334 and the first prototype An-71 AWACS aircraft was CCCP-780151. However, this does not always work, as in this case (CCCP-180151); cf. also An-124 CCCP-680125 and An-225

CCCP-480182. The meaning of the second digit, which is always an 8, is obscure; this may be a code for the OKB's experimental shop. The next two are the sequence number of the airframe (CCCP-180151 was indeed No.1) and the last-but-one digit shows the year of manufacture – in this case, 1965.)

In July 1980 the modified aircraft was ferried to Tashkent. In the assembly shop of TAPO the wing centre section of the future An-124, fitted with forward and rear fairings, was mounted atop the An-22PZ.

On 15th July this unique transport system took off from Tashkent-Yoozhnyy, the TAPO factory airfield, bound for Kiev. On its first flight the An-22PZ was accompanied by more than 100 specialists of the Kiev Mechanical Plant, including Pyotr V. Balabuyev, V. Shatalov (chief of the flight test and development facility) and O. Kotlyar (production chief) who were flying in the An-12, An-24 and An-32 aircraft. Although the An-22 with this load had made a trial flight near Tashkent the day before, the long-distance flight required courage from the crew captained by test pilot Ketov. Soon after take-off, vibration was experienced; it quickly grew worse and turned into buffeting. The buffeting was so violent that the pilots had to set their feet against the instrument panels so as to be able to discern the instrument readings. The aircraft had to make an urgent landing at a military airfield in Krasnovodsk, Turkmenistan. Inspection of the aircraft showed that the vibration was caused by a failure of the forward attachment fitting fairings: the fairings had been ripped away by the slipstream. After some discussion, the Antonov pilots decided to continue the flight. After one more intermediate landing in Mozdok, Ingushetia, the 'Carrier' made a safe landing at Kiev-Svyatoshino.

Above: This unidentified An-22 was used for testing an obscure modification, featuring a strut-mounted external stores rack with sway braces under the nose – and, interestingly, no radar at all.

Above: This model of a Batch 1 An-22 displayed at the Soviet (now Central Russian) Air Force Museum in Monino since the early 1970s carries the designation 'An-22K' which nobody seems able to explain.

In due course the airworthy Batch 1 ('glass-nosed') An-22s were retrofitted with an auxiliary power unit in the starboard main gear fairing; its nozzle can be seen immediately ahead of the radome.

Additional research made it possible to trace the basic cause of the buffeting: it turned out that the unfavourable interference between the fuselage and the special cargo mounted on top of it had previously been underestimated. Therefore, before the delivery of the next wing centre section, its mounting was modified: the cargo itself was moved slightly aft and the space between the cargo and the fuselage was closed by special fairings. On the same occasion the cargo was provided with a de-icing system which included a 1,000-litre (220 Imp gal) alcohol tank, an electrically driven pump for feeding the alcohol into the system, manifolds and nozzles. A flight from Tashkent to Kiev performed by CCCP-180151 on 13th September 1981 was a non-stop flight; it showed that the measures effected had fully reached their goal.

A different version of external mounting was developed for the carriage of the 'special cargo No.2'. The elongated outer wing panel of the Ruslan was placed along the fuselage of the Antheus and was attached to its wing centre section; in its forward and rear parts it was also attached to the floor of the cargo hold by means of a system of struts and frames. To enhance directional stability the An-22PZ was fitted with an additional centre-line fin; a stock vertical tail from an An-26 transport with the rudder locked was used for this purpose. The first aerial delivery of an An-124 wing outer panel was performed in February 1982.

On 3rd March 1983 An-22PZ CCCP-180151 received a new 'MAP-style' registration, CCCP-64459 (the 644xx series was one of several 'mixed bag' registration blocks set aside for aircraft operated by MAP enterprises). In the same year one more Antheus, '41 Red' (c/n 6340103), was returned to the OKB from a Soviet Air Force lease and converted into the second An-22PZ, becoming CCCP-64460. In 1983 regular flights were started for the delivery of the An-124 wing assemblies from Tashkent to production plants in Kiev and Ul'yanovsk; these flights lasted until 1988. In addition, in 1987-1994 six flights were made for the delivery of wing centre sections and outer panels for two examples of the An-225. The last flight of this kind was performed by the first An-22PZ (by then placed on the Ukrainian register as UR-64459), with a crew captained by V. A. Samoylov, on 23rd October 1994. In all, during the 14 years of their operation the 'Carriers' performed more than 100 flights and thus proved the versatility of the Antheus. After that, UR-64459 was withdrawn from use at Kiev-Gostomel' while UR-64460 was reconverted to standard, serving on with the Antonov Design Bureau. For the creation of this air transport system and its introduction into operation a group of employees of the Kiev Mechanical Plant was awarded a State prize of the Ukraine in 1985.

An-22Sh special cargo transporter (project)

One of the 'Carrier' versions studied in the process of calculations and research work on the 'Transport' programme was a modification of the production An-22 which received a project designation An-22Sh. To accommodate large-size cargoes, the rear fuselage of this version behind the wing centre section was enlarged to a maximum diameter of 9.6 m (31 ft 6 in); hence the Sh may stand for *shirokiy fyuzelyazh* (wide fuselage).

An-22 with a versatile external pod for special cargoes (project)

One more version of the 'Carrier' studied in the process of calculations and research work on the 'Transport' programme was a production An-22 with a versatile container for the carriage of special-type cargoes mounted on top of the fuselage.

Structural description of the An-22

Type: Four-turboprop heavy military transport. The airframe is of all-metal construction. The aircraft's crew comprises seven persons: captain, co-pilot, navigator, flight engineer, radio operator, senior flight technician for avionics and senior flight technician for paradropping and cargo handling equipment.

Fuselage: Semi-monocoque structure. The transverse members of the fuselage structure comprise 108 frames; the longitudinal members comprise 126 stringers plus beams. The main structural members are made of D16 and AK6 aluminium alloys. Highly stressed large-size integrally stamped parts of the load-bearing central part of the fuselage, the cargo hold floor sill and a number of other parts are made of V93 aluminium alloy. The flooring of the cargo hold is manufactured of a titanium alloy. The aircraft's structure also incorporates parts made of various grades of steel and of ML5 magnesium alloy. The stringers are attached to the skin by spot welding coupled with the use of the K-4S bonding agent. The U30MES-5 sealing compound is used for sealing the joints.

Structurally the fuselage is made up of four sections: the forward fuselage (frames 1-14), the centre fuselage (frames 14-59), the aft fuselage (frames 59-100) and the rear fuselage or tail section. The fuselage is of basically circular cross-section which gradually changes to elliptical with the longer axis horizontal on the aft fuselage and tail section which are flat underneath. Maximum fuselage diameter is 6 m (19 ft 8¼ in).

Above: Production An-22s built from Batch 2 onwards featured a revised nose with a forward-mounted weather radar and a chin-mounted ground mapping radar with a fairing for an optical sight ahead of it.

The navigator's station of Batch 1 ('glass-nosed') An-22s commanded a good view forward. Note the radar display mounted ahead of the navigator's seat and the map table on the left.

Above: The lowered cargo ramp of an An-22 with the rear door still closed. Two vehicle loading ramps lie folded against the surface of the cargo ramp.

Above: This view illustrates the rear fuselage structure, showing the overhead rails for the cargo hoists, the de-icing system air ducts and the 'traffic lights' on the right used for paradropping.

Three 6 x 6 army lorries (two Ural-375Ds and a ZiL-131) are driven into the cargo hold of an An-22. Most of the internal fuselage structure was covered by wall trim panels. Note the tip-up seats along the walls.

The *forward fuselage (Section F1)* includes the crew section; this is a double-deck structure with the flightdeck above and the navigator's compartment below and ahead of it. The flightdeck roof incorporating the glazing forms a flattened teardrop-shaped bulge protruding outside the circular cross-sections between frames 4 and 9. The flightdeck glazing consists of three optically flat birdproof triplex windscreen panes, plus three side windows and two eyebrow windows (all made of Plexiglas) on each side. The triangular foremost side windows are sliding direct vision windows which can be used as emergency exits on the ground. The navigator's station on Batch 1 aircraft featured a parabolic glazing frame with curved Plexiglas panels and an optically flat elliptical lower panel affording an unrestricted view in the forward hemisphere. From Batch 2 onwards this was replaced by a half-ring of transparencies allowing a measure of forward visibility and a forward pressure bulkhead kinked at approximately 80° which mounts the weather radar dish covered by a glassfibre radome; an unpressurised bay for the ground mapping radar antenna enclosed by a second radome was added beneath the navigator's compartment floor.

Placed between frames 10 and 14 is a cabin for cargo attendants accommodating 21 persons; it comprises three compartments: two on the lower deck and one on the upper deck. Two doors in the pressure bulkhead built into frame 14 provide access into this cabin from the cargo hold. One of the emergency exits is placed on the ceiling of the cabin for cargo attendants between frames 11 and 13. The second emergency exit is an escape hatch to port between frames 7 and 9 with a sloping chute (accessible both from the flightdeck and the navigator's station) used for bailing out in the air. The lower part of Section F-1 between frames 8 and 14 houses the nosewheel well.

The *centre fuselage (Section F2)* houses the cargo hold pressurised to a pressure differential of 0.25 kg/cm² (3.55 psi). Its cargo floor comprises non-slip flooring supported by transverse and longitudinal structural members. The transverse structural members include the lower parts of the fuselage frames and milled frames with tie-down fittings, the longitudinal elements are stressed H-beams. Two rails for travelling gantries are mounted on the cargo hold roof. The upper part of Section F2 between frames 39 and 49 accommodates the wing centre section. Flanking the fuselage between frames 26 and 70 are the main landing gear fairings. Their transverse framework consists of frames which, with the exception of frames 36 and 53, coincide with the planes of the fuselage frames. The longitudinal framework includes 48 stringers and several beams. The skin of the fairings has a thickness of 0.8-2.0 mm (0.0315-0.079 in). Apart from the landing gear, the fairings house some equipment items, six bag-type fuel tanks and entrance corridors with forward-hinged doors opening outwards.

The *aft fuselage (Section F3)* includes a part of the cargo hold (frames 59-63), the cargo hatch (frames 63-95) and an unpressurised section between frames 95 and 100. The cargo hatch is closed by a cargo ramp hinged to frame 63 and an upward-opening rear door segment hinged to frame 95. When this door segment is fully opened, the rails mounted on its external side join with the rails of the cargo hold. Fittings for the attachment of jacks supporting the rear fuselage during loading/unloading are mounted on the lower part of frame 63. Three vehicle loading ramps can be attached manually to the trailing edge of the cargo ramp, occupying almost its entire width. The stabiliser centre section is mounted on top of the fuselage between frames 95 and 100. The wall of the pressure bulkhead/frame 95 has a hatch for access to the unpressurised area.

The *tail section* is an unpressurised structure whose framework comprises eight frames, four beams and a number of stringers. The upper panel of this fuselage section has a hatch for access to the stabiliser. The trailing edge of the flattened tail section carries antennas, a navigation light and an illumination floodlight (to starboard).

Wings: Cantilever shoulder-mounted monoplane wings of trapezoidal planform, mounted above the fuselage to leave the interior unobstructed. Sweepback 0°, zero dihedral up to rib 26 and 3° anhedral beyond that rib, incidence +4°; geometrical camber –0°28' from the root rib to rib 13 (the No.3 production break on each side) and –2°30' outboard to the wingtip airfoil.

The wings are all-metal, stressed-skin structures; the upper skin panels are stamped of V95 alloy, the underside panels of D16 alloy. Structurally the wings are made up of seven pieces: the centre section (which is integral with the fuselage), four inner sections (SChK-I between ribs 4-13 and SChK-II between ribs 13-26; SChK stands for *srednyaya chast' kryla* – 'middle wing section') and two outer sections (OChK, *ot"yomnaya chast' kryla* – 'detachable wing section') between ribs 26 and 43. The wing/fuselage joint is covered by a fairing.

The wing centre section and all four inner sections are of three-spar construction, while the detachable outer wing sections have a two-spar structure. The wing centre section houses 14 bag-type fuel tanks; the inner wing and detachable outer wing sections accommodate integral fuel tanks. The SChK-I

Above: The An-22 has a full-width cargo hatch; note the cargo ramp uplocks. The vehicle is a TZ-22 fuel bowser (a KrAZ-258 tractor unit with a 22,000-litre/4,840-gal. trailer); the inscription reads *Ogneopasno* (Flammable).

section has a thickness/chord ratio of 16% and features a TsAGI S-5-16 airfoil. Further on along the span the airfoil changes linearly to TsAGI S-3-15 at the end of the SChK-II and to TsAGI S-3-13 at the tips.

The inner wings are fitted with double-slotted three-section flaps with a deflector, and the outer wing sections incorporate three-section ailerons, each with a servo tab and a geared tab. Flap settings are 25° for take-off and 35° for landing.

Tail unit: Cantilever structure with twin fins and rudders; no sweepback. The stabiliser comprises a centre section and outer panels and has an incidence of 0°. The centre section,

The forward bulkhead of the cargo hold. The pressure door on the right leads to the crew section. Note the overhead cargo hoists and the spare wheels. The stencil on the bulkhead reads *Ne koorit'* (No smoking).

Above: 'Wish I had a gun.' This crewman makes an interesting picture as he pops out of the tail section access hatch like a gopher from his hole. This view shows clearly the flattened fuselage tail section, the position of the fins relative to the stabiliser span and the one-piece elevators.

Left: The vertical tails are mounted in a very distinctive way, the fins being placed entirely ahead of the stabiliser leading edge. Note the de-icing air outlets immediately below the cigar-shaped fin top fairings and position of the 'An-22' titles on the fins.

the stabiliser and the fins have a two-spar stressed-skin structure. Each stabiliser outer panel carries an elevator with three servo tabs. The outermost servo tabs are locked.

The fins are mounted ahead of the stabiliser leading edge at three-quarters span and feature large cigar-shaped tip fairings protruding far beyond the leading edge. Each rudder is split into the upper and lower halves; the lower parts are fitted with gear tabs, which are locked. The upper parts of the rudders are fitted with one-piece geared tabs on the An-22 *sans suffixe* (batches 1-4); on the An-22A (batches 5-7) they are fitted with one-piece servo tabs. The elevators have 31% aerodynamic balancing, the rudders 30% aerodynamic balancing; additionally, the elevators and the rudders are mass-balanced.

Landing gear: Hydraulically retractable tricycle type, with seven independent twin-wheel struts. The forward-retracting nose unit has KT-110 brake wheels (KT = kole**so** tormoz**noy**e) measuring 1,450 x 580 mm (57.0 x 22.83 in). Each main unit comprises three tandem struts, each carrying 1,750 x 730 mm (68.9 x 28.74 in) KT-130 brake wheels, retracting upwards into large fairings flanking the centre fuselage; the mainwheels are semi-recessed when extended. The wheels are fitted with tyres featuring sidewalls of a large relative height; tyre pressure is 5 kg/cm² (71.13 psi), which enables the aircraft to operate from unpaved airfields. The steerable nose unit can turn through ±35° for taxying and is equipped with a shimmy damper. From An-22 *sans suffixe* CCCP-09315 (c/n 00340302) onwards, the forward pair of main gear struts can turn at an angle of ±7°30' to improve ground manoeuvrability. All landing gear struts have oleo-pneumatic shock absorbers and levered suspension.

The nosewheel well is closed by two lateral (main) doors, which open only when the gear is in transit, and a small rear door segment mechanically linked to the oleo strut. Each of the six main gear struts has clamshell doors rotating on axles located inside the undercarriage fairings to stow almost completely inside the fairings when the gear is down. Provision is made for retracting and extending the main gear units both all at once and in succession. On early production machines tyre pressure in all the wheels could be adjusted within the range of 2.5-5 kg/cm² (35.56-71.13 psi) to suit different airfield surfaces, but subsequently the pressure adjustment system was deleted.

Powerplant: Four Kuznetsov NK-12MA turboprops having a 15,000-ehp take-off rating and a 8,080-ehp cruise rating at 10,000 m (32,810 ft) and Mach 0.56. The engine was manufactured by the Kuibyshev Engine Factory named after Mikhail V. Frunze (now called Motorostroitel' JSC).

The NK-12MA is a single-shaft turboprop with an annular air intake with inner and outer cones connected by six radial struts, a 14-stage axial compressor, an annular combustion chamber, a five-stage uncooled axial turbine and a fixed-area jetpipe. Power is transmitted via a single-stage differential gearbox with oil cooling which also serves as the accessory gearbox. The NK-12 is the world's first turboprop engine to feature air bleed valves in the compressor section, cast turbine blades, turbine blade gap control and an integrated fuel control unit (FCU).

Engine pressure ratio 9.3; turbine temperature 1,140°K. Specific fuel consumption (SFC) at cruise power 0.158 kg/hp·hr (0.34 lb/hp·hr). Length overall 6,000 mm (19 ft 8¼ in), maximum diameter 1,150 mm (3 ft 9¹⁷⁄₆₄ in); dry weight 3,170 kg (6,990 lb) less propellers. The NK-12MA has a 4,500-hour service life.

The NK-12MA Srs 1 powering the An-22 *sans suffixe* (batches 1-4) was started by a TS-12MA jet fuel starter on the left side of the engine casing – a small gas turbine engine driving the spool directly via a clutch (TS = **toor**bos**tartyor** – turbine starter). The An-22A

(batches 5-7) is powered by NK-12MA Srs 3s featuring VS-12 air turbine starters (*vozdooshnyy startyor*). Compressed air is supplied by a twin pack of TA-6A1 APUs.

The engines are mounted in individual nacelles attached to the underside of the inner wing sections and carried in truss-type bearers; the engine attachment lugs are mounted on the forward and centre casings. Each nacelle consists of a one-piece annular forward fairing, hinged cowling panels and a fixed rear fairing incorporating a ventral oil cooler (with air intake and rear airflow adjustment flap) and a jetpipe.

The engines drive AV-90 eight-blade contra-rotating reversible-pitch automatically feathering propellers with spinners. Diameter 6.2 m (20 ft 4 in), weight 1,600 kg (3,530 lb); speed at take-off power 730 rpm, thrust at take-off power 14,800 kgp (32,630 lbst). The AV-90 has four blades in each row; the front

row rotates anti-clockwise and the rear propeller clockwise when seen from the front. The propellers are fitted with hydraulic devices for changing the blade pitch in flight and for locking the blades in intermediate pitch settings, and with an electro-hydraulic feathering system operating in both automatic and manual mode. The propeller blades feature electric de-icer cuffs. The AV-90 is developed and manufactured by the Stoopino Machinery Design Bureau.

On the An-22A, a pair of Stoopino Machinery Design Bureau TA-6A1 auxiliary power units is installed above one another in the front portion of the starboard main gear fairing for self-contained engine starting, DC ground power supply and air conditioning. The TA-6A has a three-stage axial compressor, a three-stage axial turbine and a GS-12TO DC generator/starter. Length overall 1,585 mm (5 ft 2¹³⁄₃₂ in), width 620 mm (2 ft 0¹³⁄₃₂ in), height 735 mm

The tail unit of An-22PZ UR-64459 languishing at Kiev-Gostomel', with a retired An-2 biplane and the remains of a scrapped An-72 transport prototype beyond. The rudder of the centre fin is locked in the neutral position.

The starboard main landing gear fairing of a Batch 1 An-22. The main gear fairings also accommodate the entry corridors and various equipment.

Above: The port NK-12MA Srs 3 engines and AV-90 contra-rotating propellers of an An-22A.

(2 ft 4⅝ in); dry weight (less generator) 245 kg (540 lb). The TA-6A can operate at ambient temperatures of –60°/+60°C (–76°/+140°F) and altitudes up to 3,000 m (9,840 ft); fuel consumption is 225 kg/hr (496 lb/hr). The air supply rate is 1.35 kg/sec (1.97 lb/sec) in normal mode or 1.8 kg/sec (3.96 lb/sec) in emergency mode for accelerated engine starting, bleed air pressure 4.5 kg/cm² (64.28 psi). The APUs have an upward-opening scoop-type air intake and vertically paired lateral exhausts ahead of the starboard entry door.

Control system: The aircraft has a dual mixed-type control system featuring a wide use of cable linkages. The control system of the An-22 *sans suffixe* (batches 1-4) incorporates BU-65 irreversible hydraulic actuators equipped with devices for switching them over to the emergency (servo tab-actuated) control mode. On the An-22A (batches 5-7) these functions are performed by RP-410T servos. The surfaces used as servo tabs duplicate as geared trim tabs in the main control mode. Switching over from the main con-

trol mode to the emergency mode can be effected both manually and automatically. In the latter case the transition occurs when the pressure in both actuator hydraulic systems falls to 110 kg/cm² (1,561 psi) on the An-22 *sans suffixe* or to 70 kg/cm² (994 psi) on the An-22A.

Control forces on the control columns and pedals both in the main and the emergency control mode are created by artificial-feel units in the pitch and roll channels. The electric mechanisms of the automatic load feel units are the actuating devices of the ARU-10TV automatic control force adjustment system. The automatic load feel units incorporate electric trim mechanisms which serve as actuators of automatic trimming in the rudder and elevator circuits effected by the automatic control system. The autopilot system servos are connected to the rudder, elevator and aileron control linkages. Locking of the rudders, elevators and ailerons is remote-controlled electrically; it is effected by locking devices (on the An-22 *sans suffixe*) or by servos (on the An-22A). The gust locks can only be engaged when the main landing gear oleos are fully compressed and the throttle levers are in the zero (ie, shutdown) position.

Fuel system: The fuel system comprises fourteen tanks in the wing centre section, ten integral tanks in the wings and six bag-type tanks in the landing gear fairings. They are split into four groups, one for each engine. Each of these groups has four stages (turns) of fuel consumption. The fuel from the tanks of each turn is sent by pumps into the lines supplying fuel to each engine; they are connected via cross-feed valves. Venting of the wing tanks is effected through the wing centre section tanks, which have an outlet into the atmosphere; the tanks housed in the landing gear fairings have their own venting system. The overall capacity of the fuel tanks is 127,000 litres (27,940 Imp gal). Fuel grades used are Soviet T-1, TS-2, T-2 or RT kerosene (or Western equivalents, such as Jet A-1) and their mixtures.

The wing tanks are filled through standardised pressure refuelling connectors in the starboard landing gear fairing, the tanks housed in the landing gear fairings are filled through pressure refuelling connectors in the wheel wells. The aircraft is equipped with fuel jettisoning and inert gas pressurisation systems; the latter system reduces the hazard of explosion if the aircraft is hit by enemy fire.

Electrics: The electric system caters for engine starting, propeller feathering, power supply to instruments and radio communication equipment, for the functioning of the fuel, oil and fire suppression systems, of the anti-icing and heating devices, and for the func-

The captain's and co-pilot's instrument panels of the An-22, with the engine instrument panel in between. Note the weather radar display on top.

Above: The flight engineer's workstation aft of the co-pilot's seat, with banks of engine instruments. It is equipped with a folding table and a cooling fan.

Above right: The navigator's station of a typical 'radar-nosed' An-22/An-22A offers a somewhat smaller field of view as compared to Batch 1 aircraft, but this is considered adequate. The forward/upper instrument panel is dominated by the display and controls of the RLS-P ground mapping radar; a smaller display for the RLS-N weather radar is visible on the right.

Right: The radio operator's station aft of the captain's seat.

Below Right: A section of the overhead circuit breaker panel of the uncoded camouflaged An-22A using the callsign '309'. It features controls for the fuel system, de-icing system and the like.

tioning of the landing gear steering and aircraft control systems.

The An-22 *sans suffixe* has a mixed-type electric power supply system featuring two AC generators and one DC generator on each engine. The onboard circuits include three-phase AC circuits (200 V and 36 V), single-phase AC circuits (200 V, 115 V and 36 V), and a DC circuit (27 V). The An-22A uses a three-phase AC power supply system featuring the installation of one AC generator on each engine, DC power being obtained by using a rectifier. The voltages used are 200/115 V and 36 V three-phase AC, 36 V single-phase AC

The navigator's station also houses part of the electrical equipment which is installed on racks behind the navigator's seat.

and 27 V DC. Emergency DC power supply is ensured by four 20NKBN-25 or 20NKBN-30 nickel-cadmium batteries.

Hydraulics: The hydraulic system comprises the main system and the actuator system. The *main system* includes the port and starboard systems and a system for manually operated pumps. It provides for the operation of the landing gear (retraction/extension and nose-wheel steering), the flaps, the cargo ramp and rear door segment, the wheel brakes, the entry doors and the jacks supporting the rear fuselage during loading/ unloading. The system for manually operated pumps is used during ground maintenance. Hydraulic power

is supplied by three electrically-driven pump units which ensure an operating pressure of 210 kg/cm² (3,000 psi).

The *actuator hydraulic system* comprising two independent systems (likewise, port and starboard) is used for powering the actuators in the rudder, elevator and aileron control circuits. Hydraulic power is supplied by four engine-driven pumps; the operating pressure is 150 kg/cm² (2,135 psi). All systems use AMG oil-type hydraulic fluid (*aviatsionnoye mahslo ghidravlicheskoye*).

Anti-icing system: Hot air de-icing on the wing and tail unit leading edges, engine air intakes and inlet guide vanes, oil cooler and

air/air heat exchanger air intakes, and air conditioning system air intakes located in the landing gear fairings; the air is bled from the engine compressors. Electric de-icing on the propeller blades and spinners, flightdeck windscreens and the navigator's station glazing, and the pitot heads. The heating system ensures protection of the wings and empennage from icing of any intensity at ambient temperatures down to −30°C. De-icing system of the wing and tail unit is switched on manually or automatically by an input from the RIO-2M radioactive isotope icing detector (**rah**dioizo**top**nyy indi**kah**tor obledene**nen**iya). An indicator placed on the outer surface of the fuselage near the starboard cheek window pane of the flightdeck serves for visual control of the amount of ice on the non-heated surfaces and as a back-up means of indicating the onset of icing.

Pressurisation system and oxygen equipment: The pressurisation system and the oxygen equipment ensure normal conditions in the flightdeck and navigator's cockpit, the cabin for cargo attendants and the cargo hold during flights at high altitudes. To provide breathing oxygen for the crew, the cargo attendants and the paratroopers, the aircraft is fitted with devices for collective and individual use which comprise the KP-24M and KP-56T oxygen apparatus, the KP-19 and KP-21 portable oxygen apparatus with oxygen bottles, the KP-23 bail-out oxygen apparatus and spherical bottles for gaseous oxygen with the operating pressure of 150 kg/cm² (2,135 psi).

Avionics and equipment
Navigation and piloting equipment: The flight and navigation equipment ensures automatic air navigation at any time of the year in day and night time, in visual and instrument meteorological conditions, and includes the Koopol-22 avionics suite (which includes an RLS-P ground mapping radar with a 360° field of view and an RLS-N weather radar), an ARK-UD (or ARK-U2) automatic direction finder, an RV-4 radio altimeter with dipole aerials, SD-67 distance measuring equipment and an A-711 long-range radio navigation (LORAN) system with a dorsal strake aerial on the rear fuselage. This set of equipment is used for continuous checking of the aircraft's geographical position, for spotting storm fronts and aircraft on a reciprocal heading or a collision course, for preventing collisions with obstacles and for precision paradropping of various cargoes.

Communications equipment: The radio equipment includes R-847 and R-862 communications radios (two of each type), R-802V and R-832M Evkalipt (Eucalyptus) radios (one of each type), a Peleng (Bearing) communications radio transmitter with an

R-876 receiver and an SPU-8 intercom (*samolyotnoye peregovornoye oostroystvo*).

Identification friend-or-foe system: SRO-2M Khrom (*izdeliye* 023) IFF transponder installed originally, with characteristic triple rod aerials ahead of the flightdeck glazing and under the rear fuselage. Most aircraft later had the SRO-1P Parol'-2D (*izdeliye* 62-01) IFF transponder with equally characteristic triangular aerials fitted.

Data recording equipment: MSRP-12-96 primary flight data recorder type on aircraft up to and including batch 5, replaced by an MSRP-64 primary FDR in batches 6 and 7. The FDR continuously captures 12 parameters, including barometric altitude, indicated airspeed, roll rates, vertical and lateral G forces, control surface deflection and throttle settings, as well as gear/flap transition and the like. An MS-61B cockpit voice recorder, later replaced by a Mars-BM CVR, is provided.

Lighting equipment: Port (red) and starboard (green) navigation lights at the wingtips, white tail navigation light at the tip of the fuselage tail section. Retractable landing/taxi lights under the wing leading edge outboard of the engines. Red rotating anti-collision beacons in teardrop-shaped Perspex fairings under the centre fuselage and on top of the rear fuselage.

Paradropping and cargo handling equipment: The paradropping and cargo handling equipment is intended for delivery of combat and engineering vehicles with their crews and ammunition, as well as troops (up to 227 troopers), to landing sites; for paradropping combat vehicles with the crews, cargoes and hardware items on Type 14P134 and 4P134 pallets, and paratroopers (up to 162).

Loading and unloading of self-propelled vehicles is effected under their own power, using the loading ramp; equipment items that are not self-propelled are loaded and unloaded with the help of two LPT-3000A winches installed in the mainwheel wells in the area of frames 41-43. Loading and unloading of wheelless hardware items and cargoes is effected with the help of four electric overhead gantries with a lifting capacity of 2.5 tonnes (5,500 lb) each, travelling on rails. To accommodate personnel, the cargo hold and the cabin for cargo attendants are equipped with detachable seats for troopers; the seats are installed along the sides and down the centreline of the cargo hold and are fitted with safety belts.

For paradropping the cargo hold is equipped with trooper seats, a system of static line attachment cables for automatically actuating the extractor parachutes, with devices for stowing away the static lines (only for troopers leaving the aircraft through the side doors in the landing gear fairings) and

Above: The Soviet Air Force began evaluation of the An-22 in 1967. Here a Batch 1 aircraft disgorges a theatre ballistic missile erector/launcher, with a sister ship coded '10 Yellow' in the background.

Leather-jacketed An-22 crewmembers walk to the debriefing room after a well-accomplished mission.

barriers. For dropping cargoes the cargo hold is equipped with four roller tracks, a system of lifting and suspending the extractor parachutes and with an electric system for controlling the paradropping; a P134-T powered chain-type conveyor is provided for cargoes on pallets. A centrally mounted barrier divides the paratroopers into two streams and protects them from the conveyor, while the side barriers flanking the cargo ramp protect the paratroopers from the slipstream by closing the gap between the sloping edge of the rear fuselage aperture and the ramp.

In the medevac version the cargo hold accommodates standard stretchers for 102 sick or wounded persons; the stretchers are mounted in four-tier blocks arranged in seven rows. Medical attendants are provided with

seats and specially equipped tables for medical use; a first-aid dressing station is provided on board.

Fire suppression equipment: The fire suppression equipment comprises a stationary fire suppression system and portable hand-held fire extinguishers. The engine nacelles are fitted with shields and firewalls. The APUs are installed in isolated bays and are protected by firewalls. The stationary fire suppression system comprises two independent centralised systems: the aircraft system and the system for fire suppression in the inner space of the engines. The fire extinguishers are remote-controlled electrically; they are triggered either automatically by sensors of the warning system or manually from the flightdeck.

Above: Two An-22s have already cranked up their engines while the aircraft in the foreground is about to do so.

Basic specifications of the An-22

Length overall	57.31 m (188 ft)
Height on ground	12.535 m (41 ft 1½ in)
Wing span	64.40 m (211 ft 4 in)
Wing area, m² (sq ft)	345 (3,713)
Length of cargo hold	32.7 m (107 ft 3½ in)
Empty weight, kg (lb)	118,727 (261,793)
Maximum fuel weight, kg (lb)	43,000 (94,800)
All-up weight, kg (lb):	
normal	205,000 (420,250)
maximum	225,000 (496,125)
Maximum payload, kg (lb)	60,000 (132,300)
Speed, km/h (mph):	
maximum	600 (373)
average cruising speed	580 (360)
lift-off speed	255 (158)
landing speed	240 (149)
Service ceiling, m (ft)	8,000 (2,240)
Range, km (miles):	
maximum	11,000 (6,837)
with a maximum payload	5,000 (3,108)
Take-off run, m (ft)	1,460 (4,789)
Landing run, m (ft)	1,045 (3,428)

Rescue and survival equipment: The An-22 is properly equipped to ensure the survival of the crew and cargo attendants during an emergency landing on land or a ditching. The rescue equipment comprises two escape ropes near a hatch in the floor of the upper deck cabins; two PSN-6A inflatable life rafts and 14 PSN-20AK life rafts, and ASZh-58 life vests for persons accommodated in the cabin for cargo attendants, as well as an emergency food supply. The aircraft is also provided with a PTL-100A escape chute in combination with a PSN-6A life raft.

Armament: Two KD3-226 cassette-type racks in the port landing gear fairing for carrying and dropping four radio beacons (used by incoming aircraft for homing in on the drop zone) and two KDS-16GM1 cassette-type racks in the starboard landing gear fairing for accommodating and dropping two chaff dispensers for setting up passive electronic countermeasures. From Batch 2 onwards all An-22s are fitted with an optical/IR sight with a shutter making up part of the Koopol-22 avionics suite; it is installed in a fairing immediately ahead of the chin radome.

The An-22 in action

The operational career of the An-22 has been primarily associated with its service in the military airlift units of the Soviet Air Force (and later the Russian Air Force). Officially the first squadron to be equipped with the An-22s was set up in February 1967, when the Commander-in-Chief of the Air Force issued an order to this effect; it was the 5th Squadron of the 229th VTAP (Military Airlift Regiment) based at Ivanovo-Severnyy AB in Central Russia's wheat belt and equipped with An-8s and An-12s. However, it was not until January 1969 that the squadron took delivery of its first two An-22s, CCCP-09317 and CCCP-08840 (c/ns 8340108 and 8340109). Later in that

This uncoded aircraft (formerly CCCP-09309) was the only An-22 to receive a three-tone camouflage. Note the flare dispensers atop the main gear fairings for protection against heat-seeking missiles.

year the regiment received a further four aircraft. The An-22s underwent service trials and took part in the *Vostok* (East) exercise, in the course of which they airlifted combat vehicles, military cargoes and troops.

The introduction of the An-22 into squadron service proceeded with the active participation of the Antonov OKB, which sent its representatives to Ivanovo and later to other regiments operating the aircraft. The An-22s represented an important addition to the Soviet military transport aviation fleet, significantly boosting its airlift potential.

On 26th March 1970 the Air Force C-in-C issued an order to the effect that a new military airlift regiment equipped solely with the An-22s be set up at Ivanovo. This was the 81st VTAP based on the 5th squadron of the 229th VTAP. In July 1970 five An-22 from the Ivanovo-based regiment took part in a humanitarian airlift for the people of Peru who had suffered from a devastating earthquake. A total of 60 flights were made and 250 tonnes (551,000 lb) of cargoes were carried. It was during this quake relief mission that the first loss of an Antheus occurred. On 18th July An-22 CCCP-09303 (c/n 00340207) with 26 persons on board went missing over the Atlantic Ocean en route from Keflavik airport, Iceland, to Lima with a cargo of food and medicines. A thorough and lengthy search was undertaken by NATO aircraft and a Soviet An-12, but only a few traces of the crash were found. These included a swamped life raft and remnants of packages that had contained medical equipment. The cause of the crash was never established with certainty, as the aircraft was lost in the notorious Bermuda Triangle. (Note: The registration of An-22 c/n 00340207 has also been reported as CCCP-09307 No.1; this registration was later reused for an An-22A which was retained by the Antonov OKB.)

Another An-22 *sans suffixe* crashed in December 1970. It was one of the four aircraft that were engaged in the delivery of aid to India for the people who had been made homeless as a result of a flood. The machine in question was CCCP-09305 No.1 (c/n 9340205). All four engines quit 40 minutes after take-off from Dacca (in what was then eastern Pakistan). The crew succeeded in re-activating one of the engines and bringing the aircraft to the airfield in Panagarh, India, but here their luck ended. The aircraft overshot the runway onto rough ground, breaking up, and was consumed by the ensuing fire.

The cause of the crash was traced to one of the propeller blades breaking off and severing the engine control runs. Investigation revealed faulty production methods in the manufacture of the AV-90 propellers which led to the appearance of cracks in the blade roots. In January-February 1971 all propellers

Two An-22As are prepared for a mission. Note the open APU intake door on top of the starboard main gear fairing of the aircraft in the foreground.

were removed from the An-22s and sent to the manufacturer for inspection and sorting out. Improvements were introduced into production procedures to preclude any further cases of blade separation in flight.

After the crash in India An-22 operations resumed in February 1971. The aircraft flew missions both inside the country and abroad. An example of the latter was the use of nine An-22s for the delivery of combat hardware and other military cargoes to the United Arab Republic (the short-lived union of Egypt and Syria) in the spring and autumn of 1972. The loads on these aircraft on their return flights included three Israeli Centurion tanks captured by Egyptian troops.

At the end of 1971 a second regiment operating the An-22 started its formation. The new unit, designated the 556th VTAP, was established in November 1972 at Seshcha AB near Bryansk, Russia. In October 1973, when a new Arab-Israeli war (the Six-Day War) broke out, the An-22s of the new regiment delivered combat materiel and military cargoes to the Middle East. During the same year the Seshcha-based regiment was the first to receive modified versions of the An-22.

On 3rd January 1974 the Central Committee of the Communist Party and the Soviet Council of Ministers issued a directive officially including the An-22 into the Air Force inventory. The year of 1975 saw the formation of a third regiment equipped with the An-22; this was the 8th VTAP based at Migalovo AB near Kalinin (now renamed back to Tver'). Thus, the 12th VTAD (*voyenno-trahnsport-naya aviadiveeziya* – Military Airlift Division) came to have 63 Antheus aircraft on strength. The Division's aircraft continued to fly long-range missions to destinations abroad. In November 1975 a fleet of 17 An-22s delivered cargoes with a total weight in excess of 1,000

tonnes (2,200,000 lb) for the People's Army of Angola. In March 1977, following a serious rift between Mongolia and the People's Republic of China which threatened to escalate into a military conflict, 32 An-22s performed 68 flights, airlifting 1,250 tonnes (2,756,000 lb) of combat materiel and military cargoes to an airfield close to the Soviet border with Mongolia. In November-December 1977 the An-22s of the 8th and 81st VTAPs took part in the delivery of military aid to Ethiopia.

The An-22 crews mastered their machines well, and more than once they showed high skill in coping with emergencies and unusual situations. Unfortunately, such situations did not always end well. There were several fatal accidents. One of them happened in December 1976, when the Seshcha-based first production An-22A (CCCP-09318, c/n 03340501) entered a deep sideslip when the pilot in command applied a too generous bootful of rudder. When the crew captain tried to take corrective action, the aircraft stalled and spun in from 3,000 m (9,840 ft). Human error was the cause of another accident at Seshcha AB: in June 1977 An-22 *sans suffixe* CCCP-09349 (c/n 02340405) failed to lift off during the take-off run and crashed into the forest beyond the runway; the crew walked away but the aircraft was a write-off. It turned out that the crew had tried to take off with the gust locks still engaged! Yet another Antheus – the fifth – was lost in June 1980. When An-22A CCCP-09311 (c/n 043481251, l/n 06-01) was on approach to runway 02 at Moscow-Vnukovo airport, a fire which broke out due to a malfunction and overheating of the DC batteries. Smoke poured into the flightdeck, causing the pilots to misjudge the final approach and the aircraft undershot into a field just short of the Moscow-Kiev highway, burning out completely.

A special chapter in the military career of the An-22 is associated with the type's role in the Afghan War. When the Soviet Union sent its troops into Afghanistan, the An-22s performed numerous flights alongside other Soviet military transport aircraft (primarily An-12s and IL-76s), delivering materiel, supplies and replacement troops to Soviet garrisons. On their way back the aircraft evacuated the wounded and sick personnel.

To ensure protection against heat-seeking shoulder-launched SAMs used by the Mujahideen guerrillas, special procedures had to be adopted. These included the use of a steep spiral path for climb or landing approach to stay well within the protected airfield area (a tactic similar to the 'Khe Sanh tactical approach' introduced by the USAF during the Vietnam War); this was a hard trial both for the crew's skill and the aircraft's structural strength. One more protective measure against the SAMs consisted of providing the An-22s with APP-50 flare dispensers which were mounted in boxy housings atop the main landing gear fairings. This measure was introduced after the shootdown of An-22 CCCP-08837 (c/n 7340106) in Kabul on 28th October 1984. Five machines were fitted with these devices. These dispensers were removed as unnecessary after the war.

In 1987 the Seshcha-based 556th VTAP re-equipped with the new An-124 heavy transport aircraft; the regiment's An-22s were transferred to the other two regiments based at Ivanovo-Severnyy and Kalinin-Migalovo. The 81st and 8th VTAPs retained their An-22s as late as 1997 and in subsequent years, the numbers of airworthy aircraft gradually dwindled. The An-22s of the 81st VTAP were used on numerous occasions for delivering cargoes and personnel to 'hot spots'. For example, in August 1992 this regiment airlifted the personnel of peacekeeping forces to Abkhazia during the Georgian-Abkhazi ethnic conflict and evacuated civilian population from that area. In December 1994 these aircraft took part in the deliveries of military cargoes to the Northern Caucasus in connection with the First Chechen War that had just begun. In January 1996 the An-22s airlifted Russian peacekeeping personnel to Bosnia and Herzegovina.

The An-22s were mostly operated in Aeroflot colours with civil registrations, although they never were part of the Aeroflot fleet. However, despite their primarily military role, these aircraft made a sizeable contribution to transportation jobs performed for civil purposes, whether it be cargo deliveries for the national economy or humanitarian missions of various kind. (some of which were mentioned above). For some obscure reason, unlike most Soviet civil (and quasi-civil) aircraft, the An-22s never adopted the 1973-standard fleetwide livery of Aeroflot, the two An-22PZs being the only exception. The rest of the fleet retained a rather nondescript grey/white livery as a reminder of the days when every single type operated by the Soviet airline had a livery of its own, and sometimes several. To make matters worse, many An-22s had a very weathered and untidy appearance.

The use of the An-22 in the national economy started when the first prototypes were still undergoing manufacturer's tests. For example, in March 1969 Antonov OKB crews flying CCCP-46191 and CCCP-56391 made 24 flights in the oil-rich Tyumen' region, transporting large-size single cargoes with a total weight of 625 tonnes (1,378,000 lb) for the oil industry and geological prospecting teams. In 1970 the first prototype An-22 performed numerous flights in Siberia, catering for the needs of the builders of the Alexandrovskoye to Anzhero-Soodzhensk oil pipeline. On 25th November 1970 a crew captained by I. Ye. Davydov flying An-22 *sans suffixe* CCCP-67691 No.1 (c/n 7340106) performed a unique airlift operation, delivering a 50-tonne (110,000-lb) diesel-electric power station from Leningrad to Cape Schmidt in Chukotka.

The An-22's ability to make use of unprepared airstrips became a valuable asset during its operations in the harsh conditions of Siberia and the High North. A case is on record when an An-22 made a landing on a swamp that had frozen to a depth of only 40 cm (15¾ in). The work performed by An-22s in these regions of the country proved to be a highly efficient undertaking, saving a lot of time and money for the enterprises engaged in oil extraction and other branches of economy.

Later the An-22s were used on several occasions for delivering Russian goods, including military hardware, to foreign customers. In the period between March and May 1995 the 8th VTAP delivered to Vietnam several Sukhoi Su-27 fighters purchased by the Vietnamese People's Air Force.

The An-22 has never been sold to foreign operators, but at least once it did carry a foreign registration on its fuselage. In 1992 the former second An-22PZ (CCCP-64460, c/n 6340103) was wet-leased for six months by the Bulgarian carrier SiGi Air Cargo and temporarily registered LZ-SGB, subsequently operating in the colours of cargo charter carrier Air Sofia as LZ-SFD before returning to the Ukraine as UR-64460. Piloted by Antonov OKB pilots Yu. Kurlin and V. Lysenko, it made many flights to different countries, delivering, for example, Mi-8 helicopters from Poland to the Seychelles Islands.

Over the years, several An-22s have been retired and scrapped. Luckily, the An-22 has been preserved for posterity in several aeronautical museums both in Russia and abroad. In Russia, An-22 *sans suffixe* CCCP-09334 (c/n 00340209) became part of the collection of the Soviet Air Force Museum (now called Central Russian Air Force Museum) in Monino south of Moscow. It has an interesting background. In 1987 this machine took part in airlifting a number of Mi-8T helicopters to Ethiopia and made a hard landing during a thunderstorm with no lights on the runway. The landing resulted in a failure of the middle port landing gear unit and damage to the port main gear fairing and a wing panel. The aircraft was repaired, but it was deemed inadvisable to continue its operation, and it was turned over to the museum.

Another An-22 that has found a resting place in a museum is the second prototype, which in its latter days had been operated by the Antonov Design Bureau as UR-64460. This machine was used by the OKB in various test programmes; as noted earlier, at one time it was converted into the second of two An-22PZ 'wing carriers' for the delivery of assemblies of the An-124 and, later, the An-225. In early 1998 it was offered for sale. After a lengthy period of hard negotiations it was acquired by Technikmuseum Speyer in Germany where it arrived on 29th December 1999 under its own power. Another An-22 was due for preservation at the Military Transport Aviation Museum at Ivanovo-Severnyy AB as of this writing.

The An-22 is a venerable aircraft with close to 40 years of operation to its credit (18th August 2004 mark the 40th anniversary of the rollout of the first An-22 prototype). Despite its age, it was technically capable of soldiering on well into the 21st century. In the early 1990s the service life of the An-22s was extended by a further 30 years, which – at least in theory – gave them a chance to soldier on into the second decade of the new century. In the mid-1990s there were plans to upgrade the An-22s by fitting them with modern navigation avionics, including a satellite navigation system. In 2001 a report in a military publication surmised that after 2010 the Russian Military Transport Aviation was likely to have on strength such updated aircraft types as the An-124-100, the IL-76MD-90 'and, possibly, the An-22-100' (the latter designation presumably referred to an eventual update of the An-22 on the same lines as the An-124-100). However, economic difficulties that plague the country and its armed forces seem to have shortened the aircraft's career. A report published in August 2003 stated that some 15 An-22s were still on strength with the Russian Air Force but were scheduled to be phased out 'in the nearest time'. Several examples of the An-22 remained at that time in the Ukraine, one of them being operated by the Ukrainian Air Force.

Chapter 3

Enter the Big Jets

An-122 heavy transport (project)

The advent of the world's first wide-body transport aircraft, the An-22, in 1965 marked the beginning of yet another stage in the long-lasting race between the Soviet Union and the USA for superiority in the creation of gigantic winged machines. Actually efforts to create something bigger and better had begun in the USA in parallel – or maybe even in anticipation of – the An-22's development. Thus in the early 1960s the Douglas Aircraft Company undertook project studies under the US Air Force's CX-HLS (Experimental Cargo-Heavy Logistics Support) programme. These included the Model D-906 project – a similarly sized aircraft powered by six turbofans in the 13,600-kgp (30,000-lbst) thrust class, with an MTOW of 274,880 kg (606,000 lb) and a 88,450-kg (195,000-lb) payload. The D-906 had a circular-section fuselage, shoulder-mounted wings with moderate sweepback and slight anhedral, conventional swept tail surfaces with dihedral tailplanes, three engine nacelles on evenly spaced pylons under each wing and a high-flotation landing gear comprising five independent struts, each with four wheels on a single axle (this design would later be used on the Il'yushin IL-76 transport). Straight-in loading from both ends was envisaged; to this end the entire fuselage nose, including the flightdeck, was to swing open to starboard, creating a full-width loading hatch with a vehicle loading ramp.

In April 1965 Douglas submitted the Model D-920 project as a bid for the CX-HLS competition; the aircraft was broadly similar to the earlier D-906 project, except that it was powered by four 18,145-kgp (40,000-lbst) high-bypass turbofans (to be supplied by General Electric or Pratt & Whitney) and the fuselage had a 'double-bubble' cross-section. Like the Boeing contender, the D-920 lost to the Lockheed L-500 which entered production and service as the C-5A Galaxy. This huge four-turbofan aircraft was obviously superior to the An-22 in payload and other basic performance characteristics.

This fact was not only detrimental to the prestige of the Soviet aircraft engineering; in due course of time it could result in a drastic increase in the strategic mobility of the US armed forces which were already keeping half the world under their control. Prompted by the wish to ensure an adequate response, the Central Committee of the Communist Party and the Soviet Council of Ministers issued directive No.564-180 dated 21st July 1966 and entitled *'On the main directions of the development of aircraft technology and armament in the period between 1966 and 1970'* which called for increasing the cargo-carrying capacity of Soviet military transport aircraft to 100-120 tonnes (220,500-264,600 lb). On 5th August and 13th September of that year MAP issued appropriate orders No.352 and No.413 which formed the basis for starting the design work on this subject at the Kiev Mechanical Plant (as the Antonov OKB was referred to in unclassified correspondence at that time), Chief Designer A. Ya. Belolipetskiy being put in charge of this design work. On 8th August a special ruling No.26 on this issue was also adopted by the CofM Presidium's Commission on defence industry matters (VPK).

The first attempt at creating the new aircraft reflected a natural wish to make use of the available technological reserve provided by the An-22. The proposal envisaged fitting the An-22's fuselage with new swept wings, a T-tail and four turbofans with a take-off rating of 25,000 kgp (55,125 lbst) apiece. The cargo hold measuring 32.7 x 4.4 x 4.4 m (107 ft 3¹³⁄₃₂ in x 14 ft 5¼ in x 14 ft 5¼ in) was expected to accommodate cargoes and vehicles with a total weight of 80 tonnes (176,400 lb); this load was to be carried over a distance of up to 3,500 km (2,175 miles). Designated An-122 (first use of the designation), the aircraft was expected to have a take-off weight of 270 tonnes (595,350 lb).

In October 1967 Oleg K. Antonov and V. F. Yeroshin, head of the Antonov OKB's prospective designs section, submitted an appropriate proposal to the VPK. The proposal was rejected because the aircraft's payload/weight ratio, lift/drag ratio and fuel efficiency (that is, all the characteristics that determine the degree of technical perfection) did not surpass the average level of the 1960s and the machine could not be regarded as a worthy competitor to the Galaxy.

An-126 heavy transport (project)

Having relinquished the hope of producing the new aircraft as a direct derivative of the An-22, by the middle of the following year the designers evolved simultaneously two preliminary development projects; these were the An-126 capable of carrying a payload of 140 tonnes (308,700 lb) and the An-124 with a load-carrying capacity of 120 tonnes (264,600 lb). Both of them were based on the latest achievements of science and technology and were expected to surpass the characteristics of the US aircraft as regards the flight performance and the capabilities of the surveillance and sighting system and the defensive equipment. This was especially true for the An-126 which was fitted with six underslung turbofans on wing-mounted pylons.

The cargo hold measuring 37.5 x 6.4 x 4.4 m (123 ft x 21 ft x 14 ft 5¼ in) permitted the vehicles to be arranged in two rows and made it possible to effect loading and unloading simultaneously via a rear cargo hatch and a forward loading ramp; unlike the Douglas D-906 project, however, the An-126 was to feature a T-tail and a C-5 style upward-hinging nose visor ahead of the flightdeck. It would seem that the technical solution was found; however, TsAGI specialists succeeded in convincing the Government that implementation of the project of a six-engined aircraft entailed an excessive technical risk.

An-124 heavy transport (*izdeliye* 200) (project)

After a comprehensive study of the problem the VPK took a decision to select for further development the four-engined version designated An-124 which had the in-house OKB designation '*izdeliye* 200'. The designers were faced with a task of extreme complexity: not only were they expected to achieve a two-fold improvement of the transport capacity of their previous progeny, the An-22, but they were also to reduce considerably the maintenance man-hours, increase the operational autonomy and improve a number of other important characteristics. Soon the general configuration of the machine was finalised, and a full-size mock-up was built in 1973. However, the approaches which had been adopted during the design work on the '*izdeliye* 200' were still of a too conservative nature and did not permit achieving the necessary level of perfection of the design. Bearing in mind the great leap that had to be made in the dimensions and technological level of

This crude artist's impression published in *Jane's All the World's Aircraft* was based on either satellite imagery or brief glimpses of the real thing during State acceptance trials.

the aircraft, new approaches were required for its implementation; for this reason the aircraft in the '*izdeliye* 200' version did not reach the hardware stage.

An-124 heavy transport (*izdeliye* 400) prototypes

In 1976 Oleg K. Antonov took a hard decision to rework completely the project under development; the reworked project was assigned a new in-house designation '*izdeliye* 400'. In January of the following year one more directive (No.73-23) was issued by the CPSU Central Committee and the Council of Ministers; this document endorsed the General Designer's decision and formulated new requirements for the aircraft.

To ensure the required technical level of the new An-124 aircraft which was soon dubbed Ruslan (pronounced *Rooslahn*; a Russian knight, a folklore hero immortalised by Aleksandr S. Pushkin in his poem *Ruslan and Lyudmila*), for the first time in the USSR a special comprehensive purpose-oriented programme named KTsP-124 (*kompleksno-tselevaya programma*) was evolved and implemented. It envisaged the improvement of all factors contributing to the aircraft's efficiency: aerodynamic properties, structural strength and service life characteristics, weight saving level, the engines' SFC and other specific characteristics, functional capabilities of onboard systems and equipment, man-hours required for maintenance and repairs and so on.

The adoption of this programme not only played a decisive role in the creation of the Ruslan but also gave a powerful impetus to the development of the Soviet aircraft industry as a whole. New tasks were given to engine designers and manufacturers, to avionics designers, to metallurgists, to specialists developing machine tools and, of course, to scientists working at TsAGI and other aircraft industry research institutions. In the search for an optimum combination of parameters 540 (!) possible versions of the

aircraft's layout were analysed; 185 different models, including 36 wing versions, were subjected to wind tunnel tests. A great leap was made in production methods: unique stamped wing panels measuring up to 28 m (92 ft) in length were developed; new structural materials with improved properties were created, including polymer composites; long-life fasteners were developed. As a result of the measures implemented, the aircraft's lift/drag ratio in cruise flight was increased by 20%, the payload/weight ratio was improved by 10-15%, the engines' SFC was reduced by the same factor, navigation precision was increased fourfold, and man-hours required for various kinds of maintenance were reduced by a factor of two to five as compared to the An-22 and IL-76 transport aircraft!

Dozens of enterprises and institutions within the frameworks of various ministries and government departments were involved in the implementation of the programme. To control this extremely complicated co-operation, special bodies were set up; they comprised the Central Co-ordination Council (subdivided into sections for various tasks) and the Council of Chief Designers. The sessions of these two bodies were used for discussing not only the current questions of the Ruslan's development but also scientific and technical problems that arose in the process. Co-ordination of various kinds of work within the programme and adoption of decisions on key issues were effected by Oleg K. Antonov's First Deputy Pyotr V. Balabuyev, with the General Designer conducting overall guidance of the work.

A few words should be said about the choice of the aircraft's popular name. Antonov was offered no less than six versions of the name; all of them were associated with Greek mythology in some way or other (a sequel to the Antheus precedent). This was not to the liking of the General Designer who wanted something of Slavic origin, something alluding to epic folklore heroes. Among the names seriously considered by him was even

the name Taras Bool'ba (a Cossack from a novel of the same name by Nikolay V. Gogol'), but thankfully this was dismissed and preference was given to the word Ruslan (a Russian folklore hero) owing to its brevity.

One of the key factors that had ensured obtaining the required characteristics during the transition from *izdeliye* 200 to *izdeliye* 400 was the use of wings utilising supercritical airfoils. This was the first time such an approach was practised in the USSR, and it provoked an intense clash of opinions. Usually swept wings feature a thin airfoil section; the use of supercritical airfoil sections made it possible to use thick wings, with the upper and lower skins widely spaced, without increasing the wings' aerodynamic drag. All other conditions being equal, this wing structure was lighter and less demanding to production methods as compared to thin wings; also, the resulting extra volume made it possible to house a considerable amount of fuel. At the same time the supercritical airfoil entailed a high degree of technical risk and posed a number of new requirements to onboard systems. After a thorough analysis several scientists and the majority of aerodynamics experts within the Design Bureau came to the common conclusion that the wings should retain a classic design, and only a small group of the company's specialists (ten or twelve persons) persistently argued for the need to make use of the new airfoil sections. In this difficult situation the General Designer personally opted for the wings of the new type; the wisdom of this choice was fully borne out by subsequent experience. Oleg K. Antonov himself made a drawing of the wings and made the first calculations (during the work on the *izdeliye* 200 and *izdeliye* 400 he personally did much drawing work, striving to refine the aircraft's contours).

In order to fully use the advantages offered by the supercritical wings, it was necessary to incorporate a low margin of static stability in the pitch channel; under such circumstances normal flight could be ensured by fitting the aircraft with a fly-by-wire (FBW) control system comprising a number of analogue computing devices. Another factor prompting the use of FBW controls was the sheer size of the aircraft: its big dimensions entailed correspondingly big deformations of the airframe under external stresses or as a result of thermal expansion. The use of a traditional control system in which the control inputs are transmitted to the servo by wire linkages or rods, appeared very problematic because of these deformations. In addition, the weight of this system would be prohibitive. The use of FBW controls enabled the designers to save 3.7 tonnes (8,160 lb) of airframe weight thanks to the reduced stresses on the wings and the tail unit, and a further 3 tonnes

(6,615 lb) by relinquishing the mass balance of control surfaces. This was accompanied by assigning the task of flutter suppression to servos under the control of the FBW system. Moreover, it proved possible to incorporate into the new control system an automatic stability augmentation system (SAS) which eliminated the undesirable peculiarities of the aircraft's handling at high angles of attack, as well as a device preventing the onset of extreme flight modes.

The An-124's design parameters were chosen very carefully. For example, when determining the dimensions of the cargo hold, a huge number of payload variations involving both military and civil cargoes was studied. As a result, it was acknowledged that a two-row arrangement of cargoes (vehicles) would be the optimum solution, and the width of the cargo cabin floor was set at 6.2 m (20 ft 4 in). At Antonov's initiative, for the first time in the OKB's practice a cargo-handling test rig was built, and the whole range of vehicles used by a mechanised infantry division was rolled through it in various combinations, together with other major cargo types. As a result, the General Designer personally took a decision to increase the cargo floor width to 6.4 m (21 ft).

Among the aircraft's special features mention should be made of the two cargo hatches which made it possible to ensure straight-through passage of wheeled vehicles and thus reduce considerably the time needed for loading and unloading. This rather complex procedure was made more convenient thanks to the use of a multi-wheel landing gear incorporating a 'kneeling' feature which reduced the angle of the loading ramps. The landing gear was designed with a view to reducing loads on the airfield pave-ment, thus expanding the network of operating airfields. Special attention was paid to the dynamic characteristics and rigidity of the undercarriage struts so as to avoid shimmy-type oscillations. The designers studied successively 13 variants of landing gear struts. The final version utilised two separate forward-retracting nose units side by side and five independent inward-retracting main gear struts on each side, with twin wheels on each unit. This not only reduced the huge aircraft's ground pressure but also increased operational reliability, allowing the freighter to land safely if one of the nose units or several main gear struts failed to deploy.

A double-deck fuselage of 'double-bubble' cross-section with separate pressurisation systems for the two decks was also used for the first time in the Design Bureau's practice. This feature made it possible to reduce the weight of the fuselage and increase its service life, as well as to achieve a high safety level for the crew and cargo attendants in the event of a belly landing. The designers succeeded in accommodating the greater part of the onboard equipment in special bays on the upper deck and in providing convenient access to the equipment. This made it possible to fix equipment faults promptly both on the ground and in flight, enhancing the operational efficiency of the aircraft as a whole.

The Zaporozhye-based Progress Engine Design Bureau (ZMKB Progress), then headed by General Designer V. A. Lotarev, was tasked with developing the engine for the An-124. The first project of the Lotarev D-18T high-bypass turbofan rated at 23,400 kgp (51,590 lbst) was largely based on the 18,600-kgp (41,000-lbst) General Electric TF39-GE-1 powering the Lockheed C-5A airlifter. However, the TF39 was a purely military engine which turned out to have a low service life, while the leaders of MAP wanted to have an engine suitable for commercial use (for example, on a possible growth version of the IL-86 wide-body airliner). From this point of view the Rolls-Royce RB.211-22 turbofan powering the Lockheed L-1011 TriStar wide-body airliner was deemed to be a more suitable analogue. In 1976 an MAP delegation headed by Deputy Minister A. Dondukov (who was in charge of engine construction) went to Britain for the purpose of purchasing this engine, with the intention of quietly copying it afterwards. However, the British guessed what the Soviet 'clients' had in mind, and they categorically stipulated that they would sell the engine only in numbers sufficient for equipping not fewer than 100 aircraft. As a result, the USSR never obtained the said engine in hardware form, and the development of the D-18T engine proceeded on an unbeaten track, drawing largely on the experience with the development of the smaller Lotarev D-36 turbofan which powered the An-72/An-74 and the Yakovlev Yak-42 short-haul airliner.

While we are on the subject of the powerplant, it should be noted that one of the An-124's peculiarities consisted of the use of two Stoopino Machinery Design Bureau TA-12 APUs (one in each main gear fairing). This was not so much for the sake of reliability but a safety measure dictated by the aircraft's military transport role. Doubling the amount of bleed air supplied by the APUs allowed the engines to be started simultaneously, saving time – which could be vital if the airfield was under attack and it was necessary to get out of there fast.

For the first time in the USSR a heavy military transport aircraft was equipped with an onboard automated monitoring system

The first prototype An-124, CCCP-680125, demonstrates the impressive capacity of its cargo hold. A Polish-built Jelcz coach, two AA-60 airport fire engines on a MAZ-743 8 x 8 chassis, a Bronto Skylift on a KamAZ-53212 chassis and aTZ-22 fuel bowser line up to enter the aircraft via the rear ramp. Meanwhile, the nose visor is fully open and the ramp is about to deploy, allowing the vehicles to exit that way. Note the 'Ruslan' nose titles in ancient Slavic script.

Above: Soon after the first flight, the first prototype An-124 was equipped with a long pointed air data boom supplanting the weather radar portion of the huge nose radome.

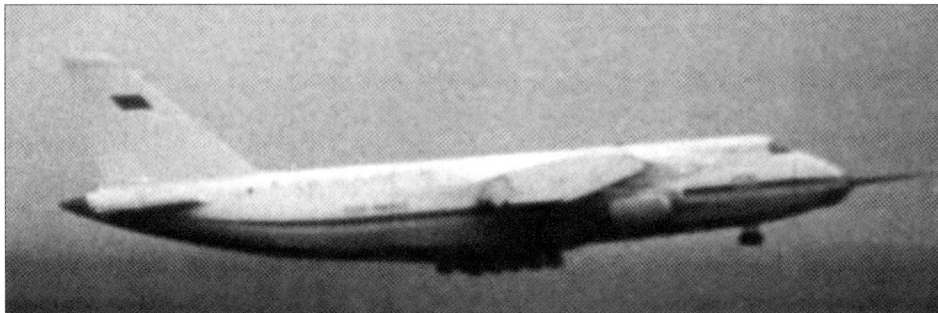

A poor-quality but interesting photo of CCCP-680125 in flight with the air data boom. The 'Ruslan' titles were carried on both sides.

(OAMS) which monitored the operational parameters of the engines, the anti-icing system, the electric supply system, the pressurisation and air conditioning system, the hydraulics, the landing gear and the like. Another important mission of the OAMS consisted of monitoring the crew's activities and, in particular, the observance of prescribed procedures, especially during take-off and landing. In addition, the OAMS came to fulfil a number of totally new tasks, such as determining the weight and CG position on the ground and in flight, the generation of data on malfunctions to be fed into the flight data recorder and into the data link equipment, determining the maximum permissible take-off weight dictated by the airfield conditions and the like.

All this, coupled with many other features, turned the Ruslan into a new-generation aircraft which was superior to the Lockheed C-5 Galaxy in many respects.

Construction of the first prototype An-124 was preceded by a vast programme for the final development and refinement of key design and layout features by means of experiments conducted on test rigs and in laboratories. The results of the work performed by numerous enterprises took the shape of some 3,500 single hardware items which were subsequently subjected to comprehensive testing. Airframe components built specially for test purposes included a prototype wing torsion box, two versions of the flightdeck glazing, a big chunk of the centre fuselage which was initially used for refining the cargo floor design and then for fatigue tests in a pressure tank. Onboard systems were tested and developed on 44 full-scale test rigs and experimental installations; these included test benches and stands for the landing gear, the main powerplant and the APU, the hydraulic system and the like. A special mention must be made of the full-scale control system test rig ('iron bird', in Boeing Company parlance) which was linked with the stand for the wing high-lift devices and was connected to the aircraft's flight simulator. The latter came to play a particularly important role in determining the Ruslan's desired stability and handling characteristics, as well as in evolving the requirements posed for its various systems. This stand fully emulated a flightdeck which was installed on a platform with three degrees of freedom, which created the effect of a real flight. The windscreen panels were emulated by a TV screen which presented the picture of the runway and the surrounding scenery. The simulator made it possible to 'rehearse' most of the flight modes, including approaches and landings, and simulate up to 75% of the situations with various possible failures. In all, the tests conducted on stands and simulators took some 135,000 hours.

For the first time in world practice, on the An-124 a full complement of static tests and fatigue tests was conducted on a single airframe which obviated the need for building yet another airframe and thus saved close to US$ 40 million. The total volume of static tests amounted to 60,000 hours. This unique work was conducted in the structural strength test laboratory of the Kiev Mechanical Plant. All the major aircraft assemblies were tested for strength in Kiev, with the exception of the landing gear units, which passed service life tests in Novosibirsk.

The prototypes of the An-124 (including the static/fatigue test airframe) were built at the Kiev Aircraft Production Association (KiAPO – **Kiy**evskoye aviatsi**o**nnoye proizvod-stvennoye obyedi**nen**iye, formerly MAP plant No.473; now known as the Aviant plant) together with the Kiev Mechanical Plant. Preparation for this work had begun long before the aircraft's technical configuration was finally frozen. For example, in 1973 construction work started on a huge production facility at Kiev-Svyatoshino with a 100-m (330-ft) spacing between the walls; from 1977 onwards the construction of this facility was closely monitored by the Central Committee of the Communist Party of the Ukraine. Detail drawings for the first prototype began to reach the plant from 1979; at about the same time the tooling up for the production was initiated.

Equipment for the aircraft was manufactured in Moscow, Khar'kov and other cities, more than 100 plants taking part in the programme, but it was the TAPO plant (the Tashkent Aircraft Production Association) that became the main partner of the two Kiev-based plants. TAPO manufactured the wing outer panels, wing centre section and large-sized transverse members of the fuselage structure; the finished subassemblies were carried piggyback from Tashkent to Kiev by the two An-22PZ special transports. The Antonov OKB branch office that had existed at the Tashkent plant since the times of the An-22 Antheus had been transformed into TAPO's own design bureau in 1973; therefore, a new branch of the Kiev-based OKB was set up, headed by I. G. Yermolayev.

The best talent of the Antonov OKB and KiAPO was engaged in the construction of the An-124; yet, even as the first prototype with the non-standard registration CCCP-680125 (c/n 01-01) was nearing completion, the engines were still unavailable. The first bench runs of the D-18T commenced barely three months before the Ruslan entered flight test. In accordance with the original plans Yuriy V. Koorlin, Merited Test Pilot and Hero of the Soviet Union, was appointed as the An-124's project test pilot. He took up his job long before the completion of the first prototype, having conducted hundreds of 'flights' in the simulator. His recommendations served as a basis for choosing many parameters of the An-124's control system. However, six months before the maiden flight a medical commission pronounced Koorlin temporarily unfit for flying; the board (top leadership) of MAP endorsed a decision to assign the role of project test pilot to V. I. Terskiy who had accumulated a lot of experience in test flights on the An-22.

On 24th October 1982 the traditional roll-out meeting attended by a host of Kiev Mechanical Plant and KiAPO employees was held in the assembly shop; after that an airport tug towed the first prototype Ruslan out into the open. For security reasons the first taxi tests and high-speed runs of CCCP-680125 were conducted during late evening hours or at night; practically from the outset it became obvious that the D-18T engines were still in a very raw condition. The Flight Research Institute's IL-76LL engine testbed fitted with this turbofan (CCCP-86891, c/n 093421628, l/n 1607A) had barely commenced its flights. In the course of the first prototype's ground checks and development work the inscription 'Ruslan' in stylised Slavic script made its appearance for the first time on the fuselage nose.

On 24th December 1982 at noon the prototype taxied to the runway of the Kiev-Svy-atoshino factory airfield and, after making several high-speed runs, stood on the runway for two hours biding its time. Then, when the sky cleared up a bit, the An-124 performed its first flight. It was flown by a crew comprising factory test pilots V. I. Terskiy and A. V. Galu-nenko, navigator A. P. Poddoobnyy, flight engineers V. M. Vorotnikov and A. M. Shu-leshchenko and radio operator M. A. Toop-chiyenko. An Aero L-39C Albatros advanced trainer piloted by S. A. Gorbik and S. V. Mak-simov flew chase during the An-124's maiden flight. The prototype easily climbed to altitude and in the course of an hour the crew fulfilled the programme for determining some stability and handling characteristics, whereupon the aircraft landed at Kiev-Gostomel'. After the touchdown strong vibrations began in the flightdeck. As it turned out later, it was caused by shimmy oscillations of the main landing gear units; this phenomenon occurred despite all the preventive measures. The crew succeeded in promptly slowing the aircraft down, but not before one of the wheel well doors and several door links had disintegrated; minor as it was, this damage upset Antonov very much. Nevertheless, the successful first flight was a victory.

The first stage of the flight testing conducted at Gostomel' lasted until September 1983, with M. G. Kharchenko and V. S. Mikhaï-lov as project engineers. In the course of that period the aircraft performed 141 flights, logging a total of 251 flight hours. This stage of the testing revealed a problem that was destined to remain the main source of trouble for the Ruslan for many years; it was the low gas flow stability of the D-18T engines, especially at take-off thrust. The problem manifested itself for the first time during the eighth take-off when one of the engines surged and then quit. At that time the runway at Gostomel' was not yet extended and CCCP-680125 had no thrust reversers yet (these were added at a later stage); therefore it was decided to continue the flight and land at Uzin AB. Ground inspection showed that the surge had caused a disintegration of the turbine disc and the runaway blades had punctured the skin of the engine nacelle. In a nutshell, the engine had become inoperative for a long time, so the crew took a decision to make the return flight to Svyatoshino on three engines. For training purposes several runs were made with one and two engines shut down, whereupon the aircraft was ferried first to Gostomel' and then to Svyatoshino where the damaged engine was replaced.

This stage of the testing saw also failures of electronic equipment. Malfunctions were noted in the system for enhancement of flight stability, although it had been assumed that the probability of such failures was extremely low. For testing purposes the landing gear units were temporarily fitted with hydraulic shimmy dampers (they were deleted later) and the rigidity of both nose and main landing gear struts was considerably increased; in addition, the steerable main units were modified (the wheel axle offset was reduced nearly by half).

Again bearing a typical 'Antonov test' registration, CCCP-680345, the second prototype of the Ruslan (c/n 01-03) made its first flight in Kiev in December 1984; the crew was captained by factory test pilot Yu. V. Koorlin.

Bearing only the CCCP- nationality prefix but no digits yet, the second prototype An-124 (c/n 01-03) is seen in an early test flight (probably its first), with the An-74 prototype (CCCP-780334) flying chase.

Above: The oldest and the (then) latest aircraft to bear the Antonov brand – but they are both equally famous. The venerable An-2 utility biplane is dwarfed by the huge An-124. By the way, doesn't that distinctive shape of the Ruslan's nose radome create the impression of a friendly smile?

The second prototype, now wearing the test registration CCCP-680345, flies over picturesque mountain scenery during tests. It was later reregistered CCCP-82002.

(Despite reports that the second An-124 was registered CCCP-680210, c/n 01-02 was in fact the static/fatigue test airframe. Some sources quote the two prototypes' construction numbers as 19530501001 and 19530501003 respectively, using the standard applied to Kiev-built production aircraft; the c/n systems are explained later.) The machine joined the manufacturer's flight test programme and was used for evaluating flight safety during various simulated failures. By 5th October 1985 the aircraft had made 163 flights and logged 289 flight hours within this programme.

In May 1985 the second prototype An-124 (by then reregistered CCCP-82002) was shown to the Soviet press for the first time. Two weeks later the huge aircraft made its international debut at the 26th Paris Air Show. This is how the true designation of the Ruslan became known to the outside world; previously some Western publications had referred to the aircraft by the erroneous designation 'An-400' – no doubt derived from the in-house designation *izdeliye* 400 which had somehow leaked to the West. After its Paris appearance the An-124 received the NATO reporting name *Condor* – a fitting tribute to its huge size, as the condor is the largest flying bird on Earth.

It would be untrue to say that the Western press was unanimous in its praise of the new 'Soviet wonder'; now and then some unfavourable or downright defamatory reports made their appearance – inspired, no doubt, by representatives of the Lockheed Company. Therefore immediately after the Paris Air Show, prompted by the desire to demonstrate to the whole world the An-124's ascendancy over the C-5A, the MAP top brass took a decision to perform several record-breaking flights on this aircraft. As early as 26th July 1985 a crew captained by V. I. Terskiy established no fewer than 21 world records in one flight on the first prototype, including the absolute payload-to-altitude record by lifting a load of 171,219 kg (386,358 lb) to an altitude of 10,750 m (35,260 ft). This was a convincing improvement on the result shown by the C-5A, which had lifted 111,461 kg (245,771 lb) to an altitude of 2,000 m (6,560 ft).

Flights within the joint State acceptance trials programme commenced in November 1983. They were conducted by crews from GNIKI VVS (the new name of GK NII VVS; the new acronym still meant 'State Air Force Research Institute awarded the Red Banner Order') with the participation of Antonov OKB test pilots. Until December 1984 An-124 CCCP-680125 performed 157 flights from Chkalovskaya AB where GNIKI VVS's military transport aviation department was based, logging a total of 304 flight hours, including 18 flights at high angles of attack. The latter

flights' mission consisted of checking the functioning of the system for preventing the onset of extreme flight modes and in determining the effectiveness of the vortex generators mounted on the wing upper surface at the roots for the purpose of precluding any possibility of the onset of stalling angles of attack. These complicated flights were performed by a mixed crew captained by Terskiy and Colonel Bel'skiy, a GNIKI VVS test pilot. Later, two more aircraft – the second prototype (CCCP-82002) and the first Ul'yanovsk-built example registered CCCP-82005 (c/n 9773054516003, l/n 01-07) joined the test programme. The aircraft operating from Chkalovskaya AB performed a total of 189 flights, logging 751 flight hours between them. During the same period flight testing of the D-18T engine was conducted on IL-76LL CCCP-86891 (this testbed made 418 flights, logging a total of 1,285 flight hours), while An-22 CCCP-09301 (c/n 9340203) made 86 flights totalling 313 hours for testing the Ruslan's flight and navigation avionics suite. The final document was signed in December 1986; called 'Act on the results of State acceptance trials of the An-124 prototype heavy long-range military transport aircraft', it opened up for the An-124 the prospects of its operational life.

In the course of the subsequent years special tests of the An-124 were conducted to determine its characteristics in conditions of natural icing and during close-formation flights; in addition, the aircraft's potential for airdropping troops and cargoes was studied. For example, in the spring of 1988 a crew captained by Terskiy, flying the first prototype of the Ruslan, performed 37 flights in search of icing hazard zones over the Barents Sea between the Novaya Zemlya ('New Land') archipelago and the Norwegian island of Björnöya. When the pilots found a suitable

cumulus cloud formation, they flew straight into the clouds, accumulated up to 90 mm (3½ in) of ice on the wings and tail surfaces and then headed for a clear sky zone to check the aircraft's stability and handling. It was then that also the first landing of a heavy transport aircraft was made on an ice-covered airfield located on Graham Bell Island, part of the Zemlya Frantsa Iosifa (Franz Joseph Land) archipelago. At that time the crew captained by Yuriy V. Koorlin (who had resumed his flying activities) performed ten flights on the second An-124 prototype in the wake of another Ruslan which had a tank with 8 tonnes (17,640 lb) of water installed in its cargo hold; the sprinkler pipes from the tank were mounted near the APU exhausts to create an icing environment for the other aircraft.

Between January 1990 and December 1992 a series of certification tests based on the NLGS-3 civil airworthiness standards for fixed-wing aircraft (***Normy lyotnoy godnosti samolyotov***) was conducted on the two prototypes and two production An-124s – Ul'yanovsk-built CCCP-82033 (c/n 9773052832054, l/n 05-07) and Kiev-built CCCP-82027 (c/n 19530502288, l/n 02-08). The tests included evaluation of flight performance, also in high ambient temperatures; determination of the optimum landing configuration; evaluation of methods of reducing the engine warm-up time at the line-up point; evaluation of flight safety during simulated failures of onboard systems; determination of noise levels and so on. It took 266 flights with a total of 732 flight hours to carry out this work. One of these flights (on 13th October 1992) ended in the first crash of the Ruslan. The crew of the second prototype captained by test pilot S. A. Gorbik was fulfilling a mission for determining the characteristics of controllability at a maximum dynamic pressure. At the moment when the ram air pressure reached its peak the

The An-124 final assembly line at the Aviastar plant in Ul'yanovsk; Tupolev Tu-204 airliners are assembled on a parallel line. Note the maintenance hatch in the An-124's nose visor just aft of the radome.

Above: Seen here at Machoolishchi AB near Minsk during a display for the CIS heads of state on 13th February 1992, '09 Black'/CCCP-82038 was the first An-124 to wear military insignia. Note the Antonov Airlines titles.

Another Ruslan in Russian Air Force markings ('10 Black', ex-CCCP-82028). It later became RA-82028.

huge nose radome collapsed; this was followed by the disintegration of the whole hinged nose visor ahead of the flightdeck. The debris caused damage to both starboard engines which became inoperative. In this situation the crew was unable to make it to the airfield, and CCCP-82002 crashed in a wooded area not far from Kiev, killing the crew. This was a heavy loss for the design team, which by then had received the name 'ANTK named after Oleg K. Antonov' (the Antonov Aircraft Science and Production Complex). This crash was due to a coincidence of several negative factors, which included, in particular, a birdstrike as the aircraft took off on its last mission. However, by that time the test were for all practical purposes completed, the aircraft had passed all checks prescribed by the Airworthiness Standards, and the crash could not undermine confidence in the aircraft. On 30th December

1992 CIS Interstate Aviation Committee's Air Register issued a type certificate as a civil transport aircraft to the An-124.

An-124 (*izdeliye* 400) production heavy military transport aircraft

Initially it was envisaged that series production of the An-124 would be launched in Kiev at KiAPO, and so it was; the first production Kiev-built example was CCCP-82006 (c/n 19530501004, l/n 01-04). In the early 1980s, however, the situation took a different turn: it so happened that the newly erected Ul'yanovsk Aircraft Production Complex named after the recently deceased Soviet Minister of Defence Marshal Dmitriy F. Ustinov (UAPK – *Ool'yahnovskiy aviatsionnyy proizvodstvennyy kompleks*) was practically standing idle. This production plant, one of the biggest in Europe, had been built specifically for manufacturing the Tupolev Tu-160

'swing-wing' strategic bomber, but the latter became a victim of the Strategic Arms Limitation Treaty (SALT) which severely limited the Tu-160's production run, leaving UAPK with nothing to build. In 1983 the Soviet Government took a decision to engage this plant in the An-124 production programme. Many specialists and workers came from Ul'yanovsk to Kiev to study the new aircraft. To ensure prompt resolution of design and production issues and to conduct the design bureau's supervision of the work on the tooling up for An-124 production, a representation of the Antonov OKB was set up at the Ul'yanovsk plant.

The first Ul'yanovsk-built production aircraft – the aforementioned CCCP-82005 (c/n 9773054516003, l/n 01-07) – took to the air in October 1985, captained by A. V. Galunenko, an OKB test pilot. According to the plan, in addition to the six aircraft of the first batch, 30 more aircraft from batches 2, 3 and 4 were to be built in Kiev, while the remaining 60 machines were to be built in parallel in Ul'yanovsk (these included three machines from the first batch).

Eventually, however, only 17 production aircraft were manufactured in Kiev. The last-but-one Kiev-built Ruslan, UR-UAP (c/n 19530502702, l/n 03-02) was rolled out of the assembly shop in 1994 and officially released by the plant on 3rd February. One more airframe (c/n unknown, l/n 03-03) sat minus engines and equipment at the Aviant aircraft plant in Kiev for several years due to the lack of a customer which would pay for the completion of the aircraft. Eventually in 2002 the Russian airline Atlant-Soyuz announced that it would buy the aircraft; with funds made available, the aircraft was finally completed in late 2003 and made its first flight on 6th October. Later, however, Atlant-Soyuz was unable to complete the purchase and the aircraft was delivered to a most improbable customer – the United Arab Emirates Ministry of Defence, wearing the Ukrainian registration UR-CCX. The rest of Batch 3 and the entire Batch 4 allocated to KiAPO were never built.

The Aviastar plant, as the former Ul'yanovsk Aircraft Production Complex has been known since 1991, completed 33 aircraft before a temporary interruption in production occurred due to lack of orders – a knock-on effect of the Russian economic crisis; the last 'pre-crisis' aircraft, RA-82078 (c/n 9773054559153, l/n 07-10) was manufactured on 18th September 1996. Lately, however, low-rate production has resumed. As of this writing, 56 Ruslans in various versions had been built, including the prototypes and the static test airframe. The latest example, An-124-100M RA-82081 (see below), made its first flight on 11th April 2004 and at least one aircraft was awaiting completion.

In May 1987 An-124 CCCP-82008 (c/n 19530501007, l/n 01-08) flown by a mixed OKB/Soviet Air Force crew captained by test pilot V. I. Terskiy performed on a non-stop flight along the borders of the Soviet Union. The aircraft covered a distance of 20,151 km (12,523.9 miles), remaining airborne for 25 hours and 30 minutes. Incidentally, the take-off weight on that occasion reached a record figure of 455 tonnes (1,003,275 lb). A world closed-circuit distance record was thus established, beating the previous achievement of the Boeing B-52H Stratofortress (18,245.5 km/11,339.65 miles).

In 1989 the same machine was equipped for paradropping; dummies and mock-ups simulating the weight of military hardware, including single cargoes weighing up to 25 tonnes (55,125 lb) were airdropped from the aircraft. While the air-dropping of cargoes posed no problems, the results of experiments with the dummies made the designers think hard. Powerful vortices behind the huge fuselage tossed the dummies about and caused the static lines of the extractor parachutes to become entangled. Finally, it was concluded that the air-dropping of people through the rear loading hatch was not safe; to enable paratroopers to leave the aircraft, it was decided to arrange an additional troop door on each side immediately aft of the main landing gear fairings, Lockheed C-130 style. CCCP-82008 was modified accordingly, but the military airlift branch of the Soviet Air Force placed no order for a similar upgrade of the machines it had on strength and the aircraft remained a one-off.

An-124-100 heavy commercial transport aircraft

The first modified version of the An-124 Ruslan to reach the hardware stage is the commercial version designated An-124-100. The need for this version arose when the An-124 military transport aircraft began operations on the commercial cargo transportation market while not possessing a formal right to do that due to the absence of a civil type certificate. Competitors fairly quickly put their finger on that weak spot and lodged complaints with the appropriate international bodies. As a result, a formal ban was placed on using the military An-124 for commercial purposes, and the Antonov ANTK had no choice but to update the machine together with the Aviastar Joint-Stock Co. and conduct costly certification tests.

To begin with, the aircraft was stripped of the military equipment for which there was no use any longer; this included certain avionics items and paradropping equipment, as well as devices for handling military cargoes. The complement of oxygen equipment was changed, radios with civil frequency grids were provided, flight and navigation instruments with scales graduated in feet and knots were installed, as were other items of equipment necessary for operations on international air routes. In addition, the maximum flap setting during landing was reduced from 40° to 30°. The rate at which the airframe's service life was used up during commercial flights proved to be 1.7 to 2.2 times quicker than in military service; hence, a new system was evolved specially for the An-124-100 for extending this critically important parameter in each individual case in a fashion that would guarantee safety even during very intensive operations. Refinements were made to the interior trim of the cargo attendants' cabin, toilets were installed, the necessary inscriptions in English were provided and so on.

Manufacture of the civil version of the Ruslan to a special order from the Antonov ANTK was started at the Kiev-based Aviant plant in 1990-91; the first two aircraft built as An-124-100s were CCCP-82027 (c/n 19530502288, l/n 02-08) manufactured on 4th December 1990 and CCCP-82029 (c/n 19530502630, l/n 02-10). After the completion of all certification tests, the Intergovernmental Ukrainian-Russian Decision No.490-93 on the An-124-100 was signed in March 1993. Then, in the period up to 1995, five more new-build An-124-100s were manufactured in Kiev (line numbers 03-01 and 03-02) and Ul'yanovsk (line numbers 07-08 through 07-10); a further 15 An-124s manufactured earlier were converted to An-124-100 standard. All of them were placed into commercial operation.

However, this important and necessary work did not address the main problem that plagued military and commercial Ruslans alike – the low margin of gas flow stability that characterised the D-18T engines from the start of series production. The Russian Ministry of Defence, the aircraft's main operator, displayed no interest in doing anything about it. Nevertheless, in the second half of the 1990s, after a lengthy search for funding sources, the Progress Engine Design Bureau that had developed the engine and the Motor Sich plant that was manufacturing it succeeded in starting production of D-18T Series 3 engines which incorporated the entire set of measures intended to improve the engine's reliability, fuel efficiency and durability. The time between overhauls (TBO) of the D-18T Srs 3 reached 6,000 hours, and there were plans to increase the designated service life to 24,000 hours. However, the price of the new engine soared to a level which most of the Ruslan's present owners could ill afford. Therefore, the operator preferred not to buy the upgraded version of engine, but to update the available engines (Srs 0 and Srs 1) to Srs 3 standard in the course of scheduled overhauls; the resulting engines were known as N-profile engines (the N stood for *nadyozhnost'*, reliability).

Changes were introduced into the aircraft's equipment to meet the ICAO requirements for operations on international routes. For example, hushkits were incorporated into the engine nacelles of the An-124-100 to make the aircraft Chapter III compliant (ICAO Annex 16/Chapter III sets the current ambient noise and pollution standards which commercial aircraft have to meet, and the even more stringent Chapter IV requirements will be enforced in 2006). Work began on fitting the aircraft with the 3M GPS satellite navigation system. In connection with the reduction of vertical separation minima (RVSM) during flights above the Atlantic Ocean to 300 m (980 ft) the necessary modifications were undertaken on the An-124-100s and a supplementary type certificate was obtained. The aircraft were also provided with the TCAS-2000 traffic collision avoidance system manufactured by Honeywell Electronics (USA). In mid-2003 installation work was completed for fitting the aircraft with the SPPZ-3 ground collision avoidance system. Detail drawings for these modifications were sent to the production plants where the machines belonging to various operators are being upgraded now.

Nevertheless, it is becoming increasingly obvious that the aircraft requires a radical upgrade: reducing the crew complement, installing new avionics and new engines. Existing plans envisage providing the majority of the new versions of the Ruslan with modern digital equipment and liquid crystal displays in the flightdeck as a joint effort by Honeywell and the Aviapribor avionics house (Russia). This would make it possible to reduce the weight of the equipment, increase its reliability, widen its functional capabilities and reduce the crew complement to three persons. In accordance with ICAO requirements production aircraft are to be fitted with a new EGPWS ground collision avoidance system and a new satellite communications system. In addition, provision is made for using on this aircraft the procedures for reducing the landing distance that had been tested on the An-70.

The table on page 52 illustrates An-124 production. In the case of Kiev-built aircraft, 195 is a code for the KiAPO/Aviant factory, 305 is a product code for the An-124 (common to both production lines), while the first two of the remaining five digits initially denoted the batch, the last three signifying the number of the aircraft in the batch. (19530501007 is an exception, being the *eighth* aircraft in Batch 1 because the seventh aircraft had gone to the Ul'yanovsk line.) Starting with line number 02-04, however, the last five digits of the c/n ceased to have any meaning – except that the very last digit

An-124 production

Construction number	Line number	Version	Registration/tactical code	Manufacture date	Notes
19530501001?	01-01	An-124	CCCP-680125		C/n probably simply 0101
19530501002?	01-02	An-124	None (static/fatigue test airframe)		C/n probably simply 0102
19530501003?	01-03	An-124	CCCP-680345, CCCP-82002		C/n prob. 0103. Crashed near Kiev 13-10-92
19530501004	01-04	An-124	CCCP-82006, RA-82006		
19530501005	01-05	An-124	CCCP-82007, UR-82007		
19530501006	01-06	An-124	CCCP-82008, UR-82008	31-12-1986	
9773054516003	01-07	An-124	CCCP-82005, RA-82005, '08 Black'		Crashed Irkutsk-2 6-12-97
19530501007	01-08	An-124-100*	CCCP-82009, UR-82009		
9773053616017	01-09	An-124-100*	CCCP-82010, RA-82010	30-12-1986	Slated for conversion into An-124VS
9773054616023	01-10	An-124	CCCP-82011, RA-82011		
19530502001	02-01	An-124	CCCP-82020, RA-82020		
19530502002	02-02	An-124	CCCP-82021, RA-82021		
19530502003	02-03	An-124	CCCP-82022, RA-82022		
19530502012	02-04	An-124	CCCP-82023, RA-82023		
19530502035	02-05	An-124-100*	CCCP-82024, RA-82024		Slated for conversion into An-124VS
19530502106	02-06	An-124	CCCP-82025, RA-82025 'Vladimir Fyodorov'		
19530502127	02-07	An-124-100*	CCCP-82026, '10 Black', RA-82026		Slated for conversion into An-124VS
19530502288	02-08	An-124-100	CCCP-82027, UR-82027	4-12-1990	
19530502599	02-09	An-124	CCCP-82028, RA-82028		
19530502630	02-10	An-124-100	CCCP-82029, UR-82029		
19530502761	03-01	An-124-100	CCCP-82066, UR-82066, 5A-DKL 'Susa'		Error, c/n should be 19530502**701**?
19530502702	03-02	An-124-100	UR-UAP, RA-82003, 5A-DKN 'Sabrata'	3-2-1994	
19530502...3	03-03	An-124	[RA-820...], UR-CCX		
9773052732028	05-01	An-124	CCCP-82012, RA-82012		
977305373203...	05-02	An-124	CCCP-82013, RA-82013		
9773054732039	05-03	An-124-100*	CCCP-82014, RA-82014		Slated for conversion into An-124VS
9773054732045	05-04	An-124	CCCP-82030, RA-82030		
9773051832049	05-05	An-124	CCCP-82031, RA-82031		
9773052832051	05-06	An-124	CCCP-82032, RA-82032		
9773052832054	05-07	An-124-100*	CCCP-82033, '21 Black'/CCCP-82033, RA-82033		
9773053832057	05-08	An-124	CCCP-82034, RA-82034		
977305...83206...	05-09	An-124-100	CCCP-82035, RA-82035		
9773054832068	05-10	An-124	CCCP-82036, RA-82036		
9773052955071	06-01	An-124	CCCP-82037, RA-82037		
9773054955077	06-02	An-124	CCCP-82038, '09 Black'/CCCP-82038		
9773052055082	06-03	An-124	CCCP-82039, RA-82039		
9773053055086	06-04	An-124	CCCP-82040, RA-82040		
9773054055089	06-05	An-124	CCCP-82041, RA-82041		
9773054055093	06-06	An-124-100	CCCP-82042, RA-82042	23-7-1991	
9773054155101	06-07	An-124-100	CCCP-82043, RA-82043		
9773054155109	06-08	An-124-100	CCCP-82044, RA-82044	10-2-1992	
9773052255113	06-09	An-124-100	CCCP-82045, RA-82045		
9773052255117	06-10	An-124-100	CCCP-82067, RA-82067, RA-82046	10-7-1992	
9773053259121	07-01	An-124-100	CCCP-82068, RA-82047		
977305...25912...	07-02	An-124-100	CCCP-82069, RA-82069		Crashed Turin-Caselle 8-10-96
9773051359127	07-03	An-124-100	RA-82070		
977305...5913...	07-04	An-124-100	RA-82071	16-10-1993	Crashed near Kerman, Iran, 15-11-93
9773053359136	07-05	An-124-100	RA-82072, UR-82072		
9773054359139	07-06	An-124-100	RA-82073, UR-82073		
9773051459142	07-07	An-124-100	RA-82074		
9773053459147	07-08	An-124-100	RA-82075		
9773054459151	07-09	An-124-100	RA-82077		
9773054559153	07-10	An-124-100	RA-82078	18-9-1996	
9773052062157	08-01	An-124-100	RA-82079		
977305...	08-02	An-124-100	RA-82080		
977305...	08-03	An-124-100M	RA-82081		
977305...	08-04	An-124-100M	RA-82082?		

Line numbers 03-04 through 03-10 and 04-01 through 04-10 were not built. Aircraft marked with an asterisk were built as An-124s and updated to An-124-100 configuration.

usually matched the last digit of the line number. Ul'yanovsk-built examples have 13-digit c/ns; 977 is again a code for the factory, the seventh and eight digits denote the quarter and year of manufacture, and the remainder is the 'famous last five' with no meaning at all. (It should be noted, however, that the 'quarter/year' digits often do not match the actual manufacture date; eg, c/n 9773054055093 suggests the fourth quarter (October-December) of 1990 but, according to official documents, CCCP-82042 was manufactured on 23rd July 1991!) The location of the c/n on the airframe remains unknown; the line number, however, is found on small metal plates on both sides of the nose loading ramp and the trailing edge of the rear cargo ramp.

An-124-100V heavy transport aircraft
The designation An-124-100V is assigned to the hushkitted An-124-100 with engine nacelles incorporating porous sound-absorbing panels which ensure that the aircraft conforms to Chapter III, Annex 16, of the ICAO standards for ambient noise levels.

Air Force An-124s upgraded to An-124-100 standard
According to a report published in June 2001, three Russian Air Force An-124s were upgraded in Ul'yanovsk to An-124-100 standard; the work on a fourth machine was nearing completion and one more aircraft was scheduled for the upgrade. The machines in question were fitted with GLONASS/ NAVSTAR equipment, TCAS and other modern systems. The aircraft were re-engined with modernised D-18RDM engines taking duly into account the lessons of the Irkutsk tragedy and affording enhanced reliability.

An-124-100M heavy commercial transport aircraft
In 1996-97 the Antonov ANTK transferred to the Aviastar aircraft plant a set of design documentation on an upgraded version designated An-124-100M (*modifitseerovannyy* – modified); it envisaged the replacement of some items of navigation and radio equipment, installation of the D-18T Series 3 engines with sound-absorbing nacelles, and the reduction of the crew from six to four.

Volga-Dnepr Airlines became the launch customer, ordering a new-build An-124-100M in July 2002 with delivery scheduled for the fourth quarter of 2003 (interestingly, the deal was signed at the Farnborough International 2002 airshow), but this schedule was not met. The An-124-100M prototype, RA-82081 (c/n unknown, l/n 08-03) was rolled out at Ul'yanovsk-Vostochnyy on 16th March 2004 and made its first flight on 11th April; it was eventually delivered to Volga-Dnepr Airlines in June. At least one An-124-100M was

Above: An-124-100 RA-82079 in the smart blue/white colours of Russian cargo carrier Volga-Dnepr Airlines.

The An-124 was often used for delivering Russian-made aircraft to foreign customers. Here, Kamov Ka-32A KF-001 for the South Korean fire-fighting service (minus engines and gearbox/rotor mast) is loaded into a Volga-Dnepr An-124-100.

ordered by Polyot/Flight Airlines, and this particular machine (c/n unknown, l/n 08-04) was awaiting completion at the Aviastar plant as of this writing.

An-124-100MV heavy commercial transport aircraft (project)
The designation An-124-100MV is assigned to the An-124-100M in the event of its being equipped with hushkits making the aircraft Chapter III compliant.

An-124-102 heavy transport aircraft (project)
This is a further modification of the An-124-100M featuring a new flightdeck data presentation system making use of multi- functional liquid-crystal displays. The crew complement is to be reduced to three (two pilots and flight engineer).

An-124-130 heavy transport aircraft (project)
This version of the An-124 was to be powered by General Electric CF6-80 turbofans. Studies

for this version were conducted from 1966 in parallel with the An-124-200 (see next entry).

A report in the Western press asserted that in July 1996 the first An-124-130 (l/n 08-03) was nearing completion in Ul'yanovsk. However, the GE company denied any deliveries of its engines to the Aviastar plant; as recounted above, the aircraft in question was eventually completed as the An-124-100M prototype. According to the said report, the An-124-130 version developed without the participation of the Antonov ANTK was to have a four-man flight crew instead of the usual six, with a Rockwell-Collins traffic-alert and collision avoidance system, global positioning system, satellite communications and ACARS data link system.

An-124-200 heavy transport aircraft (project)
Studies have been conducted on re-engining the An-124 with General Electric CF6-80C2 engines; this version is designated An-124-200.

An-124-210 heavy transport aircraft (project)

A project of a version powered by the Rolls-Royce RB211-524H-T turbofans, designated An-124-210, was submitted for participation in the tender announced by the British Ministry of Defence. Re-engining the Ruslan with RB-211s would increase its practical range by 8-10%, reduce the take-off distance considerably and enable the aircraft to take off with a greater payload in hot-and-high conditions.

The An-124-210 was not proceeded with because the British MoD succumbed to the aggressive lobbying by the Boeing Company and selected the C-17A Globemaster III (known as the Globemaster C.1 in Royal Air Force service), four of which were delivered in 2001 on a seven-year lease.

An-124-220 heavy transport aircraft (project)

Very little information exists on this version, except that it is to be powered by Western engines.

An-124-300 heavy transport aircraft (project)

In 2003 work was reported to be conducted on this version which would be capable of carrying a payload of 150 tonnes (330,750 lb); with a 120-tonne (264,600-lb) payload it would have a range of 10,000 km (6,215 miles) as against the current 4,500-km (2,797-mile) range of the An-124-100 with the same payload.

Combi version of the An-124 (project)

The various projected derivatives of the Ruslan included a combi (cargo/passenger) version. The designers of the Antonov ANTK reverted time and again to the studies of this version at different stages of the programme. During the period characterised by optimistic forecasts of passenger air traffic growth in the USSR this version was transformed into a pure airliner version intended for carrying more than 800 persons over a distance of up to 10,000 km (6,215 miles). The fuel efficiency held the promise of reaching the level of 25-26 g/passenger-km (0.0887 to 0.0922 lb/passenger-mile), a record figure for that time. The creation of such an aircraft entailed a major redesign of the fuselage, including the deletion of cargo loading hatches, introduction of entry doors, emergency exits and windows, and, most importantly, the almost two-fold increase of the pressure differential inside the aircraft. In practical terms this was tantamount to leaving only the external shell of the fuselage, while the fuselage structure would have to be totally new. The lack of a real need for such a gigantic airliner eventually led the project to be abandoned.

An-124VS ('Airborne Launch') space launch pad (project)

Development of the An-124 was associated not only with air transport operations but also with its participation in several space programmes in the capacity of a launch pad for an airborne launch of space launch vehicles (SLVs). The idea was to load a relatively small rocket on a special platform into the An-124's cavernous cargo hold. At high altitude the platform would be extracted by drogue parachutes via the rear cargo hatch and tilted into nose-up position. Then, when the carrier aircraft was out of harm's way, the rocket motors would ignite, the platform would separate, parachuting to the ground, and the rest of the launch would proceed as usual.

Optimism with regard to such proposals is based on the high level of world demand for putting into orbit lightweight space vehicles weighing up to 3 tonnes (6,615 lb); this demand is assessed at approximately 2,000 launches in the period up to 2015. Calculations show that in the event of an airborne launch the useful load placed into orbit by an SLV is increased by 20-25%, which cuts the costs associated with the launch and makes the project attractive for customers. Also, the launch can take place at the location which is the most favourable at the moment to suit the specific mission. In the Russian Federation, among the several programmes of this kind, the programme dubbed 'Airborne Launch' made the greatest headway. Together with the Antonov ANTK, the following Russian enterprises joined the project: Energiya Rocket and Space Complex, Polyot/Flight Airlines, the Samara Scientific & Technical Complex named after N. D. Kuznetsov, and others. The An-124-100 aircraft intended for participation in this programme was to be fitted with systems which catered for the loading of the transportation and launch container into the cargo hold, for air-dropping it in the launch area, for the guidance of the rocket during its flight and the monitoring of its systems, and for transmitting the information on the rocket flight parameters via a data link to the Space Flight Command Centre and to other consumers. The aircraft thus modified is referred to as An-124VS (*vozdooshnyy start*, airborne launch). In accordance with directive No.1702-r adopted by the Government of the Russian Federation on 1st December 1998 four Ruslans from the Russian Air Force's military airlift branch were to be transferred to Polyot/Flight Airlines for use in the 'Airborne Launch' project. The machines in question were RA-82024, RA-82010, RA-82014 and an aircraft coded '10 Black' (c/n 19530502127, l/n 02-07), in that order; the latter aircraft was later registered RA-82026. The first commercial launch was planned for 2003; however, due to funding difficulties the work on this pro-

gramme is proceeding at an extremely slow pace and is unlikely to reach fruition in the next few years.

An-124ARKK airborne launch aircraft (project)

This project preceded the An-124VS described above and was basically similar to it. The An-124ARKK was visualised as a component of three different aerospace systems developed jointly by the Antonov ANTK and GRTs-KBM (State Rocketry Centre – Machine-building Design Bureau) named after Academician V. P. Makeyev. All of them were intended for putting into orbit artificial satellites of varying sizes and weights using the method of airborne launch. (ARKK stands for *aviatsionnyy raketno-kosmicheskiy kompleks* – airborne space rocket complex) The first of these systems was named Rif-MA (= Reef-MA) and was built around an SLV of the same name, a derivative of the R-39 sea-launched ballistic missile. The system was intended for putting into orbit satellites weighing 950-1500 kg (2,095-3,310 lb). The other two systems had the common name Aerokosmos and differed in using different types of SLVs, respectively the Shtil'-2A and Shtil'-3A (*shtil'* is a nautical term meaning 'dead calm'). Both of these rockets were based on the R-29RM (RSM-54) sea-launched intercontinental ballistic missile known in the West as SS-N-23. The Shtil'-2A system was to launch into orbit useful loads of 430-730 kg (950-1,610 lb), while the Shtil'-3A system had a capacity for loads between 620 and 950 kg (1,370-2,095 lb).

A model of the An-124ARKK carrying a rocket in its fuselage was presented at the MAKS-93 air show in August-September 1993 as a part of the Aerokosmos system. Interestingly, it sported the designation An-124AK (obviously alluding to Aerokosmos).

There were plans for starting commercial use of the systems in 1998, but they were never put into effect.

An-124SK airborne launch aircraft (project)

The An-124SK carrier aircraft was intended for use in an aerospace system designated Space Clipper (hence the SK in which K is a Russian transliteration of the English C). Preliminary design work on this aerospace system was conducted in the Yoozhnoye KB (lit. 'Southern' Design Bureau). This system was intended for putting into orbit space vehicles weighing up to 500 kg (1,100 lb), as well as space vehicles of a greater weight. In addition to the An-124SK, the system comprised several SLVs of various sizes and types from the same 'family' and a ground production and operation facility. After the break-up of the Soviet Union the project was terminated.

An-124 airborne launch aircraft for the Oril system (project)

In 1999 an airborne launch system was under development on the basis of the An-124 and an SLV based on the ballistic missile known in the West as SS-24. This system designated *Oril* (Ukrainian for Eagle) was intended for placing into orbit useful loads up to 1,000 kg (2,200 lb).

An-124A heavy transport aircraft (project)

This version was under development for the Russian Air Force in 1996. The An-124A featured enhanced rough-field capacity enabling it to operate from so-called second-class runways. To achieve this, the aircraft was to be equipped with a number of additional landing gear units.

An-124 heavy transport aircraft with an air cushion landing gear (project)

The Antonov Design Bureau studied together with TsAGI the possibility of equipping the An-124 with an air cushion landing gear which would enable the aircraft to operate from practically any terrain.

An-124 FFR fire-fighting aircraft (project)

Studies were made of the An-124 FFR fire-fighting version which would be capable of dropping up to 200 tonnes (441,000 lb) of water on the blaze. This figure would include 70 tonnes (154,350 lb) accommodated in the wing centre section tanks instead of fuel.

An-124-XXX oversize load carrier (project)

This version of the An-124 was intended for the carriage in a 'piggy-back' fashion of bulky loads measuring up to 8.0 x 8.0 x 70.0 m (26 x 26 x 230 ft) and weighing up to 150 tonnes (330,750 lb); the loads were expected to include space vehicles with an airborne launch. Like the An-225 (described later in this book), the An-124-XXX would feature twin vertical tails. An artist's impression of this version was presented on a poster on the display stand of Volga-Dnepr Airlines at the Paris Air Show in June 2001.

Structural description of the An-124

Type: Four-turbofan heavy military transport. The airframe is of all-metal construction.

Fuselage: The fuselage measuring 69.1 m (226 ft 8½ in) in length has a 'double-bubble' cross-section, the radius of the upper lobe being 1.9 m (6 ft 2¹³⁄₁₆ in) and that of the lower lobe 3.8 m (12 ft 5³⁹⁄₆₄ in). Actually the basic fuselage cross-section is formed by three

Above: This cutaway model of the An-124VS with the port wing folded for clarity was exhibited on Polyot Airlines' stand at the MAKS-2001 airshow.

An artist's impression of a space launch vehicle with the drogue parachute deployed as it falls away from an An-124VS prior to ignition of the rocket motors.

arcs of different radii with the largest radius at the bottom; this results in a flattened underside, with characteristic chines running along the lower fuselage sides.

The fuselage features a double-deck layout. The lower deck is the cargo hold measuring 6.4 m (21 ft 0 in) in width, 4.4 m (14 ft 5¼ in) in height and 36.5 m (119 ft 9 in) in length, with 365 tie-down fittings in the cargo floor.

The unpressurised nose fairing ahead of the flightdeck hinges upwards by means of hydraulic rams to open the full-width forward cargo hatch and is secured in the open posi-

tion by an X-shaped breaker strut. The front end of the nose fairing incorporates an angled bulkhead to which two radar antennas (one for the weather radar at the front and one for the ground mapping radar at the bottom) are attached; these are enclosed by a large dielectric radome of complex shape.

The cargo floor framework is made up of transverse and longitudinal aluminium sections reinforced with composite gussets; placed on top of it is the titanium flooring with a non-slip surface. The cargo floor incorporates threaded sockets of the tie-down fittings; they are built-in flush with the floor surface and are closed by plastic plugs. The cargo floor permits the loading of all types of self-propelled and not self-propelled wheeled and tracked vehicles with a loading per axle up to 12 tonnes (26,460 lb) when arranged in one row and up to 40 tonnes (88,200 lb) when arranged in two rows.

The cargo hold has two loading hatches. The forward cargo hatch whose dimensions are identical to those of the cargo hold is closed by a three-section hydraulically actuated loading ramp which doubles as the forward pressure bulkhead when raised. Two folding circular supports are installed at the sides of the ramp's rear segment near the trailing edge, with two more on the centre segment; these supports come into action automatically as the ramp is deployed, absorbing much of the forward fuselage weight. The space under the raised ramp's rear segment serves as the common nose-wheel well.

The rear cargo hatch measuring 6.25 x 4 m (20 ft 6 in x 13 ft 1½ in) is closed by a cargo ramp, a flat rear pressure bulkhead and three cargo door segments aft of the cargo ramp.

The aerodynamically shaped outer door segments open outwards and the centre segment upwards into the roof, whereupon the rear pressure bulkhead swings upwards and aft almost entirely, propping up the centre door segment. The outer door segments are made of carbonfibre reinforced plastic (CFRP); the centre segment is a riveted duralumin structure.

The rear cargo ramp is used for loading and unloading wheeled or tracked vehicles; to this end it is equipped with several auxiliary vehicle loading ramps which are stowed manually inside the ramp's rear end. The rear cargo ramp can be used for accommodating part of the cargo. The cargo ramps forming a part of the fuselage structure feature a riveted framework made of an aluminium alloy and covered with a titanium non-slip flooring of the same type as the cargo hold floor. They have the following gradients when lowered: less than 8° on the forward ramp, 12° on the rear ramp with the aircraft lowered (ie, with the main landing gear 'kneeling' function activated) and 17° with the aircraft not lowered (ie, with the main gear in the normal position).

Access to the aircraft with the cargo hatches closed is via a port side entry door which hinges downward and incorporates airstairs. In the forward and rear parts of the cargo hold there are hydraulically-powered ladders to the upper deck which retract into the roof to permit free passage of vehicles through the hold. The upper deck of the forward fuselage houses the flightdeck. The aircraft's crew comprises six persons: captain and co-pilot up front, navigator and radio operator sitting on the port side, and senior flight engineer and electrical engineer whose workstations are located to starboard. In addition, provision is made for a loadmaster's workstation, but the duties of loadmaster can be performed by one of the flight engineers. The flightdeck glazing comprises two curved birdproof triplex windscreen panes provided with wipers and two side windows on each side. The side windows are made of Plexiglas; the foremost pair are sliding direct vision windows which can be used as emergency exits on the ground.

Located aft of the flightdeck are two compartments, each with three sleeping berths, for a relief crew, a wardrobe, a galley and a toilet. The space between these compartments and the wing centre section is occupied by an electronic equipment bay. Located aft of the wing centre section on the upper deck is a cabin for cargo attendants providing accommodation for 88 persons. It is fitted with lightweight seats four-abreast, two toilets and a galley. Four emergency exits with large downward-hinged covers are provided for the upper deck cabins; there are also two smaller exits at the front of the rear cabin.

All cabins of the aircraft can be pressurised separately as required. However, it is possible to maintain an above-zero temperature also in the unpressurised cabins, despite the lower pressure.

The fuselage structure panels are welded and bonded structures comprising a duralumin skin and stringers made of 01420 aluminium-lithium alloy; the stringers are welded to the skin after being bonded to it, while the standard fuselage frame segments made of duralumin are attached by riveting. The fuselage mainframes near the nose and main landing gear fulcrums, as well as in the wing centre section area, are manufactured from integrally stamped duralumin half-finished articles. The side panels of the main fuselage structure are made of large-size stamped panels. The floor of the upper cabin rests on transverse beams made of D16T duralumin and reinforced by composite gussets.

The space under the centre portion of the cargo hold floor is occupied by the mainwheel wells. Two large fairings enclosing the main gear fulcrums and actuators are located low on the centre fuselage sides; they also

The fully open nose visor of Antonov Airlines An-124-100 UR-82028, showing the forward cargo ramp. The nose gear units are beginning to tilt forwards to that the nose rests on two supports before the ramp unfolds.

accommodate the APU and other equipment. The main gear fairings and all wheel well doors are made of CFRP; the wing/fuselage fairings and stabiliser/fuselage fairings are made of fibreglass, as is the fuselage tailcone.

Wings: Cantilever shoulder-mounted monoplane wings of trapezoidal planform with slight anhedral from the roots; sweepback at quarter-chord 25°, span 73.3 m (240 ft 5⅞ in), total area 628 m² (6,760 sq ft).

The wings are a four-spar structure built in three pieces: the centre section mounted on fuselage mainframes, and two integral outer wing panels joined with the centre section by flange joints which cannot be dismantled in operational service. The torsion boxes of the wing centre section and the outer wing panels are assembled from large-length milled stamped panels and double as fuel tanks.

The wing high-lift devices comprise six-section leading-edge slats, three-section slotted extension flaps (each section moves on two external tracks enclosed by fairings) and 12 symmetrically placed spoiler sections. The first four sections act as air brakes during the landing run, the other four as air brakes and also as lift dumpers, enabling rapid descent before landing; the four outboard sections are used only for roll control. All spoilers are used in the airbrake mode during the landing run. Roll control is ensured by two-section ailerons; all sections are used during take-off and landing while only the inboard sections function in cruise mode.

Tail unit: Conventional cantilever swept tail surfaces. The stabiliser and the fin are conventional structures made of aluminium alloys, with the skin reinforced by scalloped metal sheets bonded underneath (to enhance resistance to vibrations). The rudder and elevators each consist of two sections. Like the ailerons, they have no mass balance; each section is held in place and moved by four actuators.

Landing gear: Hydraulically retractable tricycle type. The landing gear features two independent steerable telescopic nose struts side by side, each carrying twin 1,120 x 450 mm (44 x 17.72 in) wheels; the struts retract forward into the nose fairing to stow under the forward loading ramp. The retraction mechanisms incorporating ball-and-screw drives with hydraulic actuators incorporate a 'kneeling' feature: when the nose cargo hatch opens, the nose gear struts are retracted and the aircraft lowers its nose which rests on the aforementioned telescopic supports hydraulically connected to equate their extension before the cargo ramp is deployed. (In so doing, the nose gear units' hydraulic motors emit an absolutely hair-raising screech...)

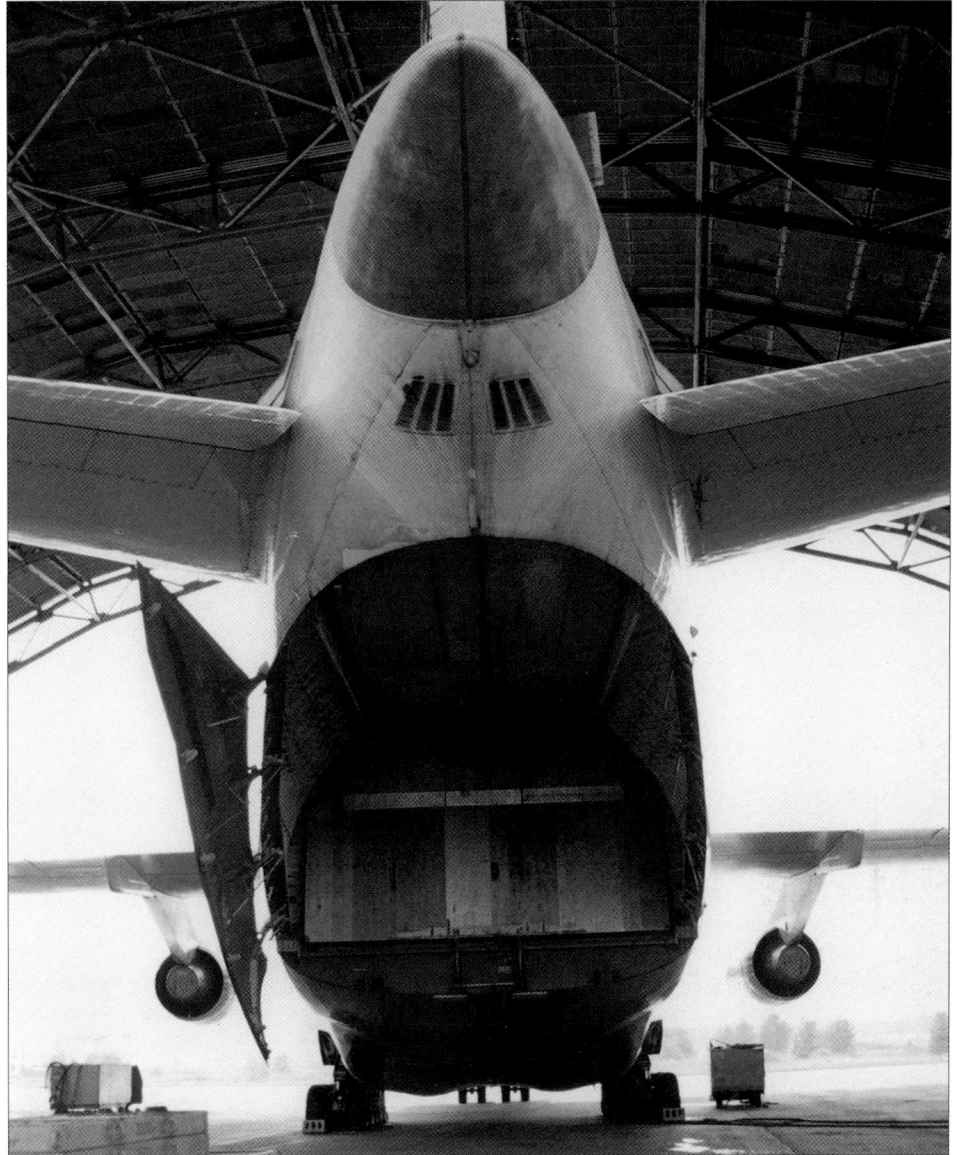

The rear cargo hatch of an An-124 undergoing refurbishment. The starboard and centre cargo door segments have been removed, revealing the rear pressure bulkhead in its in-flight position.

The main landing gear comprises five levered-suspension units on each side; each of them carries twin 1,270 x 510 mm (50 x 20 in) wheels equipped with carbon brakes and built-in cooling fans in the hubs. The main gear units retract inward and are locked in the extended position by breaker struts. They also incorporate a 'kneeling' feature lowering the aircraft to facilitate loading/unloading; this is effected by draining the fluid from the shock absorber struts into special tanks, and raising it back to normal position is done by pumping the fluid back with the help of a special hydraulic system. In addition to the common valve for retraction and extension of the landing gear there are individual valves for the retraction and extension of each landing gear unit individually.

Wide use has been made of high-strength VNS-5 steel and titanium alloys in the landing gear parts. For example, VNS-5 steel is used in the manufacture of oleo legs and shock absorber sliding cylinders; titanium is used for the wheel axles, levers, parts of bracing struts and cross members.

Each nose gear unit has two lateral (main) doors attached to the hinged nose visor and a small rear door segment mechanically linked to the oleo strut. Each of the ten main gear units has a lower (main) door and a snap-action lateral door in the main gear fairing linked to the oleo. The main doors open only when the gear is in transit.

Powerplant: Four Lotarev D-18T turbofan engines with a take-off thrust of 23,400 kgp (51,590 lbst) in ISA conditions and a cruise thrust of 4,860 kgp (10,710 lbst) at 11,000 m (36,090 ft) and Mach 0.75. The engine was developed specially for the An-124 by the Zaporozhye Engine Design Bureau.

The D-18T is a three-spool turbofan with a single-stage supersonic fan having 33 titanium blades, 60 titanium-sheathed stator

Above: A view of the An-124's cargo hold, looking towards the nose. The 'solid' section of the roof is the underside of the wing centre section.

Above: The three-section slotted flaps move on external tracks (two per section). The starboard aileron is visible on the right.

The tail unit of An-124-100 UR-82028. Note the fairings atop the stabiliser tips; these house tail logo illumination lights, a feature of many modern commercial aircraft.

vanes made of composites and a conical spinner, a seven-stage transonic low-pressure (LP) compressor with titanium blades, steel stator vanes and eight bleed valves, a seven-stage high-pressure (HP) compressor with titanium blades on the first four stages and steel blades elsewhere, a smokeless air-cooled annular combustion chamber with 22 fuel nozzles and two igniters, single-stage HP and LP turbines with cooled blades, a four-stage fan turbine and separate core and bypass nozzles. A cascade-type thrust reverser with 12 blocker doors and a translating cowl is provided on the bypass flow. A ventral accessory gearbox is provided. The D-18T has a modular construction of 17 basic modules; each spool rotates in two bearings.

Bypass ratio 5.7; overall engine pressure ratio 27.5, mass flow 760 kg/sec (1,675 lb/sec) at take-off rating and 765 kg/sec (1,686 lb/sec) in cruise mode; turbine temperature 1,610°K at take-off power. Fan speed 3,450 rpm, LP spool speed 5,900 rpm, HP spool speed 9,100 rpm. Specific fuel consumption at take-off rating 0.345 kg/kgp·h (lb/lbst·h), cruise SFC 0.546 kg/kgp·h; taking into account the fuel spent for adjustment, the SFC slightly exceeds 0.63 kg/kgp·h. Length overall 5,400 mm (17 ft 8$^{19}/_{32}$ in), width 2,792 mm (9 ft 1$^{59}/_{64}$ in), height 2,937 mm (9 ft 7$^{5}/_{8}$ in); dry weight 4,100 kg (9,040 lb).

The engines are carried on underwing pylons in individual nacelles whose fan cowl is made of glassfibre and the hot core cowl is made of duralumin and titanium. The rear part of the fan cowl is slid aft by hydraulic rams when reverse thrust is engaged to reduce the aircraft's landing run. The engines are installed in such a way that the clearance between the ground and the underside of an outboard engine even with the aircraft fully fuelled is no less than 1.4 m (4 ft 7$^{1}/_{8}$ in).

Engine thrust control is effected from the central console in the flightdeck. An electronic control system monitors the engine parameters and ensures their stability, control and surge protection; should abnormalities arise, the system introduces limitations on engine running modes. The engines are provided with built-in test equipment capable of discovering malfunctions at an early stage.

The engine running parameters are also monitored by standard measuring instruments at the captain's and senior flight engineer's workstations; engine thrust is monitored by readings from a thrust indicator.

Two Stoopino Machinery Design Bureau (NPP Aerosila) TA-12 APUs are installed in the rear portions of both main landing gear fairings; they ensure pneumatic starting of the engines in normal or accelerated mode and power supply to all aircraft systems on the ground, including the onboard cargo handling devices.

Control system: Quadruplex fly-by-wire controls. The automated manual control system (AMCS) comprises an automatic artificial-feel system (AAFS), a stability augmentation system (SAS), a trimming and balancing system (TBS), a system for changing the control gearing ratio (GRCS) and a flight mode limiter system (FMLS). All of them function on the basis of signals sent by the flight environment data system (FEDS), sensors indicating the aircraft's attitude, angular speeds and g-forces, and the pilot's control inputs. The AAFS is based on the principle of shaping the controlling command signals in conformity with control forces on the control columns and rudder pedals. Control forces are transformed with the help of a special sensor into electric signals which are transmitted through wire channels to electro-hydraulic servos installed at the end of the control chain and coupled mechanically with the slide valves of the rudder and elevator actuators. Simultaneously the same system produces load feel signals at controls in the flightdeck.

The SAS functions on the basis of signals coming from the aircraft's attitude sensors and from the FEDS. It fulfils the task of supplementing the insufficient static stability of the aircraft so as to bring it to the required level by evolving control inputs that are inversely proportionate to flight disturbances and are transmitted to the same servos; these inputs are not transmitted to the pilot. Thus, the SAS ensures that the aircraft behaves as though it possessed the standard margin of static stability. The TBS functions in response to inputs from the FEDS and the pilot and ensures automatically the necessary balancing in accordance with flight modes, while permitting the aircraft to be trimmed at the pilot's discretion.

The gearing ratio change system is intended for limiting the control surface deflection angles in cruise flight modes. To ensure the stipulated controllability characteristics in take-off and landing modes, full control authority is required. However, this amount becomes excessive at cruise flight speeds. Therefore, following an input produced by retraction of the high-lift devices, the GRCS limits the control surface deflection angles approximately by half. Conversely, during the extension of the high-lift devices the full control surface travel is restored. The pilot has a possibility of switching the GRCS from one mode to the other manually.

The FMLS system functions in response to inputs from the FEDS and angle-of-attack sensors; when the aircraft approaches the limit of the admissible AOA, the system acts first as a stick-shaker by way of a warning and then as a stick-pusher for a nose-down pitching. The force applied to the control column is so selected that the pilots can override it in case of need.

Above: The starboard main gear unit. Each of the five levered-suspension struts can retract and extend independently, maximising reliability.

Above: The twin nose gear units. Note the steering actuators/shimmy dampers.

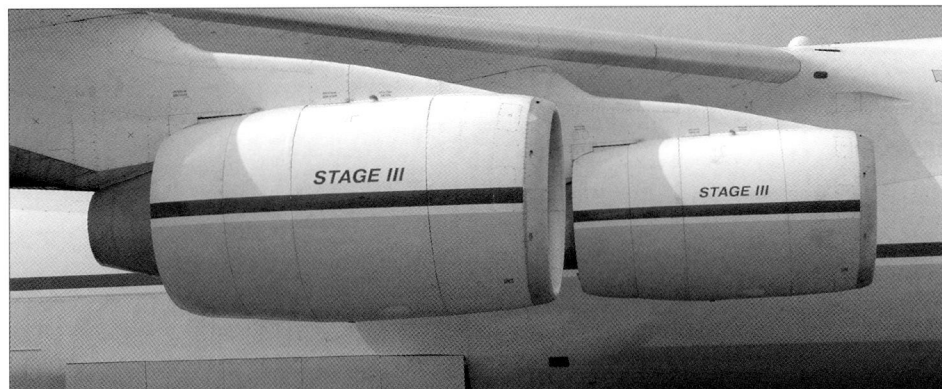

Top and above: The engine nacelles of An-124-100 UR-82028; like all other Antonov Airlines Ruslans, it is hushkitted. The D-18T's core and bypass flow have separate nozzles.

The AMCS is built up in a fashion permitting, firstly, to shape all the necessary control patterns in such a way that the aircraft possesses normal (for the pilot) stability and controllability characteristics, despite the low stability margin and non-linear momentum characteristics; secondly, to prevent exceeding the prescribed limitations. The control patterns are shaped taking into account the specific aerodynamic characteristics of the aircraft and inputs from flight mode sensors, as well as the situation in the computers of all the subsystems (AAFS, SAS, TBS, GRCS and FMLS).

To ensure the necessary safety and reliability of functioning of the AMCS, all the subsystems feature four channels distributed to both sides of the fuselage, ie, two channels run along each of the fuselage sides and are provided with a built-in monitoring mechanism. This makes it possible to pinpoint and identify any failures by means of comparisons, reduces dangers to a minimum, and enables the pilot to overcome the consequences of active failures (uncommanded actions of control surfaces) and continue his mission without limitations after the first failure in the system, with some limitations in speed and flight altitude after the second failure, to complete the flight and make a landing after the third failure and even to pilot the aircraft by applying force to controls in the event they are jammed – to pilot 'by the load feel'.

As a backup for the virtually improbable eventuality of a failure of all four channels of the fly-by-wire controls there is a fifth, mechanical channel with cable linkages; its use ensures obtaining flight characteristics sufficient for completing the flight and making a landing.

Fuel system: All fuel is housed in integral wing tanks. Fuel grades used are Russian T-1, TS-1 and T-7 jet fuel or Western Avtur equivalent. The fuel system features single-point pressure refuelling and a built-in system for warming up the fuel in low ambient temperature conditions.

Integrated hydraulic system: The integrated hydraulic system comprises four independent hydraulic systems, each of which is fed by two hydraulic pumps installed on each engine. In the aircraft's control system each

Top left: The main instrument panel of the An-124 is rather uncluttered. Note the displays of the two radars in the centre and the curious kinked shape of the control columns.

Centre left: The navigator's workstation to port also features a radar display with a rubber sunblind.

Bottom left: The senior flight engineer's and electrical engineer's workstations on the starboard side.

hydraulic system feeds its own control channel. In addition, two hydraulic systems cater for the functioning of the landing gear, loading hatches and other mechanisms, as well as the wing high-lift devices.

The landing gear wheel brakes operate from three hydraulic systems. The hydraulic systems are not hydraulically interconnected, but the use of special hydraulic transformers (reversible motor-driven pumps) makes it possible to transfer hydraulic power between the systems within two pairs of systems. In addition, every hydraulic system has a turbine pump unit which ensures the system's functioning from the aircraft's pneumatic system, should the main pumps fail.

Electric system: The electric power supply system comprises four 115 V/400 Hz AC generators, adjustment system and converters; it ensures an onboard power supply of 27 V DC and 36 V and 208 V/400 Hz AC. There are also two DC batteries, each of them housing two storage cells.

The electric power supply system likewise features four channels, with two channels functioning jointly and connected to a common distribution bus on each side of the fuselage. When the aircraft is on the ground, the buses can be connected to an airfield power source or receive power supply from the APU generators.

The emergency power supply system ensures enough power from storage batteries to enable the aircraft to complete the flight, as well as to undertake at least four attempts to start up any of the APUs.

Environmental control system: The environmental control system comprises an air conditioning system, an anti-icing system and oxygen equipment. Four subsystems for air preparation actuated by the engines cater for imparting to the original air the required temperature and pressure.

Air conditioning system: The air conditioning system ensures a pressure differential of 0.55 kg/cm² (7.82 psi) in the two upper cabins, 0.25 kg/cm² (3.57 psi) in the cargo hold, as well as the necessary temperature and air changes per hour in the cabins for people and a positive temperature in the cargo hold (in case of need), automatically maintaining the temperature values preset by the crew. The system is fairly traditional in its layout, but it features a basically new element – the fact that preparation of the air is controlled by pneumatic automatic devices.

Anti-icing system: Theoretical calculations, followed up by experiments and tests, showed that in large aircraft equipped with powered controls ice formation on the lifting surfaces virtually does not affect aerodynamic characteristics. Therefore on the An-124 de-icing is provided only on the wing outer panels on a part of their span, from the wingtip to the inboard engine, as a precaution against asymmetrical stall in icing conditions. There is a provision for anti-icing also on the engine air intake lips.

The aircraft has a traditional hot-air de-icing system fed by air tapped from the air handling subsystem. The system is turned on automatically by input from an icing sensor, or manually.

Oxygen equipment: Traditional-type oxygen equipment ensures for the crew and persons on board the necessary supply of oxygen for the duration of the flight in the event of a cabin decompression.

Avionics and equipment: The flight and navigation avionics suite has a high degree of automation and permits flight along a pre-programmed route with more than 30 waypoints in any weather conditions, including a fully automated flight mode, thanks to the availability of an inertial navigation system. The navigation suite also ensures automated landing in ICAO Cat I and II weather minima.

The communications equipment ensures all kinds of standard radio communications, including communications in automated mode.

The onboard automated monitoring system performs the functions of check and fault diagnosis. It is based on the principle of collecting once per second information from more than 1,200 various sensors placed in virtually all systems of the aircraft, processing this information in a computer and supplying the crew with information channelled to warning signals and indicators and to a display in the shape of combined pictures reflecting the functioning of this or that system, as well as to a digit-printing recorder unit and to a tape recorder for use on the ground, to an emergency recorder and to a radio communications equipment set for data transmission to the ground.

When the system shapes information pictures to be sent to CRT displays, it also produces, in case of need, recommendations to the crew to undertake this or that action.

Cargo handling equipment: The An-124 has two onboard loading gantries; each of them is fitted with two cargo hoists capable of lifting 5 tonnes (11,025 lb) apiece. The gantries travel on rails mounted on the cargo hold roof and can go beyond the rear sill of the cargo floor, making it possible to lift any kind of packed or loose cargoes with a total weight of up to 20 tonnes (44,090 lb) from the ground or from a truck bed (the gantries operate both separately and jointly). For loading non-self-propelled cargoes, the aircraft has two winches developing a pull force of 3,500 kgf (7,720 lbf) which can be installed in any place of the cargo hold, plus a system of pulleys enabling the winches to move the cargoes. In addition, a roller conveyor can be mounted on the cargo floor. All these types of equipment, including the tie-down equipment, are stowed in the space along the sides of the cargo hold and do not reduce its nominal dimensions.

The An-124 in action

Upon completion of the State acceptance trials the An-124 was gradually phased into squadron service. The first aircraft of this type entered service with the 556th VTAP at Seshcha (aka Bryansk-2) AB which made up part of the 12th VTAD, replacing the An-22s previously operated by the unit. The first An-124 arrived at Seshcha in February 1987. In the course of the following two years the regiment's complement of An-124s was built up to include 21 machines delivered from the plants in Kiev and Ul'yanovsk. The higher complexity of the new machines as compared to the An-22s, coupled with the problems posed by the rather troublesome engines and some onboard systems, necessitated a concentrated effort on the part of the aircraft industry to help the Air Force personnel in fully mastering the intricacies of the new machine and overcoming the initial operational difficulties. A large group of specialists was sent to the air base for this purpose. After a fair share of training flights the An-124 crews started flying various practical missions; the first of these were associated with the delivery of cargoes for the areas in Armenia that were devastated by the 7th December 1988 earthquake (the cities of Kirovakan and Spitak).

By 1989 the 556th regiment already had 28 machines on strength, and it was deemed expedient to undertake a reorganisation. On 25th January 1989 one more regiment, the 235th VTAP, was formed at Seshcha; it took

Basic specifications of the An-124-100

Length overall	69.1 m (226 ft 8½ in)
Height on ground	20.8 m (68 ft 3 in) *
Wing span	73.3 m (240 ft 5¾ in)
Wing area, m² (sq ft)	628 (6,760)
Maximum payload, tonnes (lb)	120 (264,600)
Maximum fuel load, tonnes (lb)	212.35 (468,230)
Max. take-off weight, tonnes (lb)	392 (864,360)
Cruising speed, km/h (mph):	
maximum	865 (537)
average	750-850 (466-528)
Approach speed, km/h (mph)	240-290 (149-180)
Range with maximum payload, km (miles)	4,500 (2,797)
Take-off balanced field length at maximum AUW, m (ft)	3,000 (9,850)
Landing balanced field length at maximum AUW, m (ft)	1,800 (5,900)

* Landing gear in normal (parking) position

over several An-124s from the 556th VTAP. On 28th March 1991 the An-124 was officially adopted for service with the Armed Forces.

Initially the fulfilment of purely military tasks did not play a significant role in the operational activities of the regiments flying the An-124; the bulk of their work was associated with civil tasks, such as deliveries of humanitarian aid, transportation of peacekeeping personnel and various cargoes for the benefit of the United Nations, export deliveries of heavy equipment and military hardware, and transportation of outsize cargoes for the national economy. In 1989 the Government officially sanctioned the use of the An-124 for performing commercial flights to any country of the world. The money thus earned was a welcome source of funding spare parts acquisition, aircrew training and housing construction for the Air Force personnel.

Air Force pilots made their contribution to the complement of world records set by the An-124s. A notable even in this context was a round-the-world flight performed by An-124 CCCP-82033 (c/n 9773052832054, l/n 05-07)

in December 1990. Starting on 1st December from Melbourne, Australia, the aircraft followed the South Pole – North Pole – Australia route with intermediate stops in Brazil (Rio de Janeiro), Morocco (Casablanca) and the Soviet Union (Vozdvizhenka). The crew comprised 14 pilots and specialists from the 235th VTAP and was headed by Lieutenant General L. V. Kozlov, chief of the Air Force Research Institute (GK NII VVS) which owned the aircraft. More than 90% of the route passed over the water expanses of four oceans devoid of any landmarks; assistance from ground navigation aids was thus almost non-existent. The flight that spanned over 50,005 km (31,078.3 miles) was performed in the course of 72 hours and 16 minutes of flight time. Seven world speed records were set during this flight. The aircraft was later coded '21 Black' but has since reverted to a quasi-civil identity as RA-82033.

Starting in 1992, the An-124 was increasingly used for fulfilling the direct tasks of the military airlift branch. Missions of this kind included the delivery of aircraft materiel from

the Transcaucasian area to Russia, transportation of military cargoes to the North Caucasian theatre of operations during both Chechen wars, and flights associated with the withdrawal of Russian troops from former East Germany. In parallel, the aircraft continued to render valuable service to the UN in airlifting peacekeeping forces, including the transportation of French personnel to what was then Zaïre (now the Democratic Republic of Congo) and Djibouti in 1994.

Pursuant to a Ministry of Defence order issued on 22nd June 1994, the 235th regiment moved to a new base at Ul'yanovsk-Vostochnyy airport. The actual redeployment began in February of the following year.

After the break-up of the Soviet Union the An-124s continued their service within the ranks of the Russian Air Force. The new situation introduced more than a fair share of difficulties associated with the maintenance and development of the aircraft and maintaining the necessary level of pilot proficiency. The difficulties were due primarily to the drastically reduced funding and the breakdown of the traditional ties with the manufacturers that had played an important role in maintaining and updating the aircraft. At one time the issue of extending the service life of the Air Force machines and their systems posed a real danger of grounding the aircraft forever. The problem was tackled, in particular, thanks to a joint effort of the Antonov ANTK, TsAGI and NIIERAT (the Air Force Research Institute for Operation and Repair of Aircraft Materiel). A concept was evolved providing for the operation of the An-124s according to technical condition; all the machines were thoroughly inspected by a joint commission which issued the necessary recommendations for their continued operation.

Yet, some problems persisted, not least the problems associated with the D-18T engines whose operation over the years had been marked with numerous failures. It is presumed that engine troubles became the cause of a tragic accident in Irkutsk involving An-124 '08 Black' (c/n 9773054516003, l/n 01-07) of the 566th VTAP. On 6th December 1997 this aircraft took off from Irkutsk-2 airfield – the factory airfield of the Irkutsk Aircraft Production Association (IAPO – *Irkootskoye aviatsionnoye proizvodstvennoye obyedineniye*) on its second mission to Vietnam for the delivery of Su-27UBK two-seat fighters ordered by that country. Immediately after take-off three of the aircraft's four engines flamed out in rapid succession. The thrust of one engine was not enough to keep the heavily loaded aircraft aloft; banking to starboard, the machine lost altitude and crashed into an apartment building near the airfield. All 23 occupants (the crew and representatives of the plants that had manufactured the Su-27s)

Above: A red-starred Russian Air Force An-124 (most probably '10 Black', c/n 19530502127) at Seshcha AB in 2002. Note the small Antonov badge below the An-124 nose titles.

Several Russian Air Force An-124s, including these two at Seshcha AB, have been converted to An-124-100s in order to facilitate flying abroad. The foremost aircraft even wears 'ANTONOV 124-100' nose titles in English!

were killed. The crash also cost the lives of 70 residents of the house, half of which was completely demolished.

Subsequent investigation tended to confirm the surmise that the uncommanded shutdown of the No.3 engine (the first to become inoperative) was caused by a surge. Thus, the 'tin kickers' (and, courtesy of the press which gave the tragedy extensive coverage, the public at large) tended to blame the engine manufacturers, although the latter contested this conclusion (as late as the beginning of 2001 the official results of the investigation were not yet submitted to the aircraft and engine manufacturers). After a period during which all Russian Air Force An-124s were grounded (commercial An-124-100 operations continued unabated in the meantime), the flights of these machines belonging to the 556th VTAP resumed on 15th May 1998. Prior to that the engines of several Ruslans were modified to increase their gas flow stability margin.

In 1998 the Military Transport Aviation of Russia was reorganised into the 61st Air Army. As a part of this reorganisation, the 235th VTAP was disbanded and its An-124s returned to Seshcha. However, the reorganisation failed to produce the desired improvement in the conditions for An-124 operations. According to some press reports, by 2001 the frequency of operational flights of the An-124s in the Russian Air Force fell drastically; this led some observers to assert that this aircraft no longer represented a major factor in the operational capabilities of the Russian Military Transport Aviation.

While the military career of the An-124 seems to have tapered off to modest proportions, in the recent years the Ruslan has succeeded in building up an enviable service record in the field of civil cargo transportation. As noted above, the aircraft belonging to the Air Force were used on numerous occasions for purely civil purposes; at the turn of the 1980s and 1990s the civil employment of the aircraft acquired a new dimension, gradually eclipsing its original basic military role. The idea of putting the An-124s into commercial service cropped up for the first time in 1988, when Christopher Foyle, a British businessman, discussed it with the Soviet Minister of Aircraft Industry A. Systsov at that year's Farnborough Air Show. In March 1989 the Antonov Design Bureau succeeded in obtaining the Government's consent for establishing the OKB's sub-division for the commercial operation of the An-124s; the revenue from these operations was to be used for financing the OKB's activities in the field of transport aircraft design. This subdivision, later known as Antonov Airlines, initially leased from the Air Force two An-124s registered CCCP-82007 and -82008. At the same time an order was

Above: The last-but-one Kiev-built Ruslan in its days as RA-82003 with Trans-Charter whose tail logo it wears; it was jointly operated with Titan Cargo. The aircraft now serves with Libyan Arab Air Cargo as 5A-DKN.

Above: RA-82077, the first An-124-100 delivered to Polyot/Flight Airlines. As with most commercial Ruslan operators, the underside of the nose visor (visible when the nose hatch is open) serves as a billboard!

Above: An-124-100 RA-82072, one of two operated by the Rossiya State Transport Co., was in the static park at the MAKS-95 airshow in Zhukovskiy.

Resplendent in the blue/white/grey livery of Antonov Airlines, An-124-100 UR-82009 is seen at Berlin-Schönefeld during one of the ILA airshows. Note the characteristic two-pronged towbar parked beside the aircraft.

placed with the Kiev Aircraft Plant for two new-build machines (CCCP-82027 and -82029), which were eventually purchased and fully paid for by the airline. After the break-up of the USSR some Air Force An-124s that were passing tests at the Antonov ANTK became the property of the Ukraine and were turned over to Antonov Airlines. The company started full-scale commercial services with these aircraft; the money thus earned was used for the development of the Ukraine's aircraft industry.

Initially the commercial cargo operations were conducted in defiance of the fact that the An-124 had not been certified as a civil aircraft. For this reason all the Ruslans were grounded in 1992, and Antonov Airlines had to invest much effort into obtaining a civil type certificate for the An-124; the certified aircraft received the designation An-124-100.

The commercial operations of Antonov Airlines got into full stride after the establishment of close ties with Air Foyle Ltd. The company's owner Christopher Foyle undertook to act as Antonov Airlines' agent in Europe and the Middle East. His company provided marketing, advertising and insurance services for Antonov Airlines. Experience showed that not all types of cargoes were equally well suited for carriage by the An-124. Antonov Airlines gradually found its niche on the cargo market: it consisted of the transportation of outsize cargoes requiring special preparation both of the cargo and the aircraft for its carriage.

The emergence of the An-124-100 on the cargo transportation market resulted in a significant growth of demand for the airlifting of heavy and outsize pieces of machinery and equipment, including single cargoes weighing as much as 120 tonnes (264,600 lb) and more. A record single cargo weighing 135.2 tonnes (298,116 lb) was delivered by an Antonov Airlines An-124 from Düsseldorf (Germany) to Delhi (India) on 23rd September 1993; it was the stator of an electric generator manufactured by Siemens AG. Some of the world's leading companies, notably in the aerospace industry, became, in fact, permanent customers of Antonov Airlines, making use of their services for the transportation, among other things, of large components of satellites and SLVs within the USA and between the USA, Europe and China.

2002 became a record year for Antonov Airlines, the operations reaching 713 flights with a total of 10,200 flight hours and a total weight of cargoes carried in excess of 44,000 tonnes (97,020,000 lb). In 2002 the Ruslans of Antonov Airlines were widely used in anti-terrorist operations, delivering more than 14,000 tonnes (30,870,000 lb) of cargoes from Germany, the UK, Poland and Italy to Afghanistan during Operation *Enduring Freedom* (the war against the Taliban militia and the al-Qaeda

terror organisation in Afghanistan).

The success story of Antonov Airlines was paralleled by the success of a similar business venture undertaken by a Russian carrier, Volga-Dnepr Airlines. This cargo airline was established as the flying division of the Ul'yanovsk-based Aviastar aircraft plant, with the participation of the Antonov ANTK, the Motor Sich engine plant, the Kiev-based Aviant aircraft plant and some banks. In 1990 this company received its first An-124 (CCCP-82042). Also in this case the operational activities of the company were based on a partnership with a British enterprise: Volga-Dnepr set up a joint venture with London/Stansted-based HeavyLift Cargo Airlines. This partnership lasted until 1st February 2001, the An-124s wearing additional HeavyLift titles to complement the Volga-Dnepr livery.

The new cargo carrier succeeded in attracting lucrative orders, the volume of operations growing steadily. In 1999 Volga-Dnepr already had seven An-124-100s at its disposal. On 3th August 2000 Volga-Dnepr obtained a registration certificate for its 10th An-124-100, RA-82079 (c/n 9773052062157, l/n 08-01). This aircraft, the first Ruslan manufactured by Aviastar after a five-year interval, was an upgraded machine with the airframe service life increased to 24,000 hours; it was equipped with an updated cabin for cargo attendants and fitted with modern navigation avionics.

In July 2002 Volga-Dnepr Airlines placed a formal order with the Aviastar aircraft plant for a Ruslan in a new version designated An-124-100M. It has an increased normal payload of 150 tonnes (330,750 lb) at a maximum take-off weight of 402 tonnes (886,400 lb). Delivery of the new aircraft was scheduled for the fourth quarter of 2003, but actually Volga-Dnepr had to wait until June 2004 when RA-82081 was formally delivered.

Here are just a few examples of the company's operations. In 1997 Volga-Dnepr An-124s ferried racing cars that took part in the Master Rally '97. Fifty-four cars could be carried in each flight; this was made possible by the installation of a lightweight upper deck suspended from the ceiling in the manner of car ferries. In that year the airline's Ruslans carried from Chicago to Yakutsk, the capital of the diamond-rich Republic of Sakha (Yakutia, the Russian Federation's easternmost constituent republic) three super-heavy Komatsu 510E quarry dump trucks, each weighing 103 tonnes (227,115 lb). The vehicles were so huge that they had to be dismantled in order to fit into the aircraft's cargo hold; the skips were dismembered lengthwise into two halves.

On 20th May 199 a Volga-Dnepr Airlines An-124-100 delivered a full-scale mock-up of

the Angara space launch vehicle from Moscow-Sheremet'yevo to Le Bourget for participation in that year's Paris Air Show. It was the first time in the history of Russia that the rocket was delivered fully assembled. Its length fully matched that of the Ruslan's cargo hold. The company undertook the transportation of US satellites to the Baikonur Space Centre; its aircraft ensured the export deliveries of Su-27SK and Su-27UBK fighters to China and Vietnam and of Su-30 multi-role combat aircraft to India. In 2003 Volga-Dnepr held more than 53% of the world's super-heavy and oversize cargo transportation market.

Antonov Airlines and Volga-Dnepr did not remain the sole civil operators of the An-124 for long. Over the years several other companies acquired a limited number of these aircraft in an attempt to gain a foothold on the cargo transportation market. These companies included the Rossiya State Transport Company (the Russian government flight), which needed a heavy transport to support the official visits of the Russian President abroad, carrying the presidential limousines and sundry other equipment (notably secure communications equipment). Other civil operators were Oryol-Avia, Magistral'nyye Avialinii (= Trunk Route Airlines), Antonov AirTrack, Trans-Charter, Titan Cargo, Ayaks (= Ajax) and Polyot/Flight Airlines. However, by 2001 all of them except the latter company either had sold their An-124s or gone out of business altogether. It turned out that the operation of the An-124 was too heavy a burden for small airlines lacking the necessary technical facilities and marketing network.

As of early 2000, the total fleet of An-124-100s in commercial operation amounted to 19 machines owned by three operators, 17 of them belonging to Antonov Airlines and Volga-Dnepr.

At present the only other Russian carrier operating the An-124-100 is the Voronezh-based Polyot (aka Flight Airlines). It received its first An-124 in 2001, a second machine joining the fleet in 2002. Two more aircraft of this type were to be transferred to Polyot from the Russian Air Force in accordance with a government directive in 2003 and 2004. The aircraft are to be used by the company for the implementation of the 'Airborne Launch' programme. The company ordered a new-build An-124 at the Aviastar plant; the aircraft (RA-82080, c/n unknown, l/n 08-02) first flew in early 2004, and another aircraft, the second An-124-100M, is nearing completion.

In the course of 15 years of commercial operation the An-124 has established a firm reputation due to its unique airlifting capabilities that are very much in demand and ensure a promising future for this aircraft for decades to come

Chapter 4

The Six-Engined Dream

An-225 Mriya heavy transport aircraft

The mid-seventies of the past century (it is still hard to get accustomed to using these words!) were marked by notable achievements in space exploration. By that time intelligence satellites deployed by the USSR and the USA had became an integral part of the military and general economic infrastructure, manned space stations had taken their permanent place on the orbits, and the first steps had been made from confrontation to international co-operation in this field. At that time everything seemed to indicate an ever-growing tempo of space exploration; this dictated the need for new, reusable means for placing useful loads into orbit. It was presumed that, if used with sufficient frequency, these vehicles would surpass traditional disposable space launch vehicles in economic efficiency.

Guided by this motto, the USA put much effort into creating the reusable space transport system dubbed Space Shuttle. Not to be outdone, the USSR soon followed suit: a decision was taken calling for the development of a Soviet system with similar characteristics. On 17th February 1976 the Central Committee of the Communist Party and the Soviet Council of Ministers issued a classified directive No.132-51 on the development of space systems known as Buran (Blizzard, pronounced *boorahn*) and *Rassvet* (Dawn) – a space shuttle and a monstrous SLV respectively; the latter was subsequently renamed *Energiya* (Energy). This programme envisaged the construction of space vehicles of hitherto unseen dimensions and weight; their various units and subassemblies were to be manufactured at enterprises located in the central areas of the USSR, and final assembly was to be effected directly at the famous Baikonur Space Centre. Thus it was necessary to deliver assembled parts of the rocket and the shuttle over a distance of 1,500-2,000 km (932-1,243 miles). Some of these parts were designed with a length of 60 m (197 ft) and a diameter of 8 m (26 ft). Furthermore, depending on the mission performed while in orbit, the Buran might make landings at airfields located all over the territory of the Soviet Union, from the Ukraine to the Far East. From there it would have to be delivered back to Baikonur, the place of the next launch.

All this looked set to turn into a major technical and economic problem. Road, rail and river transport held no promise at all for the solution of this problem because it would be necessary to build new roads and modernise existing ones, rebuild bridges, widen tunnels, raise high-voltage power lines and so on. Air transport was the only realistic alternative. Being well aware of this, the leaders of MAP addressed Oleg K. Antonov with a request to develop a dedicated aircraft for the carriage of space system sub-assemblies. At about the same time, at the turn of the years 1980-1981, Gleb Ye. Lozino-Lozinskiy, General Designer of NPO Molniya ('Lightning' Science & Production Association) which created the Buran, shared his new ideas with Antonov in the course of their working meetings. He formulated the task in a broader perspective: it was necessary to develop a reusable space transport system featuring not a vertical, but a horizontal take-off, in which the first stage was an aircraft and the second a 'baby Space Shuttle' riding an external fuel tank. In this case the aircraft ceased to be a relatively simple cargo carrier and turned into a veritable airborne space launch site, from the 'back' of which the shuttle/ET combination with a total weight of 170 tonnes (374,850 lb) was to start on its way into orbit.

It was not a matter of chance that the mentioned requests were addressed to Antonov: just then his OKB was engaged in designing the An-124, an aircraft with the world's highest load-carrying capacity at the time. The future Ruslan could just as well serve as a basis for a dedicated aircraft both for transportation of space cargoes and for use as airborne space launch platform; after all, its maximum admissible payload limited by structural strength considerations was exactly the mentioned figure of 170 tonnes. (It should be noted here that later the An-124 set a world payload record of more than 171 tonnes (377,000 lb).) The problem was that the An-124 did not exist yet. Its prototype had yet to be completed and tested, and that could take years. Moreover, the baseline version of this aircraft was not suitable in principle for the airborne launch of space vehicles because its vertical tail would be hit and very probably damaged by the jet efflux of the space shuttle's engines, and Antonov could not redesign the tail unit of the nearly completed aircraft that had been approved by all

research institutes of the customer and by the mock-up review commission. Therefore the Kiev designers undertook, as an early-stage task, an attempt to modify the renowned Antheus for the mentioned special transport role. In principle such a modification could be effected in two ways: the cargo could be carried either piggy-back or inside a considerably 'inflated' rear fuselage whose diameter was to be increased to 8.3 m (27 ft 2¾ in). The first method had to be discarded because of the difficulties with ensuring directional stability with such a big external load; the second was not feasible due to structural strength and layout problems. In short, even as a stopgap measure such an aircraft was not viable.

Under the circumstances the designers of space systems had to pin their hopes on the project of the Myasishchev VM-T Atlant (Atlantean), a derivative of the 3M four-turbojet strategic bomber that had been developed way back in the mid-1950s. It was hoped that this version would be able to tackle the problem – at least during the period prior to the completion of the first Energiya-Buran system. The modification consisted of cutting off the rear fuselage and tail unit of a production 3MS-2 tanker, reinforcing the rest of the airframe and mating it with an all-new upswept rear fuselage and twin tails, as well as installing external cargo attachment points. This extensive redesign enabled the aircraft to carry long cargoes (such as the Energiya SLV's fuel tank) on its back.

With regard to both aerodynamics and structural strength the aircraft proved to possess only a minimum safety margin: the size of some of the space cargoes turned out to be overly large for it. For example, the diameter of the Energiya's core module (fuel/oxidiser tank assembly) was 2.5 times greater than that of the VM-T's fuselage. As a result, some of the flights (in 1982-88 the two examples of the VM-T, CCCP-01402 and CCCP-01502, performed 150 flights, delivering subassemblies of the Energiya-Buran system from the manufacturers' plants to Baikonur) proved to be risky affairs and often ended in a safe landing only thanks to the courage and professional skill of the crews. Besides, the VM-T could not carry the whole range of cargoes that were required. In particular, it could lift the Buran only without the shuttle's vertical tail (for directional stability reasons) and internal equipment; hence it was impossible to jettison the shuttle in the air in the fashion of NASA's Boeing 747SCA (which was used, among other things, for 'launching' the Space Shuttle during early free flight trials). Into the bargain, the age of the two converted aircraft, which had been manufactured as 3MSs back in 1959, 30 years before the events described, was a constant reminder of the urgent need to develop a replacement for them.

Bearing in mind all these circumstances, the leaders of organisations within the Ministry of General Machinery (MOM – *Ministerstvo obshchevo mashinostroyeniya*, the Soviet space industry) framework turned to the Antonov Design Bureau once again; they were encouraged by the commencement of the Ruslan's flight tests in late 1982. Its potential transport capabilities allowed it to transport the components of the Energiya-Buran system in fully assembled condition, and the core module of the Energiya SLV could even be airlifted with its two parts (the hydrogen and oxygen tanks) joined together. However, the conventional tail unit remained an obstacle for the carriage of long cargoes.

On the other hand, by then the designers of NPO Molniya had completed one more round of studies on the re-usable transport system with a horizontal launch and came to the conclusion that the weight of the load to be separated from the carrier aircraft would be not the 170 tonnes envisaged originally but possibly as much as 270 tonnes (595,350 lb). As a result, it became patently clear that the An-124 was not suitable for use as the first stage in this system, as well as for the delivery of the Buran and components of the Energiya. A new versatile airlifter with still greater load-carrying capability had to be developed.

Projects of a future giant airlifter were promptly submitted by several organisations at once; some of them, in the opinion of specialists, did not seem to have given much thought to the feasibility of their proposals. For some reason the projects were based on the idea that the new aircraft, and a giant one at that, should be a 'clean sheet of paper' design, with all the economic consequences. However, during the last years of the 'developed socialism' the Soviet economy was already beginning to show tangible signs of overstrain, and a programme on that scale (in addition to numerous other programmes) could be the proverbial straw that broke the camel's back. Therefore Oleg K. Antonov's proposal envisaging the creation of such an aircraft with the maximum possible use of the available An-124 components proved to be the only reasonable option. It was born in the Design Bureau's PD projects department which was then headed by O. K. Bogdanov.

The first sketches of the new machine appeared on the drawing boards of the general arrangement team (headed by Oleg Ya. Shmatko) in the second half of 1983, and by the summer of the following year the overall appearance of the machine had already been finalised. It envisaged the use of the An-124's outer wing panels in their stock configuration as manufactured by the Tashkent Aircraft Production Association. The wings of the new machine featured a considerably greater span and area due to a new increased-span centre section which carried an extra pair of D-18T turbofans, as used on the An-124. The fuselage was stretched by inserting plugs in the constant cross-section area; mounted on its upper surface were external cargo attachment fittings. Bearing in mind the sharp increase in the level of stresses affecting the rear fuselage, the rear loading hatch was to be deleted. The nose landing gear units were to be reinforced and the number of main gear units was to be increased to seven on each

side, the four rearmost pairs being of a castoring type; the tail unit was provided with twin fins and rudders. The aircraft was fitted with a system for pressurising the external loads and for monitoring and maintaining constant pressure and temperature in them. Thus, a project emerged of a new giant carrier aircraft capable not only of transporting the Buran and components of the Energiya rocket with the required safety level but also of serving as the first stage of a prospective re-usable aerospace system, as well as of transporting various cargoes for the national economy.

The concept of the new aircraft took its final shape already after Oleg K. Antonov's demise in 1984 under the direction of Pyotr V. Balabuyev, the new General Designer of what was now called the Design Bureau named after O. K. Antonov, or simply the Antonov Design Bureau. After his appointment as the leader of the Design Bureau in 1984, Balabuyev organised large-scale work on the joint solution of numerous questions together with MOM enterprises on establishing production co-operation within the aircraft industry and on reaching mutual understanding with the customers that had ordered the new aerospace system.

The operational requirements for the versatile carrier/transport aircraft were approved on 16th October 1986, and by 20th May of the following year the Communist Party Central Committee and the Council of Ministers issued directive No.587-132 granting official status to the programme. The new giant aircraft was allocated the designation An-225.

Full-scale design work on the new aircraft took only three and a half years. Usually this period of a new aircraft's development is marked with the introduction of substantial changes into the PD project, but in this case the initially proposed design layout described above suffered virtually no changes. As a result, both the detail design and the construction of the An-225 prototype proceeded, generally speaking, very smoothly: that was due, no doubt, to the enormous experience accumulated by the design staff that had created a big family of transport aircraft.

Several complex technical problems were solved in the process of designing and building the aircraft; these included obtaining acceptable aerodynamic characteristics, ensuring the required structural strength, aeroelasticity and reliability of the airborne 'aircraft-plus-cargo' system. The carriage of externally mounted loads entailed a substantial increase in the aerodynamic drag of the whole system; in consequence, particular attention was paid to thoroughly refining the system's lift/drag ratio. The use of thick high-aspect-ratio wings formed by special supercritical airfoils, coupled with the cargo/aircraft arrangement featuring aft CG positions,

The An-225's rollout ceremony on 30th November 1988 began rather unusually. With the hangar doors only partly open at first, the aircraft seemed to poke its head through a hole in a fence to look out into the wide world.

Above: A few minutes later, the gates are fully opened and the many invited guests swarm around the huge aircraft like ants. Note the door aft of the starboard main landing gear fairing.

This head-on view of the An-225 on 30th November 1988 illustrates the inward-canted vertical tails. It also accentuates the huge size of the hangar the aircraft is in.

Above: Towed by a BelAZ-7420, the An-225 leaves the hangar for the first time.

careful refining of local aerodynamics and high-quality surface finish, enabled the designers to obtain a lift/drag ratio equal to 19. This value was very high not only for a transport aircraft design but for a passenger aircraft as well. Calculations and wind tunnel tests helped choose the optimum location of the external cargoes. To ensure aerodynamic stability during the transportation of cargoes

whose dimensions were similar or even superior to the fuselage dimensions, the cargoes had to be located closer to the rear fuselage. As noted earlier, the need to avoid limiting the length of externally carried cargoes prompted a decision to use twin tails. In a fashion similar to the previous work on the An-22 project, also in this case the designers had to solve a number of problems associated with ensur-

ing structural strength, flutter resistance, directional stability and controllability. They evolved a structural layout of the fuselage and the wing centre section with a system of versatile cargo attachment fitting capable of sustaining concentrated stresses amounting to several hundred tonnes.

In the course of the design work particular importance was attached to minimising structural weight within the specified values of structural strength, service life and survivability. This problem was solved through a wide use of computer calculations, coupled with the introduction of new high-strength materials and large one-piece components. Among these materials mention must be made, for example, of alloys with the addition of zirconium. In particular, as compared to traditional D16chT duralumin, the 1161T alloy possessed twice the fatigue life and destruction strength and half the crack propagation rate. It was used for the lower skin of the wing torsion box, which made it possible to obtain a very high level of design stresses (37-39 kg/cm^2; 526-555 lb/sq in). The 1973T2 alloy was especially widely used in critically important structural members. While possessing higher static strength characteristics than the V95pchT2 alloy, it had better service life characteristics coupled with high resistance to corrosion. This alloy was used for the upper

Prior to the first flight the aircraft was fitted with a long instrumented boom replacing the forward section of the radome. Note the two An-124s in the background.

wing skin panels, the horizontal tail torsion box and large-size one-piece fuselage skin panels. The 1933T3 alloy was used for the manufacture of parts from forgings and stampings; in comparison with the V93pchT3 alloy, it possessed a more advantageous combination of strength and service life properties. The landing gear made use of VT-22 high-strength titanium and 30KhGSN2MA steel obtained by re-melting in arc-vacuum furnaces. Several components were manufactured almost entirely of composite materials (CFRP, organic plastics and fibreglass). These included the landing gear fairings, cargo attachment fitting fairings, wheel well doors, wing/fuselage fairings, air conditioning system distribution ducts, engine cowlings and many other parts. To ensure high vibration fatigue and sonic fatigue strength of the wing high-lift devices, control surfaces, skin panels and tail unit leading edges, bonded structures with beaded interlayers were used.

The An-225 featured for the first time a 'power-by-wire' remote-control system for the powerplant and a system for pressurising cargoes and maintaining constant temperature in them. The multi-strut landing gear with castoring main units enabled the aircraft to operate from all types of existing airfields. The aircraft's dimensions were truly awe-inspiring: a wing span of 88.4 m (290 ft 0⅝ in), a length of 84 m (275 ft 7 in) and a height of 18.1 m (59 ft 4¹⁹⁄₃₂ in). Outwardly the An-225 resembled a scaled-up An-124, featuring the same high-set swept wings, visor-type nose cargo hatch and 'centipede' undercarriage. The main differences from the predecessor were a powerplant comprising six D-18T turbofans instead of four (three under each wing), a swept twin-fin tail unit with very distinctive arrowhead-shaped vertical tails and faired attachment fittings for external cargoes. The largest two of these fairings were located on top of the wing centre section, looking like two characteristic 'humps' side by side.

The design staff, known since the mid-1980s as the ANTK named after O. K. Antonov (the Antonov Aircraft Science and Production Complex), was hard at work implementing the project together with hundreds of other organisations. On the whole, the co-operation pattern for the construction of the aircraft was similar to the one chosen during the construction of the first Ruslans. The outer wing panels and the wing centre section were manufactured by the Tashkent Aircraft Plant, the landing gear was manufactured in Kuibyshev, hydraulics components were produced in Khar'kov and Moscow; many of the aircraft's units were manufactured by the Aviant plant in Kiev. In all, more than 100 plants participated in the An-225's construction.

Inevitably, some difficulties cropped up during the construction of such a huge air-

Above: A dream come true. The An-225 lifts off for the first time at Kiev-Svyatoshino on 21st December 1988. Note that the new inboard wing portions carrying the Nos 3 and 4 engines have no LE slats.

craft. For example, for the delivery of the wing centre section from Tashkent to Kiev it proved necessary, in parallel with the construction of the new aircraft, to re-build the first prototype An-22 which, during the 23 years of its existence, had undergone a lengthy period of tests and operation at extreme flight modes in different climatic zones and airfield conditions. The huge size and weigh of the Mriya's wing centre section installed in close proximity of the An-22's propellers dictated a prior thorough study of the airflow conditions in wind tunnel tests. It proved necessary to fit the wing centre section itself with a fairing; in addition, a special fairing of a complex geometric configuration had to be installed in the aft part between the cargo and the aircraft. In December 1987 the wing centre section attached to the upper fuselage of the An-22PZ was flown to Kiev in adverse weather conditions. The most complicated final assembly stage began.

Preparations for the first flight of the first flying prototype (c/n 01-01) proceeded in parallel with its assembly: test benches were constructed to simulate various operational situations, conditions and special piloting modes; static tests of new structural members and wind tunnel tests of models with externally mounted cargoes were conducted. The extremely complicated layout (six wing-mounted engines underslung on pylons, twin tails, gigantic dimensions and weight) dictated not only a considerable increase in the scope of theoretical and experimental research of the flutter characteristics, but also a greater precision of these studies. As a result, the designers succeeded in shaving off several tonnes of airframe weight.

On 30th November 1988, in cloudy and cold weather, the aircraft was rolled out under an official ceremony. In keeping with the already established practice of the Antonov Design Bureau the first prototype An-225 initially wore a non-standard six-digit registration, CCCP-480182; again, as in the case of the An-124, the first and last digits did not match the designation. In a departure from previous practice, however, the aircraft did not wear the customary Aeroflot livery – it was

After the maiden flight, the test crew was greeted with flowers.

Above and below: CCCP-480182 flies above the Kiev Region in the spring of 1989. These views show well the design of the tail unit – in particular, the position of the fins relative to the stabilisers.

Above and below: The An-225 is seen here at Leninsk airfield (the field serving the Baikonur Space Centre) during preparations for mating with the Buran space shuttle. The pyramidal forward support above the wing leading edge and the strut-braced rear supports aft of the wings can be seen here.

Above: Accompanied by his spouse Raïsa M. Gorbachova (third from right), CPSU General Secretary Mikhail S. Gorbachov (centre) questions Pyotr V. Balabuyev about the An-225 at Kiev-Borispol' on 20th February 1989.

white overall with a thin red cheatline. Thousands of engineers and workers, who had gathered for a meeting held on that occasion, saw for the first time the inscription Mriya (Ukrainian for Dream) which had been painted on the aircraft's side the day before. Short speeches were delivered, whereupon the many thousands of employees who had participated in the creation of the new-born giant went to their working places to celebrate its birth. The aircraft was towed to the factory airfield, and Pyotr V. Balabuyev spent much time answering questions from journalists, including questions about the aircraft's name.

On 3rd and 4th December the aircraft made its first 'independent steps' at the Kiev-Svyatoshino factory airfield; they included taxying, turns and runs up to the speed of 200 km/h (124 mph) with the lifting of the nosewheels off the runway. The machine behaved precisely as expected. After that, various kinds of additional work were performed: weighing, determining the CG position, pressure-testing the fuselage and so on. As in the case of the An-124, a modified radome incorporating a blended air data boom was installed prior to the first flight. The first flight date was set for 20th December, but foul

weather prevented the aircraft from taking to the air on that day. On the following day the weather was not of the best kind either: low clouds, head- and crosswind brought with it snow showers. Nevertheless, the aircraft was towed to the runway. After a 950-m (3,120-ft) run, the Mriya effortlessly lifted off the ground, commencing her maiden flight. The crew comprised captain Aleksandr V. Galunenko, co-pilot Sergey A. Gorbik, senior flight engineer A. M. Shu-leshenko, flight engineer V. A. Gusar, navigator S. F. Nechayev, radio operator V. A. Belo-borodov and project engineer for flight testing M. G. Kharchenko. A few days before the same crew had delivered cargoes in a Ruslan from Kiev and West Germany for the people of Armenia who had been hit by a devastating earthquake on 7th December.

During the first flight which lasted 1 hour and 14 minutes, the stability and handling of the new aircraft were determined, various aerodynamic corrections were adjusted, a check was made of the onboard systems and equipment. The flight showed that the actual characteristics of the An-225 fully met the design values and the aircraft's behaviour in the air was identical to the one simulated earlier at a test bench. Everything had proceeded so smoothly that Merited Test Pilot of the USSR A. V. Galunenko told the journalists in a jocular vein after the flight that 'if designers, production plants and pre-flight development engineers also forthwith do their job just as diligently, test pilots may quite as well become superfluous'. In short, the flight was conducted in an ideal way. The performance and handling of the An-225 were fully in accordance with those envisaged by the mathematical model and checked out on ground rigs, and the control column forces during rotation proved to be even smaller than anticipated. On 28th December the Mriya made its second flight. The manufacturer's tests began in earnest.

On 20th February 1989 CPSU General Secretary (and actually Head of State) Mikhail S. Gorbachov visited the Ukrainian capital. Immediately upon arrival at Kiev-Borispol' airport he inspected the parked An-225. Pyotr V. Balabuyev informed the General Secretary about the aircraft's mission and its basic characteristics, after which a demonstration flight took place. Gorbachov congratulated the Design bureau's staff with the new great achievement, saying: 'The Mriya is an integral part of the *perestroika*' (restructuring, ie, the democratisation of the Soviet society).

Three months after the first flight, on 22nd March 1989, the designers, testers, engineers and technicians prepared the aircraft for an unusual flight: it was to shatter world records. By that day 43 flights had been performed, in which the An-225 prototype had logged 63 flight hours. After a careful weighing of the

The crew of the An-225 receives congratulations after the flight on 22nd March 1989 in which 109 Class C-1t world records were set. Pyotr V. Balabuyev is sixth from left.

Above: Another view of the Mriya at Leninsk with the cargo mounting struts in place. Note how the ailerons and elevators 'bleed' down after engine shutdown.

Still registered CCCP-480182 but already lacking the nose probe associated with the initial flight tests, the An-225 cruises high above the clouds – oddly enough, with the landing gear extended and high-lift devices deployed. Note the video camera (a part of the test equipment) under the port fin leading edge.

Pyotr V. Balabuyev proudly upholds a model of the An-225 during one of his many press conferences.

load, which amounted to 156.3 tonnes (344,641 lb), and sealing the fillers of the fuel tanks the Mriya took to the air. Recording of the highest achievements started immediately after the take-off. To begin with, the An-225 bettered by 194 tonnes (427,770 lb) the maximum take-off weight record set by the US Boeing 747-400; then dozens more world records were beaten. Climbing to an altitude of 12,410 m (40,717 ft), the Mriya surpassed the result achieved by its elder brother, the Ruslan. The flight resulted in the establishment of not 106, as anticipated, but 109 Class C-1t records. The record-breaking flight lasted 3 hours and 45 minutes.

Soon the aircraft set about performing the job for which it was intended. On 3rd May 1989 CCCP-480182 took off from Leninsk airfield near the Baikonur space centre, carrying on its back its first cargo – the Buran aerospace vehicle weighing more than 60 tonnes (132,300 lb). In the course of the following ten days the crew captained by Galunenko performed several test flights in which the controllability of this combination was assessed and measurements were made of the speed and fuel burn. On 13th May this unique transport system performed a non-stop flight over the 2,700-km (1,678-mile) route from Baikonur to Kiev. The flight was started at a take-off weight of 560 tonnes (1,234,800 lb) and lasted 4 hours and 25 minutes.

During a short stopover in Kiev thousands of people came to take a look at this astounding combination of two flying vehicles. Photos taken during this flight were carried, probably,

by all newspapers and magazines in the USSR. When the Mriya (now re-registered CCCP-82060 in the An-124 registration block) arrived in France for the 38th Paris Air Show, carrying the Buran on its back, hundreds of thousands of spectators from all corners of the world had a chance to see them. The An-225 instantly became a world sensation.

Paris was just the beginning of an unprecedented demonstration of the Soviet aircraft industry's achievements. In August 1989 the An-225 departed for an airshow in Vancouver, Canada. Having seen the aircraft in flight, the country's Prime Minister Brian Mulroony said that Soviet airmen who came to Canada in their aircraft had presented the country's inhabitants with a grand occasion. In September the Mriya visited Prague and was put on show at an exhibition arranged by the Council for Mutual Economic Assistance (COMECON) member nations. In the following year the aircraft took part in the Farnborough '90 aerospace show and in two air shows in the USA (in Oklahoma City and in Seattle, Wash.). The world's biggest aircraft attracted the attention of a great many Americans. The participants of those flights recall that the USA had probably never seen the like of the huge queue that led to the An-225 – so numerous were those who wished to come aboard the aircraft. On 31st August – 5th September 1993 the An-225, now carrying a Ukrainian registration (UR-82060), was presented to the public at the MAKS-93 airshow in Zhukovskiy, and in December of that year it participated in the IDEX'93 show in Dubai. In

1994 the giant from Kiev drew applause in Singapore and Sharjah. Interestingly, the An-225 was far from empty when it flew to all these exhibitions and airshows: it was used for delivering the other Ukrainian exhibits.

During that period the aircraft also performed its first commercial flights. For example, in May 1990 the An-225 piloted by Sergey A. Gorbik and I. I. Bachurin delivered from Chelyabinsk to Yakutia a ChTZ T-800 caterpillar tractor manufactured by the Chelyabinsk Tractor Plant and weighing more than 110 tonnes (242,550 lb). This expedition beyond the Arctic circle, apart from its economic aspect, had major experimental significance because it provided valuable material for studying the new aircraft's transport potential and assessing its operation in the conditions of the North. Later the aircraft undertook flights to the USA and Canada, delivering hundreds of tons of humanitarian aid from these countries to Ukrainian soil.

However, the world-wide fame so quickly gained by the aircraft was but one side of the medal. For various reasons the progress of the Energiya-Buran programme was at first slowed down and then came to a standstill. The funding of the State acceptance trials began to suffer delays. The dissolution of the Soviet Union was accompanied by some elements of uncertainty in the Russian-Ukrainian relations. All these factors combined, coupled with the loss of time caused by modifications and the aircraft's participation in international airshows, led to delays in the schedule of its State acceptance trials which had been started on 15th May 1989. Until the moment of the USSR's dissolution the aircraft had made only 113 test flights with a total flight time of 253 hours and 06 minutes; of these, 14 flights were made with the Buran atop the fuselage (28 hours and 27 minutes). On the credit side was the fact that these flights were performed from airfields situated in different climatic zones of the USSR (Kiev-Gostomel', Kiev-Borispol', Akhtoobinsk (Vladimirovka AB), Baikonur (Leninsk), Moscow-Vnukovo, Petropavlovsk-Kamchatckiy (Yelizovo), Zhukovskiy, Chkalovskaya AB, Khabarovsk-Novyy). After the demise of the USSR, when the Ukraine gained sovereignty, the testing of the An-225 was resumed, but this time on a much smaller scale (due to funding shortages). After the closing down of the Energiya-Buran programme a fairly big part of the Mriya's test programme envisaging flights with ten different externally carried 'space' loads (apart from the Buran itself) was not carried out at all. The main attention was focused on studying the aerodynamically 'clean' aircraft.

In all, up to the moment when the aircraft was 'laid up' in April 1994, the An-225 had performed 339 flights and logged 671 flight hours (these figures include commercial flights and

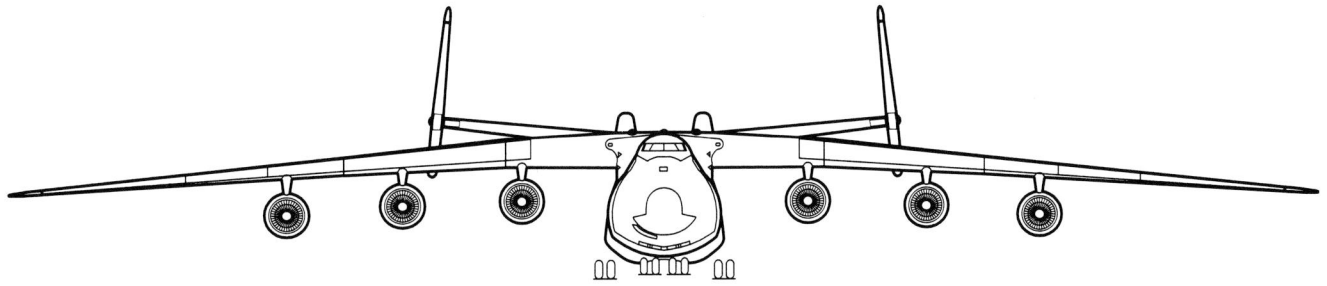

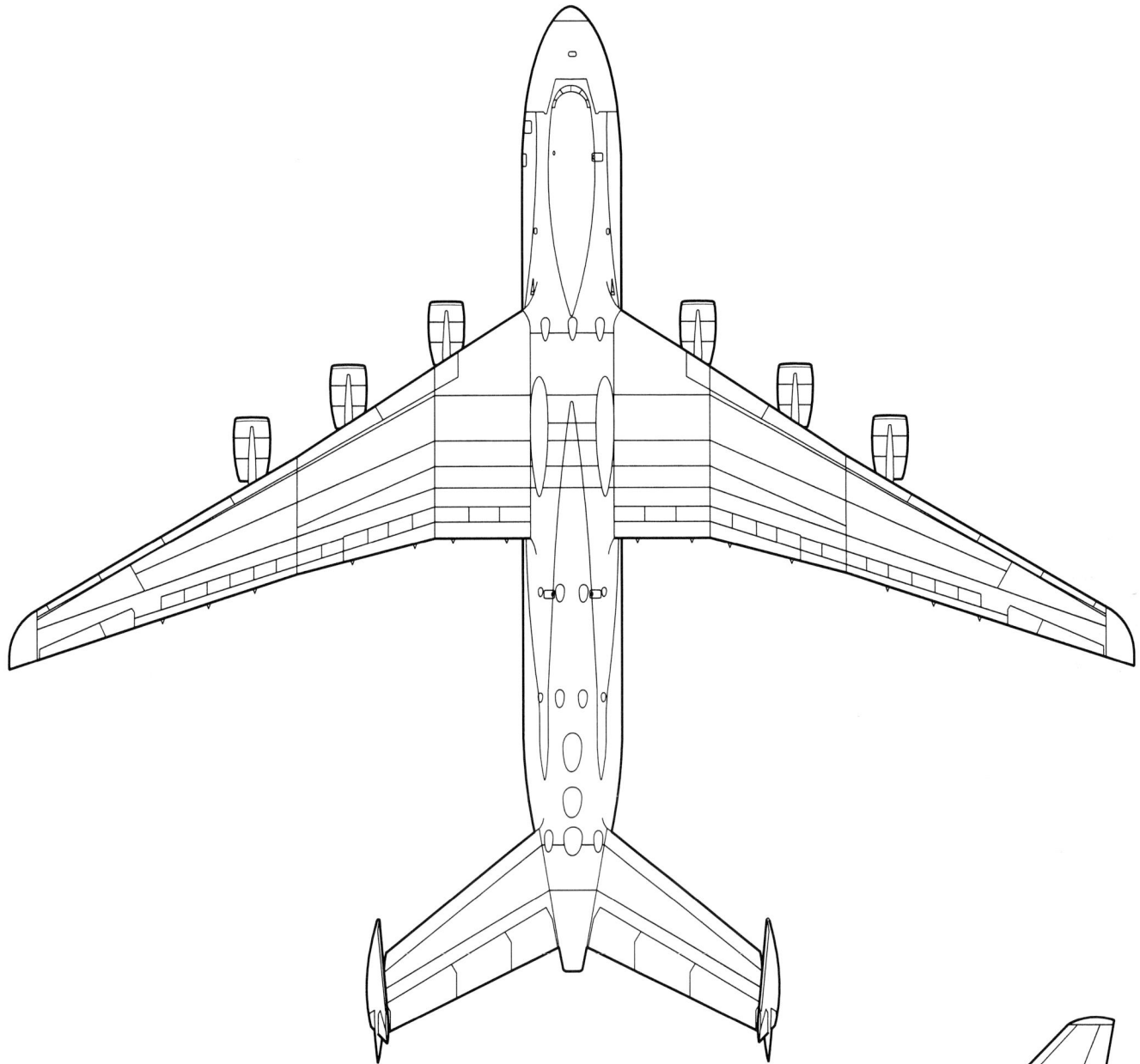

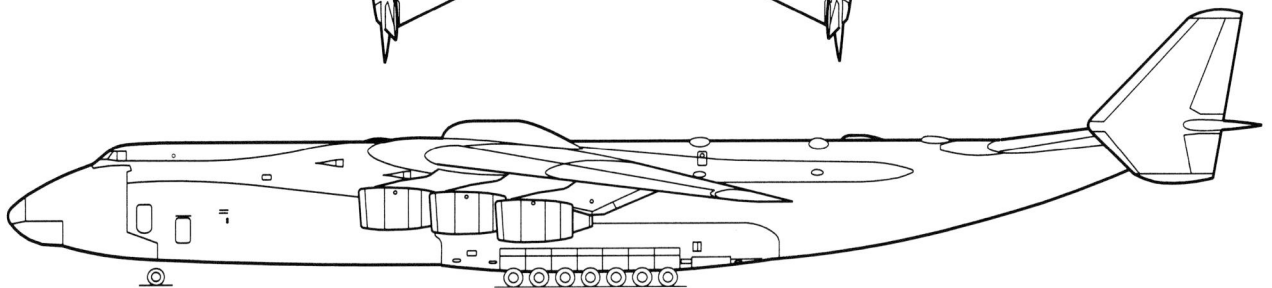

A three-view drawing of the An-225.

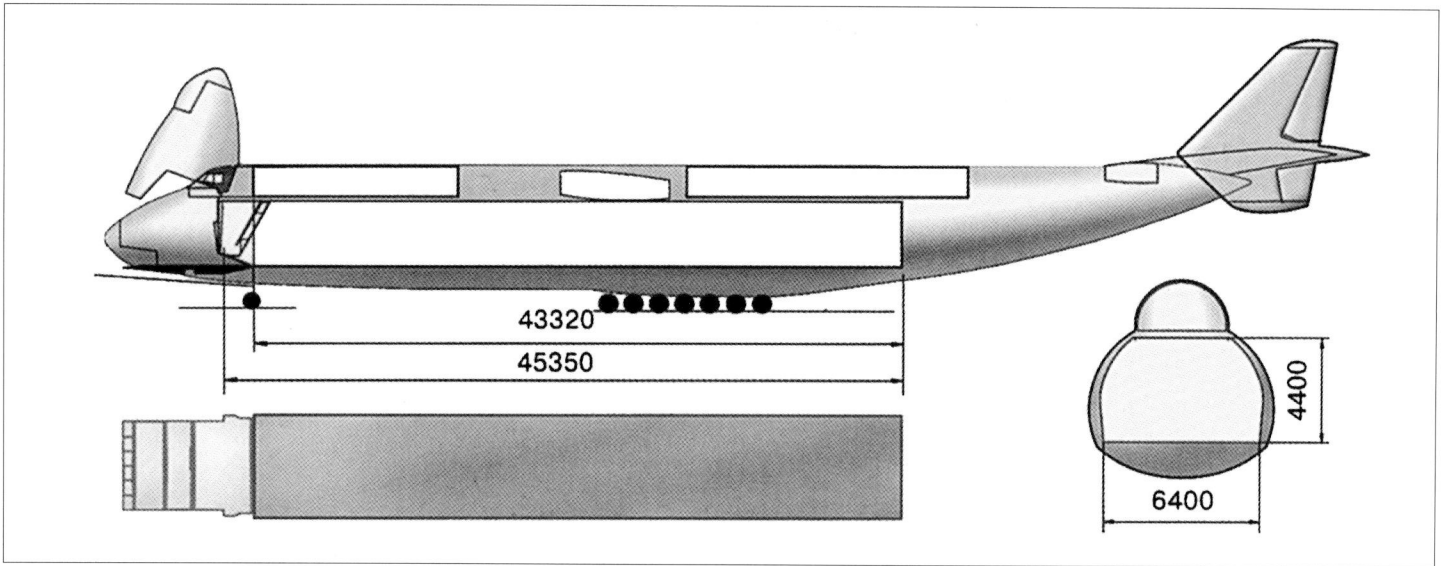

Above: This drawing illustrates the dimensions of the An-225's cargo hold in millimetres (length 142 ft 1½ in less ramp and 148 ft 9½ in including ramp).

participation in exhibitions). A protocol on the results of joint State acceptance trials of the An-225 was signed on 5th January 1996; it stated that the aircraft's characteristics obtained during tests met the stipulated performance almost entirely.

In parallel with the State acceptance trials the aircraft underwent civil certification; a large number of flights performed by it were also accepted as valid in the framework of this programme, and many flights were made specially with a view to certification. Employees of the CIS Aircraft Register (MAK) and the Aviation Register of the Ukraine, of the two countries' certification centres, as well as many independent experts, took part in this work. The certification trials were stopped when no more than 15 or 20 flights remained to be made. This was sad, but this fact was of no major importance: at that time the chances

of putting this aircraft into commercial operation were close to zero. For many years the aircraft was grounded, parked on the edge of Kiev-Gostomel' airfield.

In the course of the following seven years nothing was heard of the An-225. However, in the second half of the 1990s a favourable situation arose for the re-activation of the aircraft. The world air transportation market showed a growing demand for the carriage of super-heavy cargoes, and this prompted the idea of restoring the An-225 to airworthy condition. General Designer Pyotr V. Balabuyev signed the necessary documents, including those calling for the completion of the certification tests. However, the crash of the first prototype An-70, followed by mobilisation of all resources in order to build the second prototype of this machine, delayed the implementation of this plan by several years.

During all this time Antonov Airlines kept receiving inquiries concerning the possibility of using the An-225 commercially. The summer of 2000 saw the commencement of restoration work on the An-225. The company funded this work with its own means, aided by the Motor-Sich engine company which supplied new engines free of charge and undertook to monitor and service the engines in the course of their operational life. The share of the Zaporozhye-based engine company in the restoration costs and, consequently, in the future profits, was 30%. In addition, many other enterprises concluded contracts for their participation in this work; they supplied new equipment units, components of onboard systems and some new airframe parts or reconditioned old ones. Especially comprehensive was the range of jobs accomplished by the Ul'yanovsk-based Aviastar factory which continues to this day the manufacture of the An-124.

Fault diagnosis of the airframe and systems was completed by mid-November 2000, most of the necessary parts and equipment components were repaired or replaced by newly acquired substitutes, and installation of the engines was started. In parallel, the An-225 was being modified into a fully-fledged commercial aircraft capable of flying all over the world without limitations. The machine was fitted with TCAS, a ground proximity warning system (GPWS), equipment enabling reduced vertical separation minima (RVSM) operations, as well as new radios with a frequency grid meeting ICAO standards. In addition, in connection with the forthcoming transportation of single cargoes weighing up to 200 tonnes (441,000 lb) inside the fuselage the cargo floor and the loading ramp were reinforced. The maximum take-off weight was increased from 600 to 640 tonnes (from 1,322,750 to 1,410,930 lb). The installation of

One more view of the An-225, showing the design of the Buran's forward support.

the engines was completed in February 2001, in March all the numerous systems were brought to operational standard, and on 9th April the aircraft was rolled out of the workshop and handed over to the test personnel. Outwardly the only change was that the nose radome was now white, not dark grey.

The decision taken by Antonov ANTK General Designer Pyotr V. Balabuyev to place the An-225 into commercial operation was a difficult one, but it was inevitable. Several countries had placed new orders for cargo versions of the largest Western aircraft – the Airbus A380F and the Boeing 747-400F. In this situation the re-activation of the An-225 could provide the Antonov Airlines with a new and forcible argument for being considered a leader in this market. After all, they could handle cargoes which no other air carrier in the world could transport!

On 7th May 2001, having passed thorough ground checks and having performed dozens of taxying and simulated take-off runs at Kiev-Gostomel', the Mriya took to the air again after a seven-year break and, with a crew captained by Aleksandr V. Galunenko at the controls, performed a 15-minute flight which was immediately reported by virtually all mass media.

In the course of a month the An-225 made nearly 20 test flights without any incidents worthy of note, demonstrating sufficiently high reliability and successfully completing the certification programme; on 26th May, when the aircraft was demonstrated at the ceremony of opening a new runway at Kiev-Borispol', Chairman of the CIS Interstate Aviation Committee Mrs. Tat'yana G. Anodina handed over to its designers the type certificate. Then the Mriya went to France where it was demonstrated at the 44th Paris Air Show. The graceful flights performed by the An-225 in the skies of Paris received favourable comments from specialists and drew admiration from spectators. While representatives of the Antonov Company at the world's most prestigious air show were looking for customers, a steady flow of people queueing up five abreast was heading towards the aircraft from early morning until the evening. From 14th-19th August of that year UR-82060 took part in the MAKS-2001 airshow where it made a single demonstration flight on 15th August.

On 3rd January 2002, chartered by cargo handling agent Chapman Freeborn, the Mriya made its irst post-rebuild commercial flight from Stuttgart to Thumrait, Oman, via Cairo, delivering a 187.5-tonne (413,440-lb) load of prepared meals and clothing to the 405th Air Expeditionary Wing for US forces taking part in Operation *Enduring Freedom*. Another load of food for the US forces – 200 tonnes (440,920 lb) – was delivered from Munich to the Kyrghyz capital of Bishkek two days later.

For loading/unloading the Buran space shuttle a special gantry crane had to be erected at Baikonur – a tremendous structure that dwarfed even the mighty An-225, as these photos testify.

The An-225 became the first aircraft in aviation history to transport that amount of cargo in a single flight.

By September 2002 UR-82060 had been fitted with hushkits to make it ICAO Annex 16/Chapter 3 compliant, with appropriate 'Stage III' inscriptions being applied to all six engine nacelles. Another change to the colour scheme was the addition of 'International Cargo Transporter' titles on the forward fuselage to indicate that the aircraft was now operated by Antonov Airlines. In this guise the An-225 made a demonstration flight at Kiev-Gostomel' on 14th September 2002, the opening day of the Aviasvit-XXI airshow. The most impressive bit, however, came shortly afterwards. After the Mriya had landed, taxied in and shut down, a towbar with a special rope

Above: Overall view of the gigantic crane at Leninsk airfield (now called Tyuratam), Baikonur, as the Buran – the example which made the type's one and only orbital flight in automatic mode – is lowered onto the An-225. The aircraft was towed into the structure from the far side.

An-225 CCCP-480182 with the Buran on top – an awe-inspiring combination – taxies during early compatibillity trials. Note the test equipment video camera at the tip of the port fin. The air data boom was retained, as it was necessary to check out the aircraft's behaviour with the external load.

Above: Another view of the Mriya with the Buran orbiter on top.

The An-225/Buran combination lands after a test flight; the flaps are fully down and the spoilers/lift dumpers are deployed to help slow the machine down. A cloud of white smoke still hangs in the air where the aircraft touched down.

Above and below: The An-225 carries the Buran during an early test flight. The Mriya's high-lift devices are deployed. Note that the Buran's rear fuselage appears to be covered in dirt, with a 'colour division line', straight as if marked with a straight edge, sloping upwards from the wing leading-edge root extensions (LERXes).

Above and below: Two more views of the Mriya/Buran combination in flight. These views show the Buran's flightdeck roof windows and the forward reaction control thrusters ahead of the flightdeck; other thrusters are installed in the fairings flanking the rear fuselage.

Above: The Buran on top of An-225 CCCP-82060 at the 1989 paris Air Show – a sight that turned quite a few heads. The general reaction was that 'the Soviets have stolen the show – again'.

Above: A project which unfortunately came to naught envisaged the use of the An-225 as a flying launch platform for the British Aerospace HOTOL unmanned space shuttle, seen here in model form.

An artist's impression of the HOTOL parting company with the An-225. Note the small wings with no LERXes, the short payload bay, the rocket motor arrangement and the unusual 'rhinoceros' forward fin.

harness was attached to the nose gear units. Next, ten Ukrainian athletes strapped themselves in and, pulling (and yelling!) together, propelled the huge aircraft about 10 metres (30 ft) – an achievement which earned them a place in the Guinness Book of Records.

From then on, commercial and humanitarian airlift flights became quite a routine business for the Mriya, if not a very frequent one. One can possibly single out as something unusual the flight from New York City to Entebbe (Uganda) in early December 2002 when the Mriya delivered to that African country Christmas gifts for children suffering from AIDS. The gifts were collected by American children, many of whom came with their parents to John F. Kennedy International airport to pass the gifts with their own hands and to see the world's biggest aircraft off on its flight. A meeting was held near the aircraft with the participation of senators, popular singers and the children. The total weight of the cargo was 140 tonnes (308,700 lb), but owing to the very long distance to be covered during the flight the take-off weight of the An-225 reached 630 tonnes (1,389,150 lb)! It was the second time in its history that the Mriya took off at such a weight. In Entebbe a meeting was held, too; the Ukrainian pilots were greeted by the country's President and members of the Cabinet of Ministers.

On 23rd March 2003 the Mriya airlifted from Austria to the USA a huge industrial transformer weighing 138 tonnes (304,290 lb) and measuring 4.3 m (14 ft 1 in) in height and more than 11 m (36 ft) in length, as well as some other equipment. The total cargo weight was 175 tonnes (385,875 lb). Thereby the world record for the transportation of a single cargo set in 1995 by the An-124-100 Ruslan was bettered. The tractor-trailer combination to which the transformer was transferred in the US city of Phoenix, Arizona, had more than 50 wheels and a length comparable to that of the Boeing 747. Just a week later, on 29th March, the aircraft delivered industrial air handling units weighing 135 tonnes (297,620 lb) from Houston, Texas, to Dubai (UAE). Commercial flights performed by the An-225 have become convincing proof of the fact that the aircraft can be effectively operated not only for the unique transportation of outsize and super-heavy cargoes but also for the delivery of conventional cargoes. For example, during the recent period when transportation of humanitarian cargoes for the civilian population in the areas of military conflicts became one of Antonov Airlines' main aspects of activity, the Mriya also became involved in this work. In particular, on 10th April 2003 the An-225 delivered 168 tonnes (370,440 lb) of medical equipment to Bahrain.

Some sources credit the refurbished An-225 with the designation An-225-100.

In their plans for the future the Antonov Airlines reckon with having three An-225s in their fleet; the first step in this direction would be the completion of the second An-225 (c/n 01-02) which is still sitting in one of the factory hangars at Kiev-Svyatoshino.

Airliner version of the An-225 (project)

There was a project (reportedly inspired by an Australian citizen) of modifying the An-225 into a super-posh airliner intended to carry 328 passengers in extra comfortable conditions over distances up to 9,700 km (6,025 miles) – for example, on the London-Abu Dhabi-Singapore-Sydney route. Its three-deck fuselage would accommodate sleeping compartments, normal passenger cabins, a shop, a restaurant and a casino. In this case the aircraft was to be fitted with engines and avionics of Western manufacture.

According to some sources, there were two more passenger version projects; one of them was a combi version intended to carry 400 passengers and a number of cargo containers, the other version could accommodate 700 to 800 passengers.

An-225 as a carrier of space vehicles (projects)

In the late 1980s and early 1990s the world's leading aerospace companies initiated serious studies with a view to creating a cheap and environmentally friendly space transport means for delivering useful loads to circum-Earth orbits. A series of projects emerged; these included the NASP (National Aero-SpacePlane, USA), the Sänger (Germany), the Hope (Japan) and others. These projects made use of horizontal launch, either from the ground (NASP) or at altitude from a carrier/booster aircraft, followed by a landing in aircraft mode.

Work of this kind was conducted also in Great Britain, including, in particular, the British Aerospace HOTOL (Horizontal Take-Off and Landing) project. In accordance with the initial concept the HOTOL was an unmanned re-usable single-stage aerospace vehicle. However, due to the great technical risk and enormous costs involved the funding of the project was stopped in 1987. In May 1989 at the presentation of the An-225 aircraft at Kiev-Borispol' airport Antonov OKB General Designer Pyotr V. Balabuyev asked British journalists to recommend to specialists of the BAe company that they study the possibility of using the An-225 as the first stage for an airborne launch of their vehicle. As early as September 1990 a presentation of the Soviet-British 'An-225 – Interim HOTOL' project took place at the Farnborough '90 aerospace show.

Thanks to the mobile airborne launch this system had a number of substantial advantages in comparison with systems featuring vertical or horizontal launch from the ground. A high degree of re-usability ensured by the use of the An-225 and fully recoverable units of the HOTOL vehicle promised lower costs for placing useful loads into orbit as compared to existing means. The system met

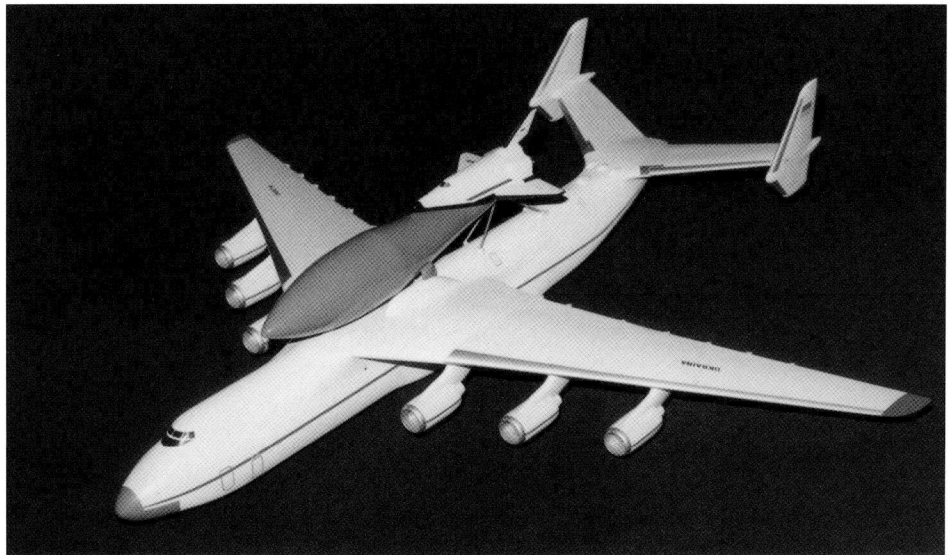

The projects envisaging the use of the An-225 in future space programmes included utilising it as a launch vehicle for the MAKS reusable transport system in manned (above) and unmanned (below) versions.

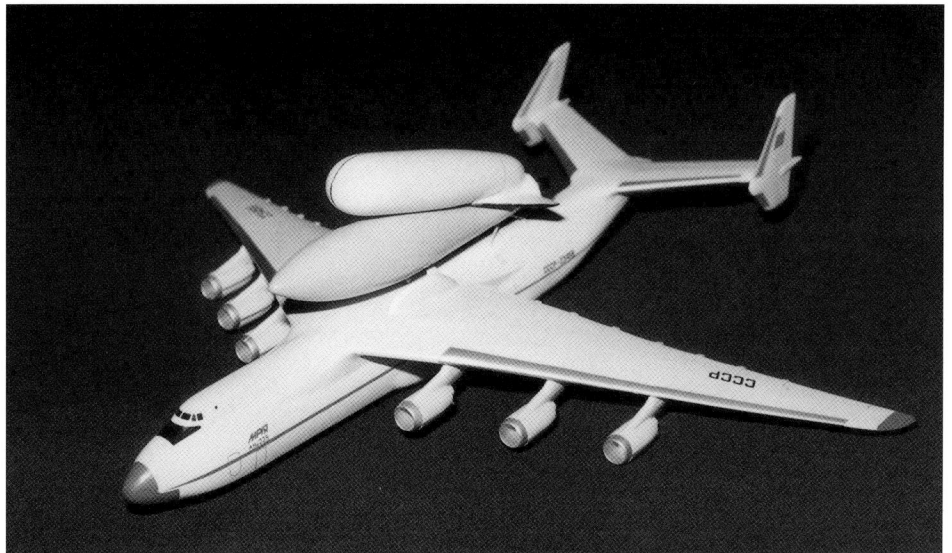

contemporary environmental requirements as regards noise levels, since the ignition of the second-stage rocket motors was to take place at an altitude of 9-10 km (29,520-32,800 ft). This permitted the use of civil airfields.

Within the framework of a joint study BAe developed the space vehicle and the onboard

An artist's impression of the An-225 carrying the Ukrainian Svityaz' suborbital launch space system.

Above: The An-225 hangared at Kiev-Svyatoshino in 2001 during refurbishment to airworthy condition with a higher payload. The aircraft still carries the Le Bourget '89 exhibit code 387.

The reborn Mriya at le Bourget again in 2001 – after all those years, now wearing the new exhibit code 410. Note the white nose radome.

complement of launch equipment to be installed in the An-225, while the Ukrainian and Russian specialists developed the carrier aircraft and the main engines for the space vehicle. In the course of 1990-91 designers from the Antonov ANTK, TsAGI and NPO Molniya together with BAe carried out a substantial volume of calculations, design and research work for the purpose of evolving the configuration of the aerospace system based on the An-225. The validity of the calculated aerodynamic properties, flight characteristics, field performance and dynamic characteristics of the carrier aircraft was confirmed in the course of testing the aerodynamic and flutter models of the Interim HOTOL vehicle as a part of the system, conducted in the wind tunnels of the Antonov ANTK and TsAGI.

The system was intended to work in the following fashion. The An-225 would take off with the HOTOL space vehicle carried piggyback. Before separation the carrier would attain the speed and altitude necessary for the launch of the aerospace vehicle. Five seconds before the launch two of the four liquid-fuel rocket motors of the HOTOL space vehicle would be ignited, and two seconds before the launch the two rocket motors would be set to preliminary thrust mode. This would be followed by the separation of the aerospace vehicle which would immediately start climbing. The carrier aircraft would deploy its airbrakes and descend, turning away in order to ensure a safe distance between it and the HOTOL. Three seconds after the separation the other two rocket motors were to be ignited, and a further three seconds later all the motors of the aerospace vehicle would achieve full thrust, speeding the HOTOL into orbit.

On 21st June 1991 a presentation of the system took place in the European Space Agency (ESA) in Paris. It was attended by 27 ESA specialists, 9 specialists from the Soviet Ministry of Aircraft Industry and 6 from the British Aerospace company. A report prepared jointly by BAe, the Antonov ANTK, TsAGI and TsIAM apparently convinced the ESA experts of the feasibility of the 'Mriya-HOTOL' project and of the lower cost of placing loads into basic orbits as compared to the Ariane-5 SLV and the Hermes space shuttle. After all, the carrier was already in existence, and TsAGI possessed a potent experimental basis for the development of space technology. Powerful engines for the Interim HOTOL were to be developed by the Voronezh-based KB Khimavtomatika (Chemical Automation Design Bureau) which had designed the main engines for the Energiya SLV.

By the mid-1990s NPO Molniya had completed the preliminary design work on a counterpart to the Interim HOTOL system. This was

Above: 'With a rebel yell...' On 14th September 2002 ten Ukrainian athletes made the Guinness Book of Records by pulling the An-225. The athletes used special 'stairs' affixed to the ground for better traction.

The ten big men pose in front of the Mriya, wearing T-shirts with the logo of the 'Brawny Men's Games' sports festival sponsored by the Ukrainian Federation of Sports and Athletics (UFSA).

the MAKS (in this case, *mnogorazovaya aviatsionno-kosmicheskaya sistema* – re-usable aerospace system) which envisaged the placing into orbit of a load of 8.5-10 tonnes (18,740-22,050 lb) in a manned version and 18-19 tonnes (39,690-41,895 lb) in an unmanned version. The system comprised the An-225 carrier aircraft and an aerospace vehicle for single or multiple use. The MAKS was intended for placing a load of 8.5 to 10 tonnes (18,740 to 22,050 lb) into an orbit of 200 km (124 miles) above the Earth. A disposable unmanned version could place a useful load of up to 18 tonnes (39,690 lb) into low orbits.

In the summer of 1999 information was published about one more re-usable aerospace system based on the An-225 Mriya carrier aircraft. Dubbed Svityaz', it comprised also units of the Zenith-2 carrier rocket and was intended for placing useful loads of up to 8 tonnes (17,640 lb) into low orbits.

Carrier aircraft	An-225	An-225	An-225
MAKS version	M-OS	M-T	M-M
Take-off weight of the second stage, tonnes (lb)	275 (606·260)	275 (606·260)	275 (606·260)
Weight of the useful load in orbit, tonnes (lb)			
H = 200 km (124 miles), i = 51°	8.3-9.5 (18,300-20,947)	18.0 (39,690)	5.5 (12,127)
H = 400 km (248 miles), i = 51°	7.0-8.2 (15,435-18,080)	17.4 (38,367)	3.5 (7,717)
stationary Earth orbit	-	4.8 (10,584)	-

i = orbit inclination

This view of the An-225 at the MAKS-93 airshow illustrates the open cargo hatch. Parked alongside is the An-32P Firekiller waterbomber prototype (UR-48004).

Aero-marine rescue system based on the An-225 and the Orlyonok (project)

Design work was conducted on a project of an international aero-marine rescue system in which the An-225 would deliver a piggy-back-mounted Orlyonok wing-in-ground effect (WIG) vehicle, or *ekranoplan* (to use the widely known Russian term) to aid ships in distress. The Orlyonok was a large *ekranoplan* developed and built by the Nizhniy Novgorod-based Science & Production Association named after Rostislav A. Alekseyev, originally known as the Central Hydrofoil Design Bureau. The Orlyonok would start from the An-225 in a fashion similar to the space vehicles; then it would alight, pick up the crew of the ship in distress and proceed on its own to the nearest seaport. Thanks to its high cruising speed this rescue system would guarantee the shortest possible time for coming to the rescue of the seamen.

Structural description of the An-225

The An-225 is a high-wing monoplane featuring a normal aerodynamic layout with swept-back wings and tail surfaces. The structure makes wide use of high-strength steel, duralumin and titanium alloys. Among these, special mention should be made of alloys containing zirconium. In the landing gear use is made of VT-22 high-strength titanium and 30KhGSN2MA steel. Some airframe assemblies are made almost entirely of composites (CFRP, organic plastics and GFRP).

To reduce costs and speed up the manufacture and testing of the aircraft, and bearing in mind the fact that the aircraft was intended to be built in small numbers, the An-225's airframe and systems make use of various units, assemblies and equipment used and perfected on its predecessor – the An-124. Substantial changes were introduced only into the tail unit, the integrated flight system, the system of automated onboard monitoring and engine control system and some indicators. Otherwise, the differences are due only to the special design features associated with the increased number of consumers and greater consumption (for example, of hydraulic fluid), with new location of units and the like.

All systems of the aircraft are highly automated and require minimum crew interference into their functioning. This is ensured by the 34 onboard computers, by a high degree of systems redundancy and their monitoring, by the reliable functioning of units and equipment items.

Fuselage: The An-225's fuselage is based on that of the An-124 but its length has been increased by 7 metres. The fuselage has a double-deck layout: the crew, equipment and cargo attendants are accommodated on the upper deck, the lower deck is occupied by the cargo hold. The cargo hold can accommodate cargoes with a total weight of up to 250 tonnes (551,250 lb). For example, it can carry 60-80 C-class ('Golf class') cars or sea-land containers. To ensure loading and unloading, the fuselage is provided with an upward-hinged nose visor and a three-section loading ramp identical to those of the An-124. The immense stresses affecting the rear fuselage made it impossible to retain the rear cargo hatch after the fashion of the An-124. The cargo hold is equipped with cargo handling devices (an overhead crane and floor-mounted roller tracks), tie-down devices and a closed-circuit TV system for monitoring the hold. The overhead cargo handling device ensures the lifting and moving of cargoes weighing up to 20 tonnes (44,100 lb) apiece; the floor-mounted cargo handling device is intended for loading and unloading non-self-propelled wheeled vehicles, self-propelled wheeled and tracked vehicles and palletised cargoes weighing up to 50 tonnes (110,250 lb). The cargo hold is pressurised and heated.

The forward fuselage houses the flight-deck providing work stations for six crew; located aft of it are an electronic equipment bay, a cabin for a relief crew with six bunks, a galley, a wardrobe and a toilet. In the event of the carriage of cargoes requiring monitoring the temperature and pressure in the cargo

Part of the An-225's crew rest area with two couches, a collapsible table and a foldaway upper sleeping berth. A second identically configured compartment is located across the aisle.

hold, the crew is augmented by an operator. The rear part of the upper cabin is used for accommodating a team which ensures loading, unloading and maintenance of cargoes carried externally.

Wings: Cantilever shoulder-mounted swept monoplane wings of trapezoidal planform with slight anhedral from the roots. The wings are assembled of integral structures (eleven integral panels in a chordwise arrangement). The structure is made of large-length (up to 30 m/98 ft) stamped panels with end fittings, and of rolled slabs. Such a structure meets the survivability criteria not only in the event of a crack spanning over two bays (which is normally considered admissible), but also in the case of a complete disintegration of one or two underside panels. The panels are joined together by titanium bolts installed with a tension of 0.8-1.2 % which ensures air/water-tightness and high resistance to fatigue. The end fitting made it possible to dispense with cut-off joints featuring thousands of bolts and to considerably simplify the assembly process.

Structurally the wings are made up of five pieces: the centre section (which is integral with the fuselage), inner wing sections and outer wing sections, plus tip fairings. The outer wing sections carrying the Nos 1, 2, 5 and 6 engine pylons are borrowed from the An-124 with insignificant changes. The inner wing sections carrying the Nos 3 and 4 engine pylons are new, featuring flaps but no leading-edge slats, and the wing centre section to which they are mated has been redesigned; the inner wings span 21.6 m (70 ft 10⅜ in), the height being 2.4 m (7 ft 10½ in). The inner wings are equipped with flaps and spoilers. Four-section leading-edge slats are provided on the outer wings only.

The galley of the An-225 with food heaters to the left of the table and storage lockers below it.

Tail unit: Twin-fin tail assembly. The cantilever shoulder-mounted swept *horizontal tail* features moderate dihedral and has a span of about 30 m (98 ft 5 in); its area comes close to the wing area of the IL-76 transport aircraft, which is 300 m² (3,225 sq ft). It is made entirely of stamped panels and rolled slabs. The *vertical tails* have a pentagonal shape, with a Vee-shaped leading edge, and are canted slightly inwards. The rudders are divided into two sections above and below the stabilisers, with aft-pointing conical fairings in between at the fin/stabiliser junctions.

Landing gear: Hydraulically retractable tricycle type; based on that of the An-124, except that the nose units are reinforced and each main unit comprises seven struts instead of five. To improve ground manoeuvrability, the last four main gear struts on each side are castoring; after lift-off the swivelling parts of

the castoring struts are locked neutral by centering devices. All the struts are independent and can be extended separately, which practically rules out a wheels-up landing. The landing gear is equipped with a system for measuring the weights sustained by it; this considerably simplifies the monitoring of the aircraft's weight and CG position. The wheels are fitted with carbon brakes; tyre pressure is 11.5 kg/cm² (164 psi).

Powerplant: Six 23,400-kgp (51,600-lbst) Lotarev D-18T turbofans in underwing nacelles and two TA-12 APUs in the aft sections of both main gear fairings. The APUs ensure independent power supply to all aircraft systems and engine starting.

Control system: The aircraft's control system comprises a quadruply redundant electro-hydromechanical manual control system and

a fly-by-wire system controlling the high-lift devices with dual redundancy. The control system also includes: an electro-hydromechanical automatic artificial-feel system in the elevator and aileron circuits, an electro-mechanical trimming and balancing system in the elevator circuit, an electro-hydromechanical stability augmentation system in the rudder and elevator circuits, and an electro-mechanical system for changing the gearing ratio in the rudder and elevator circuits. An indication system in the flightdeck shows the position of control surfaces and high-lift devices.

Remote control system: The remote control system is intended to considerably reduce control forces on the engine controls and to enhance precision in setting the operation modes. It is a twin-channel electric system. It is duplicated by mechanical linkages. The

Above: This rear view of the An-225 shows the inner faces of the fins, the flattened 'beaver tail' section of the dielectric tailcone and the absence of a rear loading hatch. The nose loading hatch is open and the ramp deployed, hence the absence of a visible gap underneath the aircraft.

main channel of the remote control system is connected to a 200/115 V AC circuit, the back-up channel is connected to a 27 V DC circuit. Each of the channels ensures the movement of the fuel flow regulator control levers with a speed of 40° per second. To increase the speed of movement during take-off and landing, both channels are switched on; as a result, the speed of movement is doubled. Normally the remote control system operates in the main channel; in the event of its failure the back-up channel is switched on automatically. If both channels suffer a failure, control is effected by means of mechanical linkages.

Fuel system: All fuel is housed in 18 fuel tanks, with single-point pressure refuelling. The fuel system comprises a number of ancillary systems, such as a venting system, a fuel consumption control system, a centralised condensate (water) draining system, a water condensate indication system, a fuel heating system and others.

Electrics: Three centralised electric power supply systems ensure the supply of electric current to onboard consumers. The primary electric power sources are functionally divided into three groups: main (engine-driven generators), auxiliary (APU-driven generators) and emergency (storage batteries). Each successive group of sources ensures, with certain limitations, the power supply to consumers in the event of a failure of the preceding group. In a fashion similar to the electric power sources there are three groups of distribution circuitry buses. When all the sources are functioning normally, each system is divided into subsystems for the port and starboard sides of the aircraft. Should any one of the sources fail, their power distri-

A side view of the An-225's tail unit; the lower rudder sections are much smaller than the upper ones. Note the many faired cargo attachment points on the rear fuselage.

bution buses are automatically backed up by the operative sources of their own or the opposite side.

Integrated hydraulic system: The integrated hydraulic system comprises four independent systems and two back-up hydraulic systems for the control of the inner and outer wing flaps, as well as leading-edge slats. All systems use AMG-10 oil-type hydraulic fluid. The main sources of hydraulic power are variable-capacity plunger pumps installed in pairs on the Nos 1, 2, 5 and 6 engines. To conserve the service life of the main hydraulic pumps, provision is made for relieving them in turn during the flight. A back-up source of hydraulic pressure for the main systems is provided by hydraulic transformers and turbine pump units. Electrically-driven pumping units are connected to the emergency power supply bus.

Monitoring system: The automated onboard monitoring system is intended for monitoring the status of the aircraft's equipment on the ground and in flight, as well as for monitoring the crew's actions. It ensures collection and processing of information about the technical condition of systems and avionics sets. The monitoring results are fed to displays and recording devices. In addition, the monitoring system sends stimulating and controlling

Above and below: The engines of the An-225 and their nacelles and pylons are completely identical to those of the An-124; thus, thrust reversers are provided on all six engines.

inputs into onboard systems and conducts a pre-programmed search of the failure location down to the line replaceable unit. All information is transmitted to displays at the flight engineer's and electrics engineer's workstations; information requiring an immediate reaction on the part of the crew is transmitted to the pilots' workstations.

The flightdeck of the An-225; note the impressive bank of throttles in the middle. The round boxes on the control yokes are part of the test equipment, housing turn angle sensors, and the rather crude-looking yokes themselves are purely provisional (compare with those of the An-124 on page 60).

The An-225 makes a demonstration flight at Kiev-Gostomel' on 14th September 2002, the opening day of the Aviasvit-XXI airshow.

Air conditioning system and environmental control system. The air conditioning system and the environmental control system create the necessary comfort in the flightdeck and the cabin for cargo attendants. In case of need a pressure differential of 0.25 kg/cm^2 (3.56 psi) is maintained in the cargo hold and heating is turned on. The air is tapped from the Nos 1, 2, 5 and 6 engines and from the APUs.

Anti-icing system: The anti-icing system protects very limited areas; research has shown that ice formation on surfaces of this size affects their lifting properties only to an insignificant extent, and the aircraft's handling remains satisfactory even after the build-up of ice accretions having the most unfavourable shapes. Hot-air de-icing on the leading-edge slats and engine air intakes, and electro-thermal de-icing for the pitot heads and flightdeck windscreen.

Thermostatic control and pressurisation system: During the transportation of certain externally mounted cargoes it is necessary to maintain a positive temperature or a positive pressure differential inside these items. In particular, the central module of the Energiya SLV is capable of sustaining only longitudi-

nally directed stresses. Since the module is transported in a horizontal position and is pressurised with an excess of pressure for the sake of structural strength, it needs to be hermetically sealed. For the first launches of this rocket its elements were delivered on an aircraft which lacked this system. Therefore the rocket fuel tanks had to be sealed just as carefully as medical ampoules. The An-225 can transport the Energiya SLV's central module in fully assembled and adjusted condition. As a result of the stresses caused by ram air pressure and vibrations, the sealing can be

damaged, resulting in decompression and loss of rigidity. To ensure safe carriage of such loads, the aircraft is provided with a thermostatic control and pressurisation system which monitors the condition of the cargoes during flight and maintains the specified temperatures and pressures in the process of their transportation.

Avionics and equipment: The navigation and communications avionics suite installed in the aircraft ensures its all-weather operation in any part of the world.

Basic specifications of the An-225

Length overall	84.0 m (275 ft 7 in)
Height on ground	18.1 m (59 ft 4$^{19}\!/\!_{32}$ in) *
Wing span	88.4 (290 ft)
Wing area, m^2 (sq ft)	905 (9,742)
Maximum all-up weight, tonnes (lb)	600 (1,323,000)
Maximum payload, tonnes (lb)	250 (551,250)
Weight of a single-unit cargo, tonnes (lb)	200 (441,000)
Speed, km/h (mph)	800-850 (497-528)
Range, km (miles:	
with a 200 t (485,100 lb) payload in the cargo hold	4,500 (2,797)
with a 150 t (330,750 lb) payload in the cargo hold	7,000 (4,350)
with a maximum fuel load	15,000 (9,323)
Runway length, m (ft)	3,000-3,500 (9,840-11,480)

* With the landing gear in normal (parking) position

Chapter 5

Propfan Promise

An-70 medium transport aircraft

In the early 1980s a decision was taken in the USSR to start design work on a medium military transport aircraft designated An-70 and its commercial derivative, the An-70T (*trahnsportnyy* – transport, used attributively); these aircraft were to supersede the An-12 which was becoming obsolescent. This decision was based on a survey of the available cargo aircraft fleet and of the prospects of cargo transportation development. The urgency of creating a new medium-haul, medium-payload commercial cargo aircraft was further enhanced by the fact that a large number of freighters – primarily An-12s, but also some early-production IL-76s – operated by the Soviet state airline Aeroflot were approaching the end of their service life.

As the reader might imagine, the early research and development work on the An-70 proceeded in utmost secrecy. The first advanced development project was completed in 1983; yet the decision to start the work on the An-70 was not officially made public until 1988. The An-70 was designed to a specification issued by the Soviet Ministry of

Civil Aviation (MGA – *Ministerstvo grazhdahnskoy aviahtsii*). The specification called for an aircraft whose flight and field performance, as well as the technical features, would enable it to replace the An-12 and, to a certain extent, the IL-76. It was envisaged that the An-70 would considerably expand the sphere of use of medium-haul and medium-payload cargo aircraft. Apart from being able to perform cargo transportation on trunk routes with an improvement in technical performance and operating economics as compared to the existing cargo aircraft, the An-70 was to be tailored for some specific tasks, such as the carriage of heavyweight containers (for example, sea-land containers), non-standard cargoes and vehicles in conditions when the network of high-class airfields was not sufficiently developed. The aircraft was also expected to surpass the An-12 in field performance, be roughly equivalent to the IL-76 in cargo-carrying capacity and possess cargo hold dimensions that would enable it to carry the whole range of cargo items that were handled by the An-22 heavy airlifter.

In addition, at that time the world market also offered a potential niche for such a medium-haul, medium-payload cargo aircraft intended for the carriage of one or two heavy containers, outsize single (unit) cargoes or heavy hardware items. Non-scheduled cargo haulage made up more than 25% of the total cargo transportation volume; at that time it was one of the most profitable branches of air transport services outside the Soviet Union. It was effected either by civil versions of the obsolescent Lockheed C-130 Hercules (the L-382) and Transall C.160 aircraft, or by cargo versions of wide-body airliners (the Boeing 747-200F and -200M (SCD), the McDonnell Douglas DC-10-30CF, the Airbus Industrie A300B4F). It was assumed that the An-70 could partly fill that cargo transportation niche.

The aerodynamic layout of the An-70 was refined at TsAGI; it ensured a high lift/drag ratio for this class of aircraft. The circular-section fuselage measured 5.6 m (18 ft 4½ in) in diameter and featured a rear cargo hatch closed by triple doors and a loading ramp.

This model illustrates the An-70 as envisaged by the original advanced development project of 1983. It looks very similar to the real thing as eventually built, major differences being the five flap tracks on each side instead of four and the absence of the fin tip fairing – and, of course, the An-70 never wore Aeroflot colours...

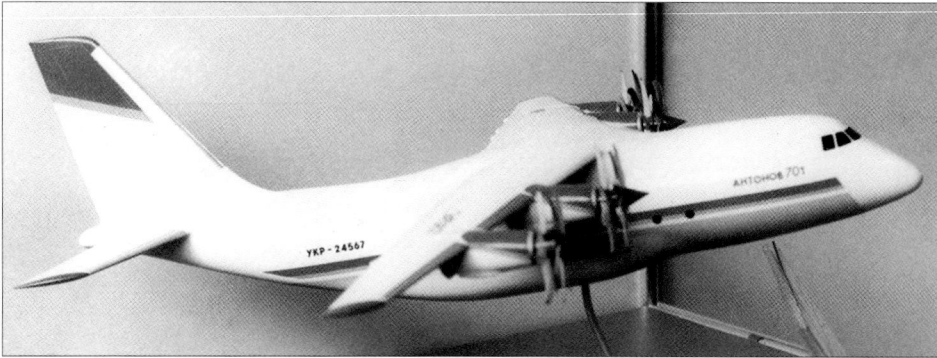

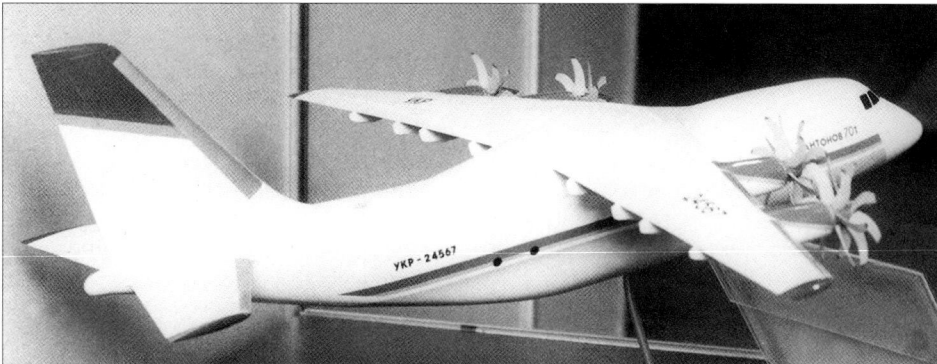

This model of the An-70 was displayed at the Aviadvigatel'-93 (Aero Engine '93) exhibition in Moscow. The number of the flap tracks is correct now but there's still no fin tip fairing and the cargo cabin window arrangement is to change yet.

The moderately swept shoulder-mounted wings with slight anhedral carried four prop-fan engines (which were under development at the time) in nacelles adhering directly to the wing underside; for the first time in the world a transport aircraft would be powered by propfan engines. The swept conventional tail unit included a fuselage-mounted horizontal tail with zero dihedral; the aircraft had a tricycle landing gear with three independent twin-wheel struts in tandem on each main unit.

According to the original ADP the An-70 would be powered by four 10,900-ehp (8,128-ekW) Lotarev D-236T propfan engines driving SV-36 tractor propfans of 4.2 m (13 ft 9¹¹/₃₂ in) diameter. Created by ZMKB Progress under V. A. Lotarev, the D-236T was a derivative of the D-136 turboshaft powering the Mi-26 heavy transport helicopter. This engine, in turn, was based on the core of the proven 6,500-kgp (14,330-lbst) D-36 turbofan powering the An-72/An-74 twinjet STOL transport

and the Yakovlev Yak-42 trijet short/medium-haul airliner. The SV-36 developed by the Stoopino Machinery Design Bureau (later renamed NPP Aerosila, ie, Aeropower Scientific & Production Association) was a contra-rotating propfan featuring eight blades on the front and six on the rear row. These ran at 1,100 and 1,000 rpm respectively; the 100-rpm difference was intended to reduce noise and vibration. The straight blades with slightly raked tips were made of glassfibre with a hollow composite spar and integrated electric de-icing threads.

Tests of the D-236T began in 1987. The engine was put through its paces on two flying testbeds operated by LII in Zhukovskiy – the IL-76LL4 (CCCP-76529, c/n 073410308, l/n 0807), where it was fitted instead of the port inboard engine, and the Yak-42LL (alias Yak-42E, CCCP-42525, c/n 11030703), where it was mounted on a special pylon instead of the starboard engine.

As of September 1983, the An-70 was to have an overall length of 41.4 m (135 ft 10 in), a wing span of 47.5 m (155 ft 10 in) and stand 14.4 m (47 ft 3 in) tall on the ground. The maximum take-off weight was set at 93,100 kg (205,250 lb); the aircraft was to have a never-exceed speed of 600 km/h (372 mph), a maximum cruising speed of 550 km/h (341 mph) and a minimum control speed of 170 km/h (105.5 mph). The cruise altitude was 9,000-11,000 m (29,530-36,090 ft) and the service ceiling was 11,300 m (37,070 ft), decreasing to 9,800 m (32,150 ft) with one engine inoperative. In the commercial version the crew consisted of four persons – two pilots, a flight engineer and a loadmaster; there was also room for two cargo attendants.

However, many aircraft have a tendency to grow in the course of design. Soon the customer submitted a revised specification, requiring the An-70's MTOW to be increased to 123,000 kg (271,164 lb). This was too much for the D-236T engines, which apparently had no reserves for uprating. The Antonov OKB was forced to rework the project accordingly. By 1990 the aircraft featured a new power-plant consisting of four 14,000-eshp (10,290-kW) D-27 propfans developed by ZMKB's new Chief Designer Fyodor M. Muravchenko and driving Aerosila SV-27 contraprops of 4.5 m (14 ft 9⁵/₃₂ in.) diameter. The need to use a 'clean sheet of paper' engine instead of one based on proven components undoubtedly contributed to the An-70's subsequent development problems.

Again, the propfans had eight blades on the front and six on the rear row but the blades were scimitar-shaped; this ensured high cruising speeds while providing a 30% lower fuel burn as compared to contemporary turbofan engines. In late 1990 a prototype D-27 engine was fitted to IL-76LL CCCP-76529; prior to that, the engine had run for many hours on a ground test bench).

Thanks to the high-set wings the air intakes of the D-27 engines were placed high above the ground (5.5 m/18 ft); the outer propfans' blade tip clearance was also big (3.2 m/10 ft 6 in). Thereby the blades were well protected from foreign object damage. Coupled with the multi-wheel undercarriage, this enabled the aircraft to operate from dirt, gravel and grass airstrips. The high-set wings also allowed the maintenance vehicles to move freely around the aircraft. The fuselage parameters were thoroughly optimised as regards aerodynamics and the structural layout; this made it possible to create within the dimensions of a medium-sized aircraft an aerial cargo hauler with the cargo hold dimensions close to those of heavy transport machines. As a result, the list of cargo items that could be carried by the aircraft was enlarged by a factor of 1.5-2, which made the

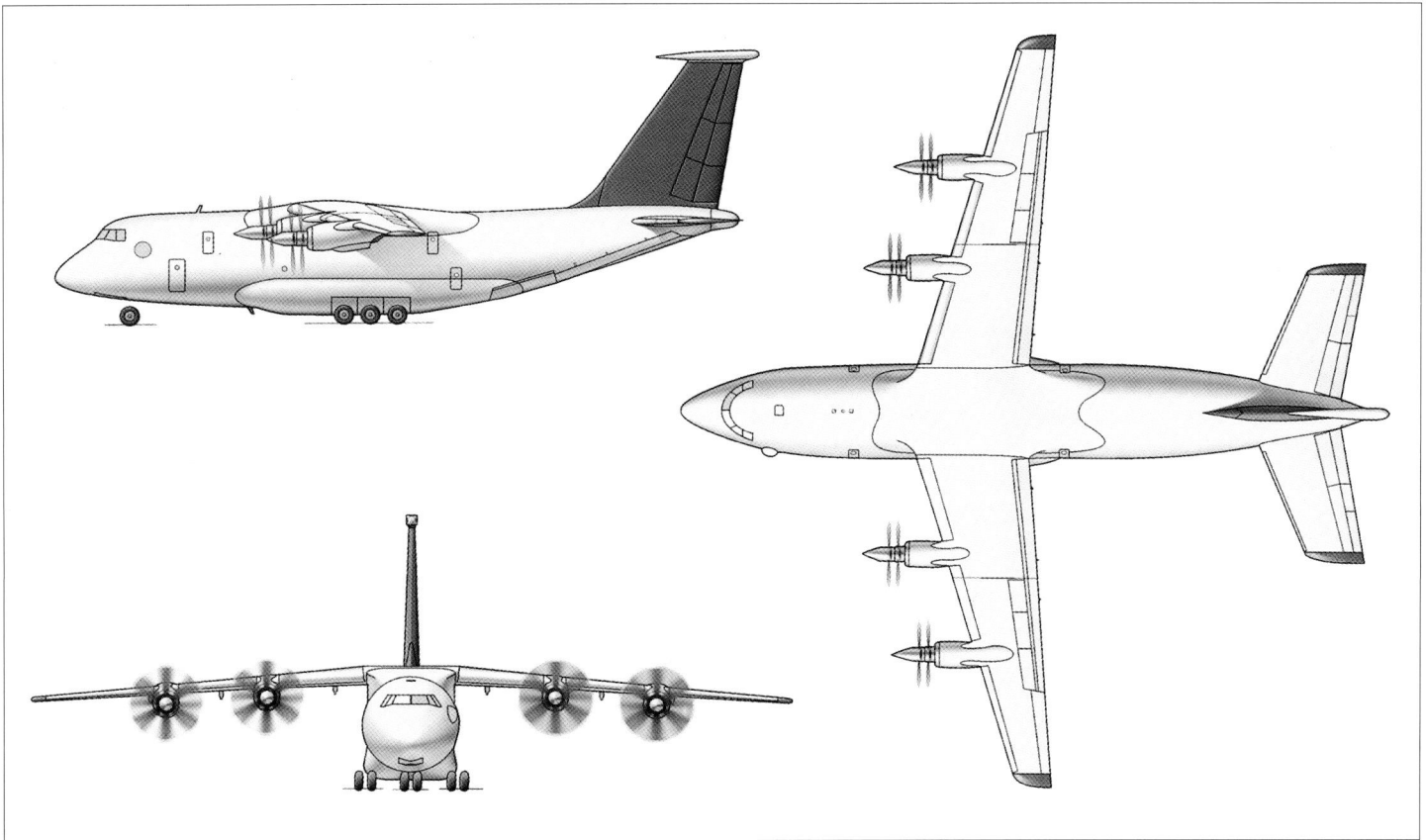

A three-view of the An-70 as eventually built. Note that the flap track fairings do not protrude beyond the wing trailing edge.

utilisation of the aircraft more intensive, increasing the number of hours logged and the profitability of operation.

Being a new-generation transport aircraft, the An-70 was superior to the An-12 in all parameters, possessing a 1.8 times greater maximum payload, a 1.3 times higher cruising speed, a 1.5 times higher cruise altitude, thrice the cargo hold volume and a 10 times longer range with a 20-tonne (44,100-lb) payload.

The volume of the An-70's cargo hold surpassed that of the IL-76 by one-third and was three times greater than that of the basic ('short') Lockheed C-130 and the Transall C.160; it could accommodate virtually all types of armament and army vehicles of the CIS and NATO countries. Moreover, as distinct from Soviet and foreign transport aircraft, the width of the cargo hold made it possible to accommodate vehicles and other hardware in two rows. The cargo hold could accommodate 300 fully equipped troops or 206 stretcher patients with medical attendants; in the 300-seat troop carrier (non-paradropping) version a lightweight upper deck with seats was suspended from the ceiling, a feature found previously on the military versions of the IL-76. The An-70's systems enabled it to operate independently from unequipped airfields in the course of 200 hours thanks to the APU which catered for electric power supply and air conditioning, to the onboard automated monitoring system and the necessary amount of spares kits on board and to the onboard mechanised cargo handling devices. The high technical potential of the An-70 made it possible to develop within short time limits a whole family of

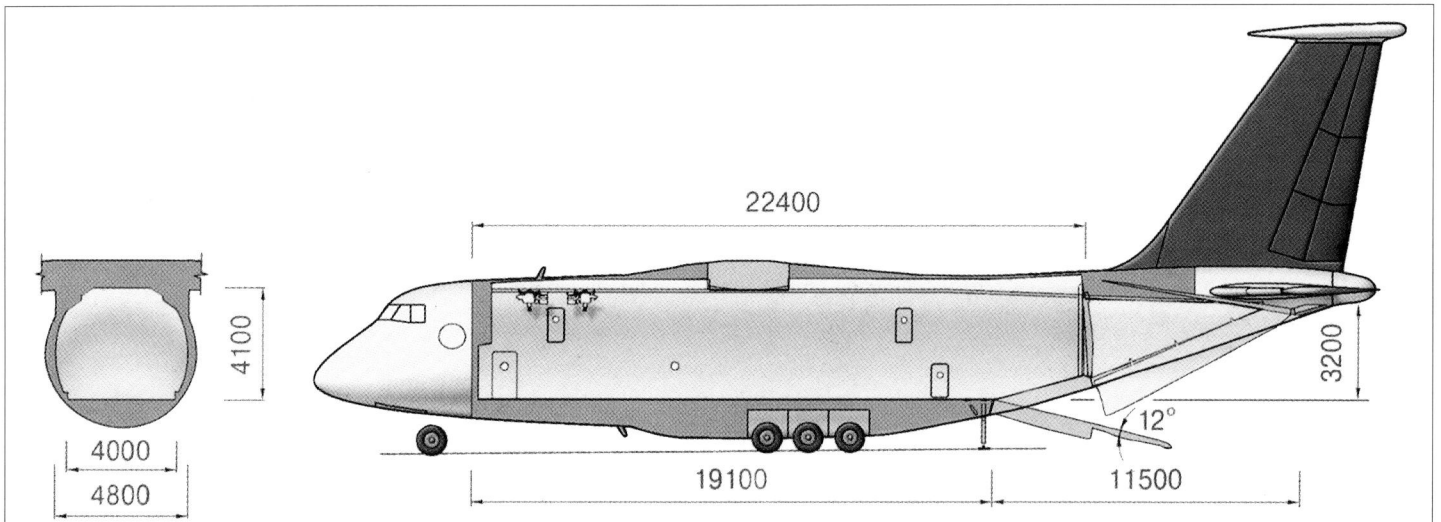

This drawing illustrates the dimensions of the An-70's cargo hold in millimetres.

Above: Bearing only the UR prefix, the first prototype An-70 sits in front of the Antonov ANTK hangar at Kiev-Svyatoshino. Note that the aircraft carries an Uzbek flag in addition to the Ukrainian and Russian flags; originally it was envisaged that the TAPO plant in Tashkent would participate in An-70 production.

special-mission aircraft, such as an airborne early warning and control (AEW&C) aircraft, an airborne command post, a patrol aircraft, an in-flight refuelling tanker and a maritime search and rescue aircraft for the Navy.

The An-70 became the first aircraft developed in the CIS countries to feature a digital multiplex interface meeting the US MIL-STD-1553B standard (even the most up-to-date Russian fighters, the Mikoyan MiG-29M and the Sukhoi Su-35, have avionics of less advanced architecture). Representatives of the Antonov company claim that this enabled the designers to reduce the length of onboard wiring by 70% and its total weight by 40%. The use of the MIL-STD-1553B databus was expected to simplify the integration of the An-70's avionics with systems of Western manufacture in due course.

The crew of the An-70 was reduced to three persons. The flightdeck was equipped with six multifunctional colour CRT displays and with the SKI-77 head-up display; the latter facilitated landings on short runways.

Navigation and radio navigation systems met the ARINC 700 standard. The flight control system catered for optimising the fuel burn, choosing the optimum glide path, for navigation and the fulfilment of standard procedures during flight in an airfield or airport area. It comprised an onboard digital computer, an inertial navigation system based on laser gyros, and a short-range radio navigation (SHORAN) system which ensured automated blind landing in ICAO Cat II and IIIA conditions. The onboard radio equipment was intended for operation in the HF and VHF bands.

The An-70 was provided with a three-channel digital FBW control system and a six-channel analogue FBW control system. The airframe featured a large proportion of composite materials (in particular, the vertical and horizontal tail surfaces were made of composites).

The design of the An-70 incorporated features giving it a service life of 45,000 flight hours, 20,000 landings or 25-30 years of operation. The aircraft's operational and technical characteristics were expected to ensure an annual utilisation of 3,000 flight hours, with the possibility of increasing this figure to 3,500 hours after three years of operation. The aircraft's systems and structure were designed with ease of monitoring in mind and featured a high degree of redundancy, which made it possible to operate the machine according to its technical condition. The aircraft was equipped with the BASK-70 automated onboard fault diagnosis system (*bortovaya avtomatizeerovannaya sistema kontrolya*) which had been developed by the Antonov OKB together with the St. Petersburg-based Leninets Holding Co. The system is capable of recording and analysing up to 8,000 parameters, the information being channelled to multi-functional displays in the flightdeck. The BASK-70 included a ground-based PC which analysed the flight information, registered all malfunctions and also determined the requirement for spare parts proceeding from the real condition of the aircraft and its onboard systems.

On 14th July 1994 the articles of incorporation and other documents were signed for the establishment of an international consortium for the purpose of implementing the programme of the An-70 and An-70T aircraft powered by the D-27 engines. The consortium comprised the Antonov Aviation Scientific and Technical Complex (Kiev), Aviaprom JSC (Moscow), the Motor Sich aero engine plant (Zaporozhye, Ukraine), the Tashkent Aircraft Production Association named after Valeriy P. Chkalov (TAPO), the Avi.S JSC (Samara), the Aviant State Aircraft Factory (Kiev), the Aviapribor JSC (Moscow), the Electropribor plant (Kiev), Rosaviafond (the Russian Aviation Foundation, Moscow), the Aokima JSC (Moscow), Aviabank (Moscow), Prominvestbank (Kiev), UkrNIIAS (the Ukrainian Scientific Research Institute for Aircraft Systems, Kiev) and the Leninets Holding Co. (St Petersburg). The aircraft created much stir, and the press even went as far as to report that TAPO in Tashkent had already launched large-scale (!) manufacture of

The first prototype An-70 becomes airborne on its maiden flight on 16th December 1994. Note the red-painted radome incorporating an air data boom, the port side observation blister aft of the flightdeck and the open APU air intake in the port main landing gear fairing.

wings for the An-70 (naturally, nothing of the sort had happened in actual fact) and that later on the enterprise would manufacture structural members for the fuselage and engine mountings. It was envisaged that the manufacture of other parts and the final assembly would be effected at the Aviant factory (formerly MAP plant No.473) in Kiev and the Aviakor factory in Samara (formerly MAP plant No.18).

Here it should be noted that the countries of Western Europe could not put up with a situation when the prospective Russian-Ukrainian aircraft would be the sole contender for transport aircraft market; in consequence, in the early 1990s seven European countries formed the FTA (Future Transport Aircraft) consortium which announced a tender for the creation of a prospective medium transport aircraft for the NATO. The aircraft was tentatively dubbed FLA (Future Large Aircraft). Above all, the Europeans wanted to find an alternative to their dependence on the USA which was pressing its NATO allies into buying the McDonnell Douglas (now Boeing) C-17A Globemaster III high-capacity airlifter at an exorbitant price. An alternative that came into consideration was provided by the proposal submitted by the Airbus Industrie concern, envisaging the development of the A400M aircraft. A company named Airbus Military was formed for the manufacture of this aircraft; it announced its participation in the international tender, the results of which were to be made public in early 2000.

While arguments raged in Western Europe as to which way to go, construction of the first prototype An-70 was nearing completion in Kiev. On 20th January 1994 at 15.39 local time the first An-70 military transport (c/n 0101 – ie, Batch 1, first aircraft in the batch) was rolled out at Kiev-Svyatoshino, wearing a striking four-tone blue/white colour scheme and the Ukrainian nationality prefix UR but no individual registration letters. The rollout ceremony was attended by Russian Air Force Commander-in-Chief Air Colonel-General Pyotr S. Deynekin, Ukrainian President Leonid Kravchuk, Kazakh President Nursultan N. Nazarbayev and other high-ranking officials.

After many months of preparatory work and ground testing of aircraft systems, on 16th December 1994 the still unregistered An-70 prototype performed its maiden flight, piloted by a crew captained by Sergey Maksimov. For the initial flight tests the standard radome had been replaced by a modified one incorporating a huge blended air data boom and painted bright red. After the first flight the An-70 remained grounded for almost six weeks, parked at Kiev-Gostomel' airfield while specialists tried hard to find the cause of the unsatisfactory running of two D-27 engines during the flight. The cause was

eventually traced to the faulty functioning of the reduction gearbox designed by ZMKB Progress. The faults in the reduction gears were rectified, and on 8th February 1995 the aircraft made its second flight, followed by the third flight on 9th February. During these flights there were numerous malfunctions in the control system; in addition, during the third flight one of the flaps failed to extend.

Under the terms of the test programme, 250 flights were to be performed in the course of two years. Within this time frame the preparations for series manufacture of the aircraft at the plants in Kiev and Samara were expected to be completed. But these plans were shattered when the first prototype An-70 crashed on 10th February 1995 during its fourth flight, killing all seven crew. The mission for that flight was simple: calibration of the airspeed indicators on the An-70 relative to the speed readings on the An-72G chase aircraft registered 72966 (sic – no prefix; c/n unknown, f/n 11-04) and video filming of the An-70 through the An-72G's starboard-side cargo cabin emergency exit at a distance of 100 m (330 ft) between the two aircraft and an altitude of 3,000 to 3,500 m (9,840-11,480 ft).

Approximately at 17.30 local time, when executing a manoeuvre not envisaged by the mission assignment, the An-70 collided with the An-72G that was flying ahead of it. The An-70 fell into a wood near Velikiy Lis ('Great Forest' in Ukrainian) settlement, 40 km (25 miles) from Kiev, disintegrating utterly. Before the collision the crews maintained a distance slightly in excess of 100 m; this was 'a standard test procedure'. While executing a manoeuvre, the An-70 suddenly approached from below in the An-72G's starboard rear quadrant and struck the chase plane's fuselage with its fin near the emergency exit hatch through which the video filming was made. As the An-70 pressed on relentlessly, its fin and port stabiliser ripped away the An-72's starboard flap and crushed the starboard main landing gear fairing and the struts stowed within. As a result of the collision the An-72G sliced off the An-70's port stabiliser and half the fin, which were made of composites. Thereupon the An-70 entered a deep sideslip and then dived nearly vertically into the ground from an altitude of more than 3,000 m (9,840 ft), impacting at an angle of 87°. The crew of the An-72G, notwithstanding the damage sustained by the wings (the flaps were destroyed) and the undercarriage, succeeded in landing their machine at Kiev-Gostomel' from where both aircraft had taken off.

On the following day search teams sent to the crash site managed to recover the An-70's flight data recorder. Its titanium body was heavily marked by melting caused by the post-crash fire, but the metal tape carrying information on 296 flight parameters was

intact, albeit the recording required restoration before it could be analysed.

Almost the whole crew of the ill-fated aircraft were the persons who had been the first to take it into the air. The crew comprised the Antonov Design Bureau test pilot Sergey Maksimov (captain), V. Lysenko, V. Nepochatykh, P. Skotnikov, A. Kostrykin, M. Berezyuk and A. Goryltsov. The crew of the An-72G comprised six persons, including captain V. Terskiy and co-pilot Ye. Galunenko.

The loss of the first prototype was only the beginning of the An-70's subsequent vicissitudes. Just think that there were plans to launch production as early as 1996, which would have created 27,000 jobs for highly skilled personnel in the Ukraine and more than 50,000 jobs in Russia in the period between 1996 and 2007. A week after the tragedy, on 18th February, the head of Russia's State Committee for Defence Industry Viktor Glukhikh, who had arrived in Kiev on that day to take part in a conference on the problems of interaction between Russia and the Ukraine in the field of aircraft and aero-engine construction, stated that the work on the An-70 transport aircraft would continue in accordance with the Federal programme of support for the aircraft industry.

Under the terms of the intergovernmental agreement between Russia and the Ukraine 'On co-operation in ensuring the establishment of joint series production and deliveries for operational service of the An-70 military transport aircraft and the An-70T commercial transport' signed on 24th June 1993 by Leonid D. Kuchma and Viktor S. Chernomyrdin, the then Prime Ministers of the Ukraine and Russia respectively, the Samara-based Aviakor plant and the Kiev-based Aviant factory were designated as chief enterprises responsible for the series manufacture of the An-70. However, notwithstanding all the resolutions and 'good intentions', up to the autumn of 2000 the Aviant factory, for example, had not received a single grivna to finance the tooling up for production.

A decision was taken to convert the static test airframe, which had been built in parallel with the crashed prototype, to flight test status. In December 1996, after the testing and refinement of the onboard systems and equipment, the second An-70 prototype (c/n 770102; 77 is presumably a product code) was rolled out, bearing a totally different white/blue/grey colour scheme patterned on that of Antonov Airlines. Preparations for the resumption of the flight tests were commenced by a crew comprising Aleksandr V. Galunenko (Antonov Design Bureau) and Colonel Anatoliy V. Andronov, Merited Military Pilot of Russia, chief of the military transport aircraft flight test department of the Russian Air Force's 929th State Flight Test Centre

Above: Gleaming with fresh paint, the second prototype An-70 (c/n 770102) sits in the Antonov ANTK's prototype assembly hangar at Kiev-Svyatoshino shortly before the rollout. The Ukrainian and Russian flags have yet to be applied on the nose.

This view of the second prototype emphasises the almost non-existent wing sweep and the wide spread of the engines along the wing span.

named after Valeriy P. Chkalov (formerly GNIKI VVS). In 1996 the expenditures on the programme amounted to 100 million grivnas, out of which 60 million was the money owed by the Antonov ANTK to subcontractors. 93% of the invested money was ANTK's own funds; contribution from the State made up only 7% (Russia, 6.4%; the Ukraine, 0.6%). The price of one machine was set at about US$ 50 million.

In its design the second prototype was virtually identical to the first one, except for the location of hydraulic systems which were transferred from the stabilisers and the fin into the fuselage. This modification was prompted by the bitter experience of the crash suffered by the first machine when the chase aircraft severed the stabiliser accommodating four hydraulic systems.

On 24th April 1997 the second prototype An-70 (again carrying only the UR prefix as yet) made its first flight from the Kiev-Svyatoshino factory airfield. The aircraft was flown by a crew comprising project test pilot Aleksandr V. Galunenko (captain); 929th State Flight Test Centre test pilot Colonel A. V. Andronov (co-pilot); V. I. Soroka (navigator); V. M. Chepil' (flight engineer); I. G. Minayev (radio operator) and A. M. Zagoomennyy (project engineer for flight testing). The flight lasted 26 minutes, terminating at the Kiev-Gostomel' flight test facility.

The take-off run during the first flight of the second machine was 850 m (2,790 ft); the flight was performed at an altitude of 3,500 m (11,480 ft). The mission consisted of checking the functioning of the engines and equipment, as well as stability and controllability. An Aero L-39C Albatros advanced trainer was used as a chase aircraft. On 28th May the An-70 returned to Svyatoshino where it was demonstrated to Viktor S. Chernomyrdin, Russia's Prime Minister. The high-ranking guest was able to observe the take-off of the machine which, in the presence of spectators, departed for Gostomel' for a further round of tests. In all, An-70 c/n 770102 had made 12 flights by 11th June 1997.

Later the second prototype received the 'custom' registration UR-NTK (the 'NTK' indicating that the aircraft belonged to ANTK (Aviation Scientific and Technical Complex) named after Antonov) and the exhibit code 354 with which it was to make its public debut at the 42nd Paris Air Show (15th-22nd June 1997), although the aircraft failed to make its way to Le Bourget on that occasion. The machine featured a standard radome (as distinct from the first prototype) and was fitted with five data recording video cameras pointed at the propellers and flaps. A rather unorthodox location was chosen for the data recording equipment – it was accommodated on a shortened upper deck section sus-

pended at the front end of the cargo hold, leaving most of the hold free for people or vehicles.

On 19th-24th August 1997 the aircraft had its public debut at the MAKS-97 international air show in Zhukovskiy, featuring both in the static park and in the flying display. The demonstration flights made a lasting impression not only on the general public but on many specialists as well; the An-70 demonstrated surprising agility for an aircraft of its size, quite apart from the very distinctive rolling roar of the four D-27 propfans which was quite unlike the sound of any contemporary aircraft.

On 20th September 1997 the President of the Ukraine issued decree No.1061/97 according to which decorations were awarded to test pilots for their personal courage and high professionalism displayed during the testing of the An-70 military transport aircraft. Crew captain Aleksandr V. Galunenko, counsellor of the Antonov ANTK's General Designer, was awarded the order 'For Merits' (3rd Degree), and co-pilot A. V. Andronov, colonel of the Russian Air Force, received the order 'For Courage' (3rd Degree).

In January and February 1998 the testing of An-70 UR-NTK proceeded with a high degree of intensity. Eleven flights were made (in all, the second prototype had made 61 flights by that time). On 13th February test

Bearing the custom registration UR-NTK, the An-70 made its first public appearance at the MAKS-97 airshow where it did a lot of flying. Here the aircraft enters a port turn immediately after taking off from Zhukovskiy's runway 30 on 20th August 1997.

Above: UR-NTK makes a flypast in 'clean' configuration at the MAKS-97 airshow. The An-70 is a fairly elegant machine for an airlifter. Note the Le Bourget exhibit code 354 above the entry door (despite the fact that the An-70 did not go to Paris that year); note also that only the Ukrainian and Russian flags are carried now.

The An-70 produces a puff of smoke as it touches down on runway 12 at Zhukovskiy during the MAKS-99 airshow, with the control tower in the background. The aircraft now wears a new Le Bourget exhibit code, 375, from that year's Paris Air Show where the type made its Western debut.

Above: The An-70 makes a high-speed pass at the MAKS-97 airshow. The four D-27 engines with that multitude of propfan blades churning up the air make a very distinctive sound.

The An-70 displays surprising agility for an aircraft of its size. Outwardly UR-NTK differs from the first prototype only in having an ordinary (albeit large) window on the port side of the flightdeck instead of an An-26 style faired observation blister. Note the 'anti-soot' panels on the flaps' upper surface in line with the engines.

An artist's impression of the Airbus Industrie A400M, originally known as the FLA. Apart from the tail unit, the similarity to the An-70 is obvious.

parachute jumpers of the Feodosia-based Ukrainian State Aviation Research Centre (GANITs – *Gosoodarstvennyy aviatsionnyy naoochno-issledovatel'skiy tsentr*) performed parachute jumps from the An-70 for the first time under the direction of Lieutenant-Colonel I. I. Kurzhumov acting as jumpmaster. After the dropping of dummies the first jump was made by Warrant Officer D. N. Sokolov through the emergency escape chute; he was followed by Major I. M. Sila and Senior Warrant Officer A. A. Rogov who made their jumps through one of the entry doors and the emergency escape chute respectively.

On 3rd June 1999 two flights were made on the An-70 with Peter Henley, a British test pilot, in the co-pilot's seat. He had mastered 66 types of aircraft and had logged more than 9,000 flight hours during his service in the RAF and at BAE Systems. Prior to the flights, Mr. Henley had passed a preparatory course on an An-70 simulator. The crew was captained by Antonov ANTK test pilot Aleksandr V. Galunenko. After the landing Henley said in his interview to the ANTK press-service that the An-70 was an impressive military transport aircraft and that it possessed excellent controllability in the FBW mode. He was much impressed by the An-70's short-field capabili-

ties. Aleksandr Galunenko demonstrated to the British pilot that the aircraft's landing run on a normal paved runway could be as short as 300 m (980 ft). Peter Henley noted that he had flown many aircraft designed by Airbus Industrie which featured a side-stick controller, but, in his opinion, the option with the control column chosen for the An-70 was more convenient for aircraft of that class, especially for pilots who had previously worked on conventional transport aircraft. In the British pilot's opinion, in its handling the An-70 was similar to the C-130. Both aircraft were provided with automatic protection in the event of an engine failure, the onset of stall and the like. However, the An-70 was considerably superior to the C-130 as regards the payload and, as Henley put it, 'this aircraft (the An-70 – *authors' note*) will enjoy great success'.

Much comment was provoked by the presence of the An-70 at the 43rd Paris Air Show held at Le Bourget on 12th-20th June 1999 where it made its Western debut. Bearing the new exhibit code 375, the aircraft performed four demonstration flights in Paris, showing to advantage its outstanding capabilities. After the end of the air show the An-70 paid a visit to Köln where it was inspected by

members of the Bundestag. On 17th-22nd August 1999 the aircraft was displayed again statically and in flight at the MAKS-99 air show in Zhukovskiy and its cavernous cargo hold was shown to the public, albeit no one was allowed inside. Two days earlier, the An-70 had been on show at Chkalovskaya AB (seat of the 929th State Flight Test Centre's transport aviation branch) during the 'open house' on occasion of Aviation Day celebrated on the third Sunday of August.

In the course of four years a considerable volume of flight testing had been conducted on the second prototype An-70; the testing confirmed the validity of most of its design features. The aircraft repeatedly took part in international exhibitions in the CIS republics, as well as outside the Commonwealth of Independent States, and performed flights in widely varying climatic conditions.

Joint State acceptance trials and certification tests of the An-70 commenced in 1999; by January 2001 Stage A of the programme was virtually completed. In accordance with the approved joint State tests programme the flight tests in low ambient temperature conditions were to be conducted in January and February. For this purpose the machine, along with a team of testers and engineers from the Antonov ANTK, was sent to Yakutsk, which is just about the coldest place in Russia. The aircraft carried close to 1,000 kg (2,200 lb) of equipment that was necessary for the conduct of the testing. On 26th January, at about midnight local time, the An-70 made a scheduled refuelling stop at Omsk-Tsentral'nyy airport. Having refuelled the aircraft with 38 tonnes (83,790 lb) of kerosene and made the necessary pre-flight checks, in the morning of 27th January the crew captained by test pilot Vitaliy Gorovenko began the take-off. Suddenly the engine indication

Ukrainian servicemen prepare to board the An-70 in the course of the aircraft's State acceptance trials.

and crew alerting system (EICAS) indicated the failure of starboard inboard engine; 20 or 30 seconds later the port outboard engine cut as well. By that moment the aircraft had gained an altitude of 40 m (130 ft) and was just beyond the end of the runway. In this situation the crew had no choice but to land the aircraft straight ahead of them; luckily, lying beneath the aircraft was a snow-covered field (during that winter the snowfalls had been 2.5 times heavier than usual). Fortunately, the belly landing did not result in a fuel fire and explosion, and there were no fatalities among the 33 occupants. Only four members of the test team suffered more or less serious injuries; two of them were taken to a hospital in Omsk. The aircraft, however, was rather worse off, sustaining considerable damage: it broke its back aft of the wings, the underside of the fuselage was crushed, and the port outer wing and the port side propfans were also damaged.

On the same day a commission headed by V. Voskoboynikov, chief of the Board of the civil aircraft engineering development programme of the Rosaviakosmos (Russian Aerospace) agency, started an investigation of the accident. The commission comprised specialists from the 129th State Flight Test Centre of the Russian Ministry of Defence, from the leading research institutions of the aircraft industry (TsAGI, TsIAM, LII and GosNII GA), representatives of the main companies that had participated in the development of the aircraft as a whole, its powerplant, systems and equipment. A group of 55 Antonov ANTK specialists headed by General Designer Pyotr V. Balabuyev arrived from Kiev.

There were three main theories as to the causes of the accident: engine malfunction, fuel contamination (ie, water crystallisation) and illegal interference (deliberate actions which resulted in the crash landing). The possibility of sabotage was considered because the relationship between Russia and the Ukraine was not always a sunny one, and a good deal of anti-Ukrainian sentiment existed in Russia. To all appearances, UR-NTK looked like a write-off and it seemed that the aircraft embodying the pride and hope of the Ukrainian aircraft industry (which had cost the Antonov ANTK US$ 80 million) was doomed once and for all.

At first, the specialists were sceptical about the possibility of repairing the machine. Nevertheless, Balabuyev conducted negotiations with the management of the 'Polyot' (Flight) Omsk Aircraft Production Association (OAPO 'Polyot', former MAP aircraft factory No.166) with which the Antonov Design Bureau had long-standing co-operation ties. After the necessary preparations for evacuation the machine was dismantled and moved piecemeal to OAPO at Omsk-Severnyy air-

field where it was rebuilt to flying condition, making use of parts and units manufactured in Kiev, including a chunk of the centre fuselage to replace the portion where the crack was. According to some sources, the repairs cost US$ 2 million.

The accident investigation panel completed its work in March 2001; the results of the investigation were made public by Dmitriy Kiva, Deputy General Designer of the Antonov ANTK, in Kiev on 15th March. He stated that the accident with the An-70 in Omsk had been caused by a failure of the No.3 (starboard inboard) engine. Immediately after the takeoff an overspeeding of the No.3 engine's propfan occurred, and the full authority digital engine control system (FADEC) shut the engine down. In so doing the second row of propfan blades failed to feather due to a broken pipeline supplying oil to the blade pitch control mechanism in the propfan hub. This row of blades continued its rotation due to windmilling, thus creating a negative thrust of some five tonnes (11,000 lb). The crew increased the power output of the other three engines, but at that moment the FADEC shut down the No.1 (port outboard) engine because of the unstable functioning of the sensor monitoring the rpm of the free turbine. With only two engines running, at low airspeed, coupled with the presence of negative thrust and airflow separation on the wing section aft of the unfeathered propfan blades, continued flight was no longer possible.

The commission concluded that the crew had acted competently and professionally when it made a wheels-up landing on the snow-covered field near the village of Chukreyevka not far from Omsk-Tsentral'nyy.

Specialists of the Antonov ATK and the Russian-Ukrainian STS consortium (**sredniy trahns**portnyy samol**yot** – medium transport aircraft) created for the purpose of building the An-70 were of the opinion that the accident with the An-70 near Omsk would not affect the plans for the development of the machine and its series production. However, the Ufa Engine Production Association (UMPO – Oo**fim**skoye mot**or**ostroitel'noye proi**zvod**stvennoye obyedi**neniye**) took a decision to postpone its participation in the D-27 engine production programme until 2006. The Samara-based Motorostroitel' (= Engine builder) Joint-Stock Co. engine plant decided to join the programme instead of UMPO. According to estimates made by specialists, the refinement of the D-27 engines alone would require US$ 30 million.

By the time of the accident Russia had already invested more than US$ 300 million into the An-70 project, and Il'ya Klebanov, Deputy Prime Minister of Russia, declared that 'the accident would under no circumstances entail the closing down of the pro-

gramme for the development of the aircraft.' In his opinion, this was 'one of the most promising aircraft in the world' and it was exactly the work on the An-70 that had to be pursued further. The designers of the aircraft also reckoned with large-scale exports of the An-70's military version: the NATO's transport aircraft fleet had reached obsolescence by the mid-1990s and required renewal, and the characteristics of the An-70 made it eminently compatible with the doctrine of re-equipment of the European air forces.

It still remained to be decided who would build the aircraft in Russia. Yuriy N. Koptev, General Director of the Russian Aerospace Agency, signed a document announcing a tender for the manufacture of the aircraft. Earlier, as already mentioned, it was presumed that the production of the aircraft would begin at the Aviant factory in Kiev and the Aviacor plant in Samara. However, the Samara plant, which had experienced serious difficulties in the course of the recent years, was simply not prepared for participation in this project. Besides, the plant's management was dead set against the An-70 for some reason – which, interestingly, did not stop Aviacor from building the An-140 regional airliner, which was just as Ukrainian. The decision to issue a tender meant that the leading role of Kiev and Samara in the assembly of the An-70 – a role that had seemed indisputable merely a short time before – was called into question. According to Yuriy Koptev, some ten enterprises vied for the assembly of the An-70.

Plans to display the An-70 at the 44th Paris Air Show were thwarted when the organisers of the show banned the rebuilt aircraft from flying to Paris on the grounds that it was 'unsafe'. The second prototype was on display again at the MAKS-2001 airshow (14th-19th August 2001). Yet the designers of the aircraft were in for yet another unhappy experience. When the aircraft was being readied for a training flight at Zhukovskiy on 13th August, problems arose with the No.4 engine. The machine was towed away to the parking apron of the Myasishchev Design Bureau on the south side of the field where it sat for some time waiting for a replacement engine. Eventually the engine was delivered and installed, but the demonstration programme was ruined. The An-70 made only a single demonstration flight (on 15th August in a unique formation with the first production An-140, UR-PWO, and the An-225). The fact that the aircraft had undergone extensive repairs was pretty obvious, as the main landing gear fairings and part of the belly (just aft of the wings where the fuselage had been spliced) were painted up in the wrong shade of grey. Two of the test equipment suite's video cameras had been relocated ahead of the port main gear units and ahead of the cargo ramp (in connection with rough-field operation trials and paradropping trials respectively).

The unsatisfactory state of affairs with the An-70's powerplant inevitably affected Russia's participation in the joint programme. The Russian military, as distinct from politicians, began to claim that it would be much more profitable to make an investment into the stretched IL-76MF military transport powered by proven Solov'yov PS-90A76 turbofans that would be dependent virtually entirely on Russian manufacturers. In the end their viewpoint apparently prevailed, and Russia practically stopped funding the An-70's development programme. (It should be noted that many high-ranking Russian military, including Russian Ministry of Defence weapons department chief Colonel General Anatoliy Sitnov, were opposed to the An-70. This was not merely a case of the 'not invented here' syndrome but hard feelings against the Ukrainians for keeping a regiment of IL-78 tankers at Uzin AB (which left the Russian Air Force rather short of flight refuelling capability), for appropriating the naval bases on the Black Sea, for the ostensible declarations about the Ukraine's intention to join the NATO and so on; the critics seem to forget that development of the An-70 had begun long before the Ukraine gained independence and that the IL-76 is also built outside Russia, after all!) Now the management of the Antonov ANTK was in for hard times, but it continued its struggle for the survival of the programme.

In an effort to attract orders and secure much-needed funding for the An-70, the Antonov ANTK began courting the Czech Air Force. First, a model of the An-70 in CzAF colours was shown at the IDET-2001 defence trade fair; next, the second prototype was demonstrated to the military top brass and high-ranking statesmen at Prague-Ruzyne airport on 1st-4th July 2002. The aircraft made two demonstration flights and showed its ability to swallow various military vehicles. CzAF pilot Stefan Rucka was given a chance to fly the An-70 and was extremely pleased, saying it was the 'best aircraft he had ever flown.' Czech Deputy Minister of Defence Stefan Fule also spoke highly of the An-70, stating that the Czech Republic 'needs these aircraft not only due to the forthcoming reform of the Armed Forces but also on the assumption of the military strategy of the Czech state approved by the government.' As a result, the Czech Republic took out an option on three An-70s; the Hungarian Air Force also showed an interest in acquiring the type.

The Ukraine hoped that it would be able to make use of the MAKS-2003 airshow (19th-24th August 2003) for mitigating the tensions that had arisen in Russia around the An-70 at the turn of the century, but these hopes were also frustrated. On the eve of the show the Russian military, claiming that the aircraft was not ready for demonstration flights, tried to ban it from participation in the air show. Then they consented to this participation, but stipulated that the Antonov enterprise show its progeny only in the static park. Commander-in-Chief of the Russian Air Force Colonel-General (at that time) Vladimir Mikhaïlov, a key figure in the 'anti-Antonov lobby', declared that flights of this aircraft were unsafe due to poor engine reliability and that he would 'pray every day lest the An-70 should cause trouble at the airshow.' When the leaders of the Antonov ANTK got wind of it, they addressed the Ukraine's Prime Minister Viktor Yanukovich, who in turn addressed his Russian colleague. Mikhail Kas'yanov promised that the An-70 would take to the air at Zhukovskiy. Despite sceptical forecasts, the An-70 put up an excellent display during the first and the last days of the air show. However, the An-70 was barred from flying during the 'Presidential' part of the demonstration flights, although the machine was readied for the flight. It made a lift-off only when the President of Russia had left the site of the air show in his aircraft. 'Our take-off was prohibited – said crew captain Vitaliy Gorovenko at a press-conference, answering numerous questions from journalists – and I want everybody to know this.'

Thus, the demonstration flights did not have the expected effect, and no change occurred in the attitude of some high-ranking Russian officials to this aircraft after MAKS-2003. Moreover, on 25th August some mass media carried a news item asserting that the then Russian Prime Minister Mikhail Kas'yanov had signed a document stipulating that no funding of the work on the An-70 should be provided in the Russian budget for 2004. It turned out to be a hoax, but the negative effect produced by this could not but aggravate the persisting problem.

Faced with this situation, the Ukrainian Government, in the absence of positive moves from the Russian side, approved on 10th September a bill on a State programme for the development of the An-70 military transport aircraft and its purchase under defence procurement orders. In a break during a Cabinet of Ministers session Anatoliy Myalitsa, the Minister of Industrial Policy of the Ukraine, informed journalists that this programme comprising two stages was intended to cover the period up to 2006 and was to be financed from the State budget, the volume of funding being more than one million grivnas. 'Regardless of how the work in Russia proceeds, we are adopting a law, ensuring the funding and we shall buy production aircraft for our army – the Minister emphasised. We reckon with a long life for the An-70, and there is a sufficient market for this.' In particular, as shown by the aerospace shows held in September 2003 in Zhuhai (China Aerospace '03) and Kuala Lumpur (LIMA-2003), military authorities of China and Malaysia displayed much interest in this aircraft.

According to press reports, the Ukrainian Air Force has a requirement for up to 65 An-70s and the initial order is for five machines. Other sources say the UAF plans to acquire only five An-70s, though this figure appears a bit low, considering the size of the

Mission	Commercial versions			Military versions	
Version	An-70T	An-70T-100	An-70TK	An-70-100	An-77
Number of engines (D-27 or CFM56-5C4)	4	2	4	4	4
Crew	2-3	2	2-3	2	2-3
Runway length, m/ft	1,900-1,300 (6,230-4,265)	2,500-1,300 (8,200-4,256)	1,900-1,300 (6,230-4,265)	1,700-600 (5,580-1,970)	1,700-600 (5,580-1,970)
Load (tonne/lb) – range (km/miles)	35-3,800 (77,160-2,360)	30-1,000 (66,140-620)	35-3,800 (77,160-2,360)	35-3,800 (77,160-2,360)	35-3,800 (77,160-2,360)
SFC, g/tonne-km	145	130	145	150	150
Mission type variations	1. Cargo transportation 2. Forest fire fighting 3. Environment monitoring		Commercial carriage of cargoes up to 30 tonnes (66,150 lb) and 150 passengers	1. In-flight refuelling 2. Early warning 3. Search and rescue	

Ukraine's military airlift component and the number of high-time An-12s that are due for retirement or sale on the civil market. According to UAF Commander-in-Chief Lieutenant-General Yaroslav Skalko, two An-70s were nearing completion in mid-2004 and the first production aircraft was due for delivery by the end of the year.

There are indications that the Russian political leaders, as distinct from the military, are still trying to keep the joint An-70 project afloat, not least for political reasons; the final outcome is hard to predict.

Listed below are some of the versions of the An-70 that have been studied.

An-70T commercial transport (project)
The An-70T is a version of the An-70 military transport aircraft capable of carrying 35 tonnes (77,175 lb) and powered by four D-27 engines; it is intended for use on the civil air freight market. The main changes incorporated in the An-70T in comparison with the baseline An-70 *sans suffixe* consist in adapting its equipment and systems to civil aviation requirements and in some simplification of the airframe structure.

The An-70T will be able to operate not only from airfields with concrete runways 1,800-2,000 m (5,900-6,560 ft) long but also from small airfields with runways 1,300-1,400 m (4,264-4,592-ft) long, as well as from unpaved runways. Making the aircraft capable of operating from paved and unpaved runways with a length of 1,300-2,000 m (4,264-6,560 ft) will considerably expand the airfield network available to the aircraft. Transportation of cargoes to small airfields will increase the speed of their delivery and guarantee that they will be delivered safely intact. As a result, the profitability of the An-70T will be considerably increased.

An-70-100 medium military transport aircraft (project)
The An-70-100 is a version of the An-70 with updated equipment and reduced crew complement.

An-70T-100 medium commercial transport aircraft (project)
The An-70T-100 is a version of the An-70 with a lower take-off weight, powered by two D-27 engines. Its design envisaged the use of a smaller number of main landing gear struts and changes to some systems and units. When operating from runways with a length of 2,500 m (8,200 ft), the aircraft was expected to carry a 30-tonne (66,150-lb) cargo over a distance of 1,000 km (622 miles) or 20 tonnes (44,100 lb) over 4,300 km (2,672 miles) with an extremely high fuel efficiency of 130 g/tonne-km.

Like the baseline version, the An-70T is intended for operations from runways with a length of 1,300 m; in that case it would possess performance comparable to that of its predecessor, the An-12.

An-70TK medium cargo aircraft/airliner (project)
A convertible cargo/passenger version designated An-70TK (*konverteeruyemyy*) is intended to accommodate up to 150 passengers or 30 tonnes (66,150 lb) of cargo.

An-70T-200 medium commercial transport aircraft (project)
The An-70T-200 is a version of the An-70T with a cargo-carrying capacity of 35 tonnes (77,175 lb), powered by two Kuznetsov NK-93 contra-rotating integrated shrouded propfans on underwing pylons.

An-70T-300 medium commercial transport aircraft (project)
The An-70T-300 is a version of the An-70T-100 with a cargo-carrying capacity of 35 tonnes powered by two CFM International CFM56-5C4 turbofans.

An-70T-400 medium commercial transport aircraft (project)
The An-70T-400 is a version of the An-70T with a cargo-carrying capacity of 35 tonnes powered by four CFM56-5C4 turbofans.

An-77 medium military transport aircraft (project)
The An-77 is a version of the An-70 military transport with a cargo-carrying capacity of 35 tonnes powered by four CFM56-5C4 turbofans.

An artist's impression of the An-70 in Czech Air Force colours.

Specifications of military transport aircraft

Aircraft type	An-70	Tu-330*	FLA*
Wing span	44.6 m (146 ft 4 in)	43.50 m (142 ft 8¹⁹⁄₃₂in)	42.90 m (140 ft 9 in)
Length overall	40.76 m (133 ft 8⅖ in)	42.00 m (137 ft 9⁷⁄₃₂ in)	41.30 m (135 ft 6 in)
Height on ground	16.38 m (53 ft 9 in)	14.00 m (45 ft 11¾₆ in)	14.00 m (45 ft 11¾₆ in)
Cargo hold dimensions:			
length	18.75 m (61 ft 6 in)	19.50 m (64 ft)	17.25 m (56 ft 7⅛ in)
width	4.00 m (13 ft 1½ in)	4.00 m (13 ft 1½ in)	4.00 m (13 ft 1½ in)
Maximum take-off weight, tonnes (lb)	133.0 (293,265)	103.5 (228,217)	107.0 (235,935)
Maximum useful load, tonnes (lb)	35.0 (77,175)	35.0 (77,175)	32.0 (70,560)
Cruising speed, km/h (mph)	750 (465)	850 (528)	n.a.
Cruising Mach number	n.a.	n.a.	0.72
Practical ceiling, m (ft)	11,000 (36,080)	11,000 (36,080)	n.a.
Practical range, km (miles):			
with a load of 20 tonnes (44,100 lb)	7,400 (4,600)	5,600 (3,480)	n.a.
with a load of 25 tonnes (55,125 lb)	n.a.	n.a.	3,700 (2,300)
with a load of 30 tonnes (66,150 lb)	n.a.	3,000 (1,865)	n.a.
with a load of 35 tonnes (77,175 lb)	3,500 (2,175)	n.a.	n.a.
Ferry range, km (miles)	8,700 (5,407)	n.a.	n.a.

* Design performance

An-170 heavy commercial transport aircraft (project)

The designation An-170 refers to studies of a heavy transport aircraft with a cargo-carrying capacity in excess of 50 tonnes (110,250 lb) which is a derivative of the An-70.

An-171 medium/heavy transport aircraft (project)

This derivative of the An-70 carrying 45 to 50 tonnes (99,225 to 110,250 lb) was proposed in the late 1980s as a replacement for the IL-76; it differed from the baseline An-70 in having a stretched fuselage and greater wingspan, as well as more powerful engines. However, it lost out to another contender, the IL-106 (which, ironically, was eventually shelved, too).

An-7X medium military transport aircraft (project)

The possibility of using the An-70 as the main prospective military transport aircraft was considered not only within the framework of the CIS but even in some leading NATO countries as well. The Defence Ministries of Germany, France and Great Britain voiced their interest in the new aircraft being developed by the Antonov ANTK. The hypothetical possibility of using the An-70 was considered even by the US military (!), and earlier at that. For example, in 1994 the then director of the Advisory Group on Aerospace Research and Development (AGARD) noted that the An-70 and An-124 ought to be considered as possible candidates for filling the gap and meeting the needs of the USAF if the C-17 Globemaster III is purchased in smaller numbers than originally planned. Also, such long-standing partners of Russia in aircraft engineering and air transport business as China and Iran showed their interest in the An-70.

In October 1997 the Presidents of Russia and the Ukraine Boris N. Yeltsin and Leonid D. Kuchma sent jointly signed letters to Federal Chancellor of the Federal Republic of Germany Helmut Kohl and French President Jacques Chirac. In these letters they proposed that 'our countries join efforts in the creation of a European advanced military transport aircraft based on the An-70' and thereby demonstrate to the whole world the advantages of European co-operation as exemplified by the German-Russian-Ukrainian-French production of this aircraft. Yeltsin and Kuchma were convinced that co-operation of that kind would not only improve the aircraft's technical qualities but would also reduce unit costs.

In their joint answer Kohl and Chirac reacted positively to this proposal and promised to study 'the feasibility and prerequisites for co-operation with Russia and the Ukraine on the basis of the An-70 in the course of 1998.' This study was expected to give an answer to two questions: does the Ukrainian-Russian An-70 project correspond in principle to the technical notions and requirements laid down in the European Safety Regulations (ESR), and how the co-operation of interested states can be organised at the industrial level? After all, up to now there was no appropriate example for co-operation on such a large-scale project between former Cold War adversaries. The answer to the first question was found relatively easily. Yeltsin and Kuchma had pointed out in their proposal that the advantages of this machine 'have been recognised by European aircraft manufacturing companies taking part in the creation of a similar aircraft in the framework of the FLA project.' The meaning of this rather vague hint becomes clear when one compares the parameters of the FLA project at its initial stage and those of the An-70. One becomes aware of a striking similarity not only in the outward contours, but also in the expected transport capacity and dimensions of the cargo hold. Designers of the FLA came to the same conclusions as their Ukrainian colleagues; it should be noted, though, that the An-70 programme was many years ahead of the FLA programme.

In the summer of 1998, in the course of a CIS summit in Chişinău (Kishinyov), the capital of the Republic of Moldova, Presidents of Russia and the Ukraine Boris Yeltsin and Leonid Kuchma signed one more joint appeal to the leaders of Germany and France with a proposal for joining forces in the creation of a hitherto unsurpassed medium transport aircraft. Yevgeniy Shaposhnikov, the Russian President's assistant on aeronautical matters and former Chief Executive Officer of Aeroflot Russian International Airlines, said that he saw three ways in which Europe could solve the medium transport aircraft problem. The first way was to buy American aircraft that would be inferior in their characteristics to the An-70; the second way was to spend several years and US\$ 7-8 billion on the creation of an indigenous European aircraft in accordance with the FLA programme; and the third would be to join Russia and Ukraine for the speediest construction of the An-70. It was also said that waiting for investors to come along could take forever; consequently, it was necessary to speed up the An-70's production entry, as typical customer philosophy was 'if you'll build it, I'll buy it'. A project was prepared for the establishment of a new consortium named STS (or MTA – Medium Transport Aircraft) which included banking institutions for the purpose of attracting private funding. At the same time it was noted that neither Russia nor the Ukraine had any intentions to promote the launching of the An-70 into production in Western Europe.

A special study conducted by the Daimler-Chrysler Aerospace (DASA) jointly with the Russian-Ukrainian STS consortium on the question of the technical suitability of the An-70 noted a positive result. Here are some excerpts from this study:

'In all its aspects (materials, structure, corrosion protection etc) the airframe (of the An-70 – *authors' note) is solidly built and based on a weight-saving principle. The engines' efficiency is on a part with world standards. Most of the subsystems meet the ESR requirements. The primary flight control systems possess a high level of redundancy. Development methods and procedures corre-*

spond to Western programmes.' Of course, proceeding from the Western notions, numerous changes – either absolutely necessary or desirable – were recommended in certain areas. Nevertheless, the final conclusion concerning the technical suitability was unequivocal: the aircraft met the Western ESR requirements, and the experience accumulated by the Antonov ANTK (fuselage, wing and systems design) and ZMKB Progress (engine design) gave good chances for the successful development of the transport system.

Yet, the answer to the question concerning the possible patterns of industrial co-operation between the East and the West remained controversial. The jointly formulated part of the study contained a proposal for setting up a limited liability company whose shares would be divided equally between the Russian-Ukrainian consortium and the Western companies involved (DASA, Aérospatiale, Alenia and CASA). This joint stock enterprise was to become the main contractor. However, in a special statement DASA pointed out that it would not be in a position to assume responsibility in this capacity and was prepared to act only as a subordinated customer (backed up by a guarantee). Apparently DASA, like its other Western partners, regarded the economic and industrial risks of co-operation with a world alien to it as an aggravating factor. But it is quite possible that this attitude was prompted to some extent by surmising that the implementation of the FLA project within trustworthy aircraft industry structures could become a reliable and attractive solution for the participating companies.

On 17th June 1998 Mr. Norman Ray, the NATO Secretary General's assistant on defence matters, and Mr. Richard Williams, chief of NATO's International secretariat for the planning of armaments, programmes and defence support policy, paid a visit to the Antonov ANTK during their official visit to the Ukraine. Naturally the guests were interested primarily in the An-70 which was then being considered as a possible replacement for several aircraft types used by the air forces of NATO countries. Mr. Ray, a former airman with a 30-year service record, carefully examined the An-70 and sat in the captain's seat for a while; in his comments he gave a high appraisal to this product of joint Ukrainian-Russian efforts.

Between 30th November and 2nd December 1998 a delegation from the Federal Republic of Germany's Ministry of Defence paid a working visit to the Antonov ANTK. In the course of this visit, on 1st December, a check-up paradrop of dummies equipped with standard parachutes of the German airborne troops from the An-70 was conducted at the Antonov ANTK at Kiev-Gostomel'. The tests conducted at the suggestion of the German side showed good results.

At the end of January 1999 the STS consortium completed preparation of a technical proposal on the An-7X aircraft (a version of the An-70 modified to meet NATO requirements) for participation in a tender organised by West-European states. The proposal was sent to the Ministries of Defence of Russia, the Ukraine, Germany, France, Italy and Spain from whom the STS had received official applications. In the period between 18 and 22 January the Antonov ANTK hosted an official visit by a group of European aerospace industry representatives; as a result of this visit, seven companies from the Federal Republic of Germany expressed their readiness to join the programme to create a European aircraft based on the An-7X. These companies included the BMW Rolls-Royce team whose sphere of activities encompassed work on aircraft powerplants; Fairchild-Dornier, one of the world's leaders in the post-sale support of aircraft; VDO-L and BGT, prominent in the design and production of instruments. These companies were prepared to take part in adapting the An-7X to the requirements of European air forces and then start manufacturing its airframe assemblies and various equipment items. The DASA multinational concern took a final decision concerning its participation in the An-7X programme later; it proved to be a 'thumbs-down' decision which was taken before other European countries were approached for participation in the programme.

On 31st March and 1st April 1999 a Ukrainian-Russian-German meeting on the An-7X programme at the political level was held in the Antonov ANTK. The delegations were headed by Yevgeniy I. Shaposhnikov, the Russian President's assistant on aeronautical matters; V. I. Gureyev, Minister of Industrial Policy of the Ukraine; and R. Schreiber, chief of Armament department of the German Ministry of Defence. In the course of this meeting questions pertaining to the promotion of sales of the An-7X on the European market were discussed.

On 20th May 1999 the potential German participants in the An-7X programme announced that they had formed the Airtruck GmbH consortium which assumed full responsibility for the participation of German companies in the project. The first task facing Airtruck GmbH was the preparation, jointly with the STS, of documents that were required for adopting a decision on the possible purchase of the An-7X by the armed forces of the Federal Republic of Germany. It had been calculated that NATO's European nations needed some 288 An-7X aircraft. In addition, the world export market for these machines, in the opinion of experts, amounted to no less than 500 aircraft. General Designer of the Antonov ANTK Pyotr V. Balabuyev believed that an An-7X modified to suit NATO requirements could be flown in 2001. The flyaway price of the An-7X, according to calculations, would be roughly US$ 50 million. The price of the other contender offered by the Airbus Industrie consortium (it was this consortium's project, designated A400M, that was adopted as the basis for the FLA) was nearly twice as high, reaching some US$ 90 million. The programme for the An-7X manufacture was intended to cover a 16- to 18-year period with the subsequent operation in the course of 30 to 40 years.

On 16th June 1999, during the 43rd Paris Air Show, a presentation of the An-7X project to armament experts of 17 NATO countries was arranged at the French Ministry of Defence; the presentation was made by Pyotr V. Balabuyev, head of the STS consortium and General Designer of the Antonov ANTK. At this presentation M. Weise, chief of the Armaments Department of the French MoD, gave a high appraisal to the project, emphasising in particular the thorough preparation of its economic aspect. During the Paris Air Show the subject of the An-7X was discussed with the French Minister of Transport M. Guessot, the head of the French part of the Ukrainian-French commission on military technology matters General Panier, the chief of France's General Armaments Board M. Helmer, Secretary of State of the German MoD Mr. Stütze, Chief of the Armaments Department of the Ministry of Defence of the FRG Mr. Kämpf, chief of the Materiel and Maintenance Service Command of the Luftwaffe Mr. Leil and other statesmen. All of them spoke highly of the aircraft and were optimistic as to its chances to win the tender. In the framework of efforts aimed at creating a unified structure for the manufacture of the An-7X specialists of the Antonov ANTK conducted numerous talks with representatives of many Western European aerospace companies.

At the turn of the century, however, the prospects for the Russian-Ukrainian project suffered a setback. Under the pressure of political and economic factors Western European countries took a decision to speed up the work on the A400M and reject the possibility of any participation in the Russian-Ukrainian project. Well, what else could you expect? Get real.

Thus, the Ukraine and, in particular, the Antonov ANTK were placed in a difficult situation: not only Russia, but the West European countries as well effectively declined to participate in the project of a prospective medium transport aircraft.

Above: The forward fuselage of the An-70. The high-set flightdeck and the sharply sloping nose ahead of it give a good field of view.

Structural description of the An-70

Type: Four-propfan medium military transport. The airframe is basically of metal construction, some major structural assemblies being made of composites – glassfibre reinforced plastic (GRP) and carbon fibre reinforced plastic (CFRP).

Fuselage: Semi-monocoque stressed-skin structure of circular cross-section, with a beam-and-stringer construction, the trans-verse framework consisting of frames. The greater part of the fuselage is pressurised; the pressurisation system maintains a minimum cabin pressure equal to atmospheric pressure at an altitude of not more than 2,400 m (7,870 ft).

The fuselage is built in three sections. The *forward fuselage* accommodates the flight-deck, a cabin for cargo attendants and the foremost portion of the cargo hold. The flight-deck is located at 'first floor level' and accessed from the freight hold via a sloping stair; this offers better visibility and enhances crew survival in the event of a crash landing. The space under the flightdeck floor houses an avionics bay and the nosewheel well.

The flightdeck glazing comprises two curved birdproof triplex windscreen panes provided with wipers, two side windows on each side and a large circular window (or a faired observation blister) to port. The side windows are made of Plexiglas; the foremost pair are sliding direct vision windows which can be used as emergency exits on the ground. An escape hatch with a window is provided in the flightdeck roof.

The crew section is separated from the cargo hold by a pressure bulkhead which allows the flightdeck to double as a safety wall protecting the crew in the event of the cargo becoming dislodged during an emergency landing. At the front the crew section is delimited by the sloping forward pressure bulkhead which is flat and mounts the weather/navigation radar dish covered by a glassfibre radome.

The flightdeck is intended for a crew consisting of two or three persons. Its layout (the pilots are seated side by side, the flight engineer is seated near the central control pedestal) ensures the best possible conditions for crew interaction in flight. The flight engineer's instrument panel is located on the starboard side; provision for a navigator's station is made on the port side near the circular window (or blister). The crew enjoys a good view both outside and inside the flightdeck. The control columns are fitted with very compact control wheels.

The bulk of the instruments and information displays is located on the central console and overhead instrument panel and in the centre portion of the main instrument panel – that is, in the area which affords all crew members the possibility to mutually check each other's actions and render mutual help.

The use of a highly automated FBW control system, advanced navigation and technical flight support, the wide use of multi-function information display systems and dialogue-type control panels makes it possible to control the aircraft effectively while maintaining the crew workload at an acceptable level. All seats are equipped with electrically-powered adjustment devices ensuring comfortable postures for the crew members both during work and when having a rest, as well as catering for safety in the event of an emergency landing.

Two forward-hinged entry doors with circular windows and integral two-section boarding ladders are located at the rear of the forward fuselage section; they open outward through 90° manually or hydraulically (the latter option is exercised in flight for paradropping personnel). A ventral escape hatch with

The rear fuselage underside, showing the two telescopic circular supports built into the cargo ramp and two more immediately ahead of the ramp.

a sloping flightdeck escape chute is located immediately aft of the nosewheel well; its forward-opening hydraulically actuated door acts as a slipstream deflector when the crew bails out.

The *centre fuselage* is occupied by the cargo hold. The cargo hold roof features guide rails for movable overhead hoists and attachment points for a removable upper deck for carrying troops; the latter is suspended on the same level as the flightdeck floor. Six emergency exits with circular windows are provided in the hold: two at main deck level at the rear end of the hold and two pairs at upper deck level fore and aft of the wings. Two more circular windows are provided to admit daylight into the hold.

The space under the centre portion of the cargo hold floor is occupied by the mainwheel wells. Two large fairings enclosing the main gear fulcrums and actuators are located low on the centre fuselage sides; they also accommodate the APU and other equipment.

The *rear fuselage* is cut away from below; the cutout is a loading hatch closed by a cargo ramp, a flat rear pressure bulkhead and three cargo door segments aft of the cargo ramp. The outer door segments open outwards and the double-hinged centre segment upwards into the roof, whereupon the rear pressure bulkhead swings upwards and aft almost entirely, propping up the centre door segment. The overhead hoist guide rails continue across the rear pressure bulkhead and the roof of the cargo hatch, allowing the hoists to travel beyond the sill of the ramp. Their long travel to aft makes it possible to carry out the loading of large-size cargoes and containers.

The cargo ramp is used for loading and unloading wheeled or tracked vehicles; to this end it is equipped with four auxiliary vehicle loading ramps which are stowed manually inside the ramp's rear end. The ramp incorporates two hydraulically-powered circular telescopic supports side by side near the trailing edge; two more supports of the same type are built into the fuselage underside immediately ahead of the ramp hinge line. These supports are extended to stop the aircraft from falling over on its tail during loading and unloading of heavy items.

Wings: Cantilever shoulder-mounted monoplane wings of trapezoidal planform with slight anhedral from the roots; sweepback at quarter-chord 14°, total area 202.6 m² (2,181 sq ft).

The wings are a two-spar structure built in three pieces: the centre section (which is integral with the fuselage) and one-piece wing panels, plus detachable raked tip fairings. The wing/fuselage joint is covered by a fairing. Aerodynamically the wings are based on the use of new TsAGI P-202 supercritical

Above: The open cargo hatch of the An-70 at the MAKS-99 airshow. The cargo ramp is fully lowered, resting on the supports, and four vehicle loading ramps are attached to the ramp's trailing edge.

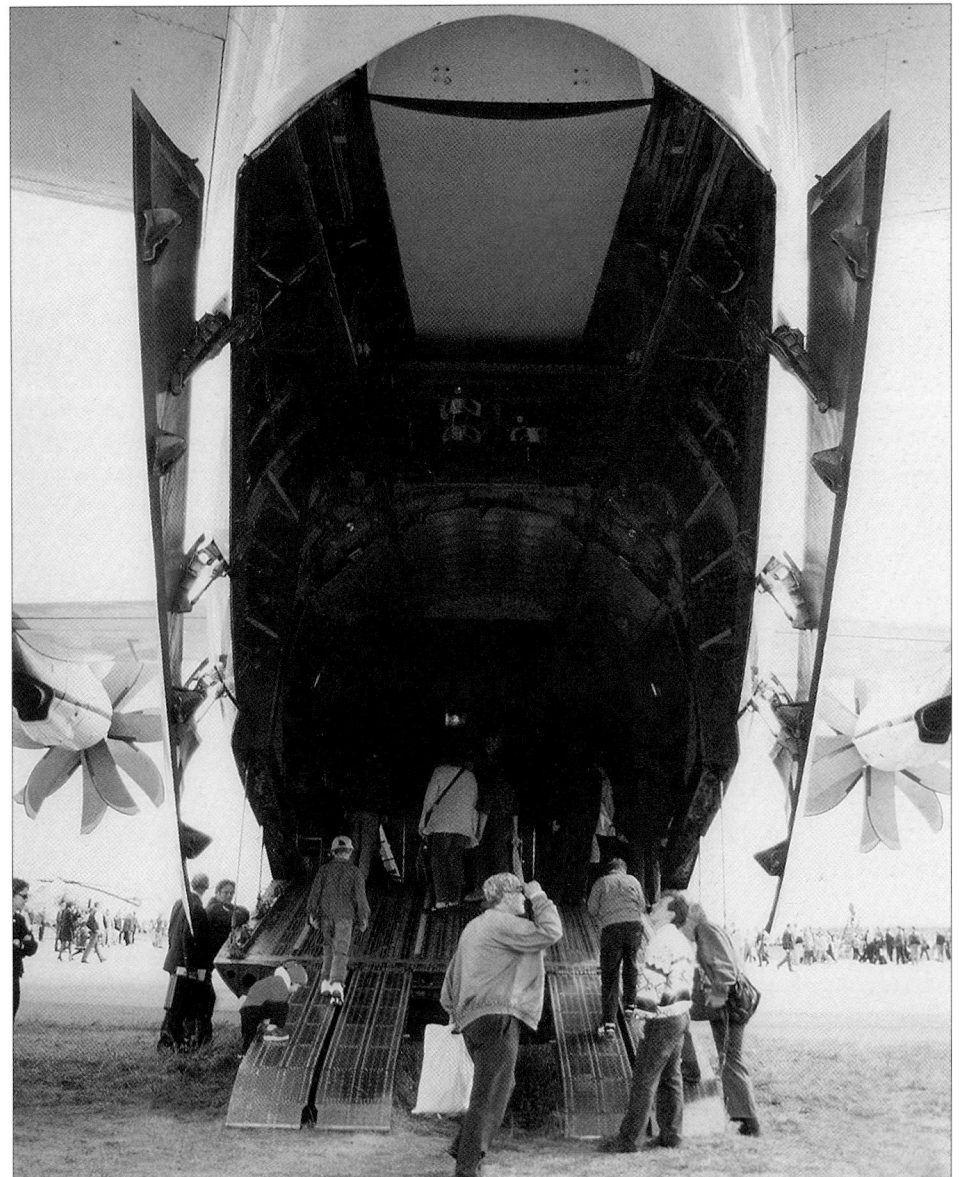

This view shows the cargo door design (note the two-piece centre segment), the rear pressure door opened into the roof and the overhead cargo hoist rails. There are three hydraulic rams for each side door.

Above: The cargo hold of UR-NTK, looking aft, with the rear pressure door in its vertical closed position. The hooks of the four overhead hoists are attached by straps to cargo tiedown fittings to keep them from swaying.

Above: The cargo hold of UR-NTK, looking forward. Note the tip-up seats along the walls and the neat wall trim panels; the An-70 is generally characterised by a high manufacturing standard.

The test equipment is located rather unconventionally – on a segment of the detachable upper deck. Note the overhead hoists and the long cables leading to their remote control boxes.

airfoil which ensures high lift both in cruise flight and in take-off and landing modes.

The wing leading edge between the fuse-lage and the inboard engine nacelles is fitted with leading edge flaps; three-section leading edge slats moving on curved tracks are utilised on the rest of the span (one section between the engine nacelles and two sections outboard). The trailing edge is fitted with two-section double-slotted extension flaps occupying 75% of the span, with ailerons outboard of them; the flaps move on external tracks enclosed by fairings (two on each section). Spoilers divided into sections of roll control spoilers, air brakes and lift dumpers are installed ahead of the flaps.

Tail unit: Conventional cantilever swept tail surfaces. The *horizontal tail* has no dihedral; it is manufactured of CFRP. The elevators are double-hinged, with the segments mechanically interconnected, and are each divided into two sections; each elevator section is connected with the control system actuators by mechanical linkages.

The *vertical tail* is also manufactured of CFRP and has a four-spar structure. The rudder is double-hinged, the two segments being mechanically interconnected, and consists of three sections. The fin is topped by a large cigar-shaped fairing housing aerials.

Landing gear: Hydraulically retractable tricy-cle type; wheel track 5.2 m (17 ff 0¾ in), wheel base 18.15 m (59 ft 6½ in). The forward-retracting nose unit is fitted with twin non-braking wheels; it has a combined steering mechanism/shimmy damper and features electro-hydraulic remote control by means of twist knobs on the pilots' side control consoles. The main units retract inward; each main unit comprises three independent twin-wheel struts. The mainwheels are equipped with single-disc brakes made of carbon-based composite materials and built-in cooling fans in the hubs.

All landing gear struts have oleo-pneumatic shock absorbers and levered suspension; the landing gear enables operations from unpaved and semi-prepared runways. The main units incorporate a 'kneeling' feature – the oleos are compressed on the ground to lower the tail and reduce the ramp angle when vehicles are loaded; the same feature allows the mainwheels to be changed singly without jacking up the aircraft. The landing gear is provided with a system for measuring the aircraft's weight and CG position when parked on the ground.

The nosewheel well is closed by two lateral (main) doors and a small rear door segment mechanically linked to the oleo strut. Each of the six main gear struts unit has a lower (main) door and a curved lateral door in the main gear fairing linked to the oleo. The main doors open only when the gear is in transit; this prevents mud, water and slush from entering the wheel wells.

Powerplant: Four ZMKB (Muravchenko) D-27 propfan engines with a take-off rating of 14,000 ehp and a cruise rating of 6,750 ehp designed by ZMKB Progress in Zaporozhye.

The D-27 is a two-spool engine with an annular air intake, low-pressure (LP) and high-pressure (HP) axial compressors with a centrifugal final stage axial compressor, an annular combustion chamber, a three-cascade turbine (HP and LP compressor turbines plus a power turbine) with active blade gap control and monocrystalline blades, and a fixed-area jetpipe with a conical centrebody. Power is transmitted via a single-stage differential gearbox with a built-in torque meter. Provision is made for tapping bleed air from the engine in all of its operation modes for the needs of aircraft systems (air conditioning system, equipment cooling system, anti-icing system and others).

Three accessory gearboxes (one dorsal and two ventral) are provided; the accessories include a hydraulic pump serving as the main source of hydraulic pressure and an AC generator. The engine is started by an air turbine starter fed by the APU, ground supply or cross-bleed from other engines; the start-up procedure is automated. A closed-type lubrication system and a fire suppression system are provided.

The engines are noted for their high fuel efficiency, the fuel burn in take-off and cruise mode being 170 g/ehp·h (0.37 lb/ehp·h) and 130 g/ehp·h (0.29 lb/ehp·h) respectively. Engine pressure ratio 22.9 at take-off power and 29.7 at cruise power; mass flow at take-off rating 27.4 kg/sec (60.4 lb/sec). Turbine temperature is 1,640°K at take-off power and 1,450°K at cruise power. Length overall 4,198 mm (13 ft 9¼ in), width 1,260 mm (4 ft 1⅝ in), height 1,370 mm (4 ft 6 in); dry weight minus propfan 1,650 kg (3,640 lb).

The engines are mounted in individual nacelles attached directly to the wing underside and carried in truss-type bearers. Each nacelle has two hinged cowling panels affording almost unrestricted access to the engine and a fixed rear fairing with an orifice for the jetpipe (which is angled slightly downward).

The engines drive SV-27 contra-rotating propfans of 4.5 m (14 ft 9⁹⁄₃₂ in) diameter developed and manufactured by NPP Aerosila. The SV-27 is a reversible-pitch and fully feathering propfan with hydro-mechanical pitch control. It weighs 1,100 kg (2,425 lb) and features 14 blades (eight in the front row and six in the rear row); the blades are made entirely of composite materials, their structure incorporates a hollow spar and integral electric

Above: The port main landing gear unit. Note the perforations in the wheel hubs admitting air for the integral brake cooling fans. The APU exhaust is visible on the right beneath the port main deck emergency exit.

Above: The main gear units seen in mid-retraction; each unit can be retracted or extended independently. The ventral anti-collision light is visible ahead of the wheel wells; there are two dorsal ACLs fore and aft of the wings.

The nose landing gear unit with a towbar attached. Note the test equipment sensor measuring the oleo compression near the towbar attachment lug and the ventral escape hatch just aft of the nosewheel well.

Above: The No.1 engine of An-70 UR-NTK. This view shows the relatively short engine nacelle and the shape and position of the oil cooler housing, as well as the extraordinarily long spinner of the SV-27 propfan.

Another view of the No.1 engine's SV-27 propfan, showing the scimitar shape of the blades.

de-icer threads. The engines and propfans are controlled by a full-authority digital engine control (FADEC) system.

An NPP Aerosila TA-12-60 auxiliary power unit is installed in the rear portion of the port main gear fairing for self-contained engine starting, AC ground power supply and air conditioning. The APU has a two-piece intake door (the forward half opens inward and the rear half upward), a one-piece cowling and a lateral exhaust surrounded by a heat-resistant steel panel. Electric power 60 kVA, bleed air supply rate 1.6 kg/sec (3.5 lb/sec), fuel consumption 250 kg/hr (550 lb/hr), weight includ-

ing generator 335 kg (740 lb). The TA-12-60 can run at altitudes up to 7,000 m (22,965 ft) and ambient temperatures of −60/+60°C (−76/+140°F).

Control system: The manual control system used on the An-70 is a fly-by-wire system having no mechanical linkages between the flightdeck and the hydraulic control surface actuators. It includes a quadruplex FBW (electric remote control) main system and a hydraulic remote control (back up) system. The FBW system ensures piloting the aircraft in both manual and automatic mode. The high-lift devices control system is used for controlling the flaps, leading-edge slats and spoilers.

Fuel system: The fuel is housed in integral wing tanks. Each engine receives fuel independently from its own group of tanks. Fuel transfer to a service tank section of the wing and fuel delivery from the service section to the engine is performed automatically by electrically driven pumps.

Single-point pressure refuelling is effected through twin international standard connectors located in the front end of the starboard landing gear fairing; refuelling by gravity through fillers on each tank is also possible. When using single-point refuelling, the fuel flow rate is 2,700 litres (594 Imp gal) per minute. Refuelling for a typical commercial flight takes 15 minutes. The aircraft is equipped with a special system for scavenging the refuelling piping after the completion of refuelling. Provision is also made for centralised defuelling and for pumping the fuel from one tank to any other during the aircraft's stay on the ground.

Single-point refuelling, the scavenging of the refuelling piping, and centralised draining of fuel condensate is controlled from two control panels installed in the front end of the starboard landing gear fairing.

Hydraulic system: The hydraulic system comprises four independent hydraulic systems. They use AMG-10 oil-type fluid. Nominal pressure in the systems is 210 kg/cm^2 (3,000 psi). The main source of pressure in each hydraulic system is an engine-driven hydraulic pump of variable capacity. In each hydraulic system there is a provision for a back-up power source; the back-up sources are hydraulic transformers installed in each system, turbine pump units installed in two systems and an electrically driven pump unit installed in the third hydraulic system. In addition, the aircraft is equipped with a ram air turbine pump unit as an emergency source of hydraulic power.

The landing gear retraction and extension system features a hydraulic system with a

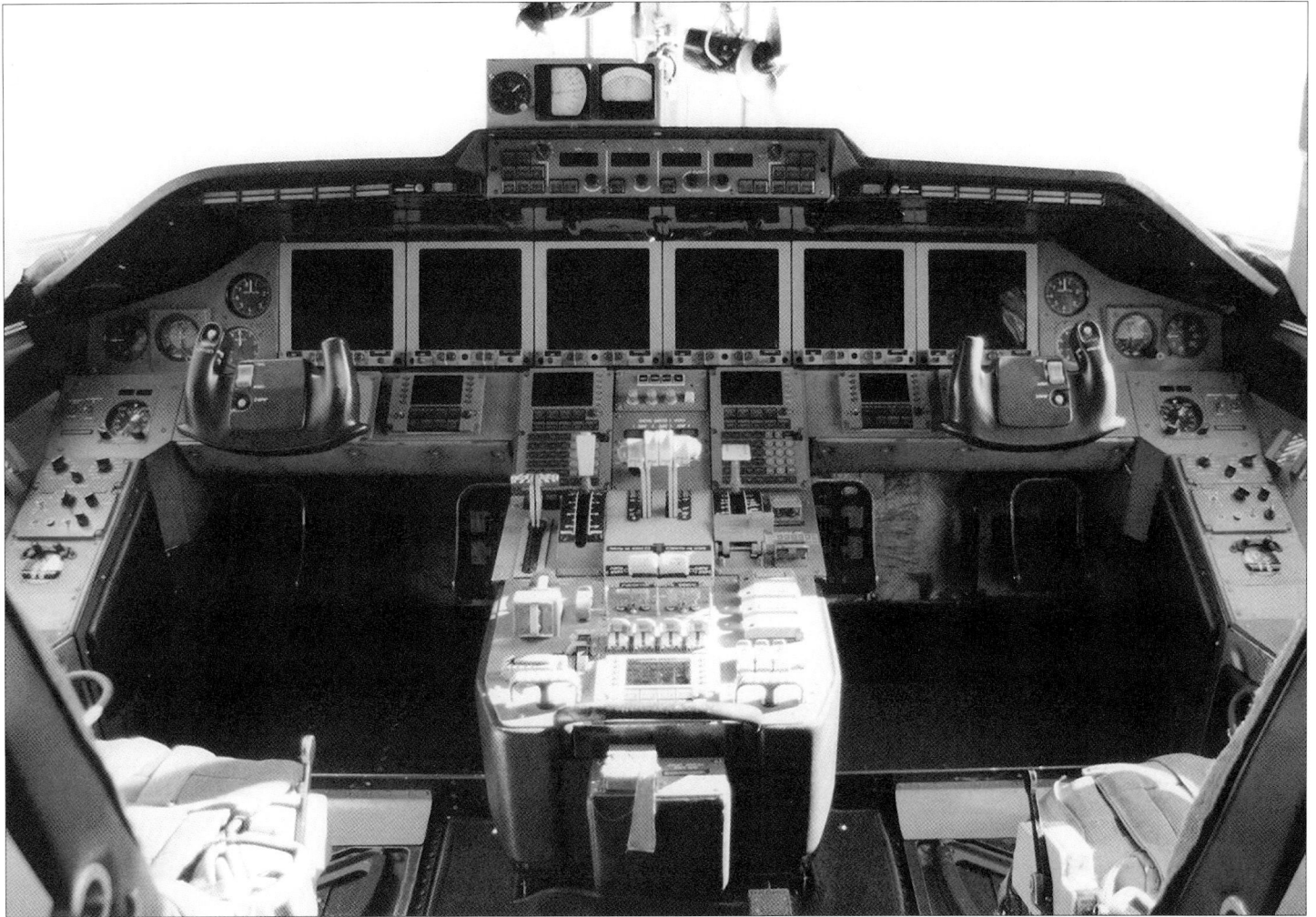

Above: The main instrument panel of the An-70 is dominated by six CRT displays – two primary flight displays for each pilot and the engine information and crew alerting system screens. Note the four input/output modules below the PFDs and EICAS screens. The small control wheels slide into and out of the panel for pitch control.

Above, left and right: Four more full-size CRT displays and three I/O keypads are provided at the flight engineer's station on the starboard side. Note the full-size keyboard below the pair of displays on the side wall allowing text commands to be entered. The panel shown on the right faces aft.

Two more sections of the flight engineer's extensive instrument panel with vertical strip gauges and banks of caution/warning lights.

Basic specifications of the An-70

Wing span	44.06 m (144 ft 6⅝ in)
Length overall	40.73 m (133 ft 7¹⁷/₃₂ in)
Height on ground	16.38 m (53 ft 9 in)
Fuselage width, m (ft)	4.80 (15 ft 9 in)
Wing area, m² (sq ft)	202.6 (2,181)
Propeller diameter, m (ft)	4.50 (14 ft 9⁵/₁₆ in)
Cargo hold dimensions	18.75 x 4.0 x 4.1 m
	(61 ft 6 in x 13 ft 1½ in
	x 13 ft 5¹³/₃₂ in)
Cargo hold volume, m³ (cu ft)	425 (15,011)
Maximum AUW, kg (lb)	133,000 (293,265)
Maximum payload, kg (lb)	47,000 (103,635)
Cruising speed, km/h (mph)	750-800 (466-497)
Cruising flight altitude, m (ft)	9,000-12,000
	(29,520-39,360)
Ferrying range, km (miles)	8,700 (5,407)

manually operated pump intended for pressing the main gear struts into 'down and locked' position and for replenishing the hydraulic fluid tanks from a reserve tank of the hydraulic system.

Avionics and equipment: The aircraft is equipped with systems and avionics suites whose performance meets the standards of the 21st century. The systems and avionics suites make use of digital electronics, as well as multiplex data exchange channels and a full-colour CRT indication and warning system which gives the pilots recommendations on tackling and overcoming failures.

Collection, transmission and processing of information inputs for control, monitoring and indication of the general aircraft equipment is effected by the control system. Presentation of information to the crew is handled by the CRT indication system.

The introduction of digital electronic control systems and the sending of their information flows through a multiplex data exchange channel of the system controlling the aircraft's equipment will make it possible to raise the degree of automation of these systems, reduce the area of the control panels and information displays in the flightdeck and reduce the crew workload.

Air conditioning/pressurisation system: The air conditioning system ensures life support, maintaining the necessary conditions in the flightdeck and cargo cabin. It feeds engine bleed air into the air conditioning units and maintains cabin pressurisation. It is possible to maintain a low temperature in the cargo hold, which permits the carriage of perishable goods. There is a provision for connecting a ground source of compressed air, as well as a ground air conditioning unit, to the air conditioning system through an onboard coupling.

Cargo handling equipment: A versatile set of cargo handling equipment enables efficient loading and unloading of the aircraft at airfields lacking adequate ground equipment. The cargo handling equipment enables the aircraft to carry rigid and flexible pallets, containers, including sea-land containers, outsize and large-length cargoes, wheeled and tracked vehicles. The cargo handling equipment is compatible with similar equipment used abroad. The aircraft can be operated from equipped and unequipped airfields abroad.

The cargo floor features numerous threaded holes used for installing cargo tie-down lugs and cargo handling equipment (such as roller conveyors). Four interlinked electrically driven hoists travelling on overhead rails are used for lifting and loading heavy items; they can be moved beyond the cargo ramp's trailing edge for lifting loads straight off a truck bed. The cargo hold can be equipped with a modular upper deck for personnel carriage; this is built as easily removable sections which can be mounted in any number and arrangement depending on the mission.

The An-70's way into production has been long and arduous, but now it looks like this promising programme is taking off after all.

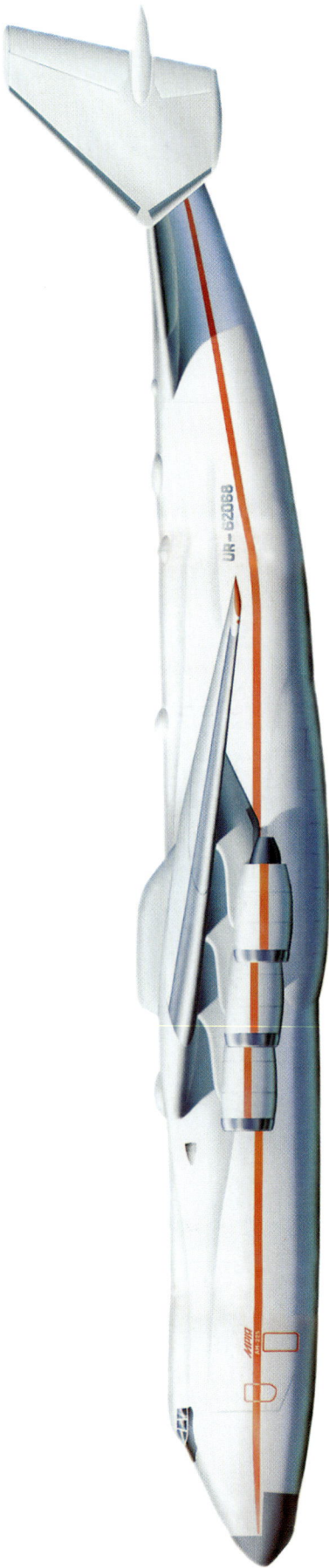

The An-225 Mriya prototype.

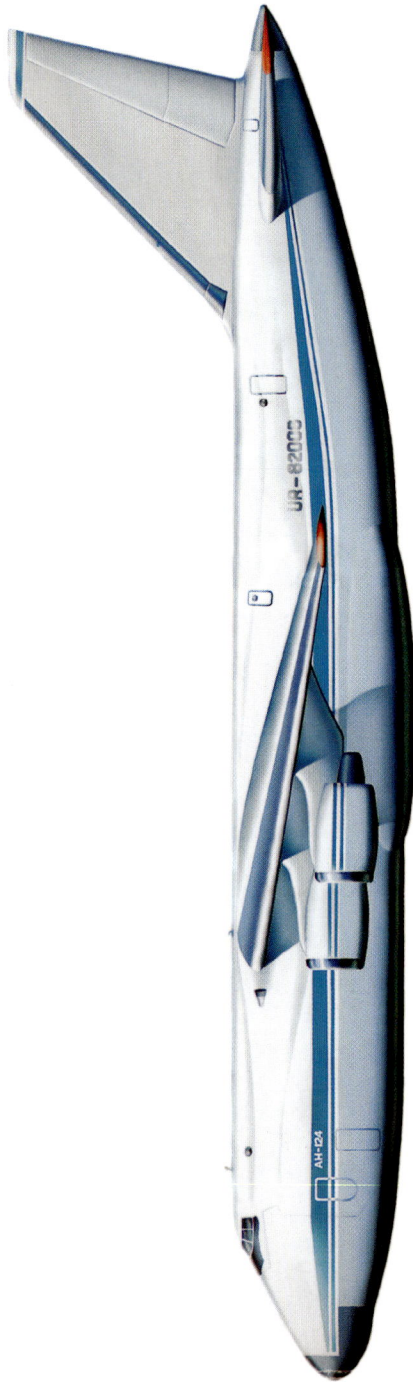

An-124 UR-82008 prior to the application of Antonov Design Bureau tail colours.

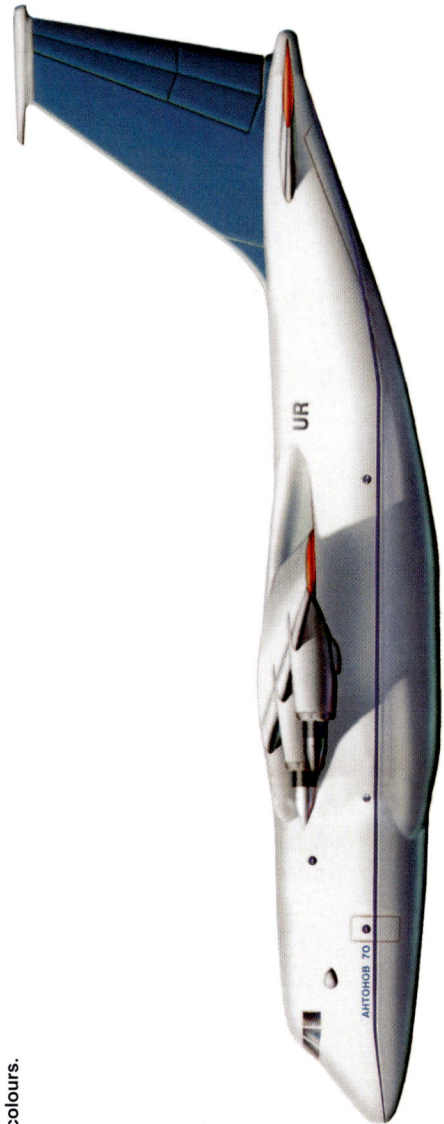

The second prototype An-70

Above: An-22 *sans suffixe* CCCP-09333 caught by the camera at the point of rotation on take-off at a civil airport. The An-22s seemed to be finished with paint of singularly poor quality, with the result that they quickly assumed a very weathered appearance.

An An-22 coming in head on, growling at you from a sullen sky, sure is an impressive sight – and sweet music to the ears of the aviation fan.

Above: The fuselage of a Sukhoi Su-27 on a special dolly is about to be loaded aboard An-22A RA-09343 which will take it to a repair plant. The curious angle of the fighter is due to the fact that otherwise the load would be too wide to fit into the hold. Note the IRCM flare dispensers under the An-22's tail section and on the main gear fairings.

The cavernous hold of the An-22 looks rather gloomy, with very limited lighting. The vertical beams where the hold is at its narrowest are the three heavy-duty fuselage mainframes to which the wing spars are attached. The crewman marshalling the lorry onto the hold is standing in line with the entry corridors.

Above: The four-tone camouflage scheme worn by An-22 c/n 043481250 (l/n 05-10) certainly does the Antheus justice. Too bad that no more An-22s were painted like this; at any rate, this colour scheme would probably have been more weatherproof!

Another aspect of RA-09343 parked in brilliant sunshine on a snowbound ramp. No, the aircraft is not rusty; the white paint on the upper fuselage has been removed altogether by the elements, revealing the yellow shade of the electrochemically coated duralumin. In contrast, the rudders seem to have had a fresh coat of paint.

Above: An-22 *sans suffixe* RA-09306 was one of the many that stayed operational long enough to see the demise of the Soviet Union and receive the Russian prefix. It is seen here at Vladimirovka AB in Akhtoobinsk, the seat of GNIKI VVS's main facility, in the mid-1990s.

An-22A UR-09307 was one of three An-22s operated by the Antonov Design Bureau and the only one of the three to wear full house colours. It is seen here at Kiev-Svyatoshino in September 2000 during the Aviasvit-XXI airshow. This machine is unusual in having a non-standard chin radome of much smaller size.

Above: Wearing the Le Bourget '85 exhibit code 321 on the nose, the second prototype An-124 (in its definitive guise as CCCP-82002) is seen here during a test flight. Test equipment video cameras in small orange fairings can be seen under the starboard wingtip and the starboard tailplane root.

Above: Boldly displaying the Russian Air Force's red star insignia, An-124 '09 Black' (c/n 9773054955077, l/n 06-02) makes a flypast during one of the Aviation Day displays. The registration RA-82038 (used as a radio callsign) is painted in small digits beneath the tactical code.

At least one Russian Air Force An-124 (RA-82021) wore this revised Aeroflot livery with a blue/white vertical tail. Introduced by way of experiment in the mid-1980s and worn by several Soviet types (mainly military or industry-operated aircraft), this colour scheme saw very limited use.

Above: Seen here 'cleaning up' after take-off, An-124-100 UR-82008 displays an interim version of Antonov Airlines' livery with 'Antonov Design Bureau' tail colours but an Aeroflot cheatline. This was the only An-124 to be retrofitted with paratrooper doors aft of the main gear fairings; they are barely discernible in this view.

Seen here taxying to its hardstand at Moscow-Vnukovo after a training flight in 1996, RA-82072 was one of two An-124-100's operated by the Rossiya State Transport Co. (the Russian federal government flight) in this stylish livery. This aircraft and sister ship RA-82073 were sold to Antonov Airlines as UR-82072 and UR-82073.

An impressive air-to-air of RA-82043, the second An-124-100 delivered to Volga-Dnepr Airlines.

Above: A livery to be seen no more. Originally built for Antonov AirTrack as UR-UAP, An-124-100 RA-82003 wore this simple but nevertheless pleasing livery when it belonged to Trans-Charter and was operated jointly with Titan Cargo. Both airlines are now dead and gone, and the aircraft has been sold to Libya.

Special ramps with a very small gradient have to be erected in front of the An-124's nose hatch for loading very bulky and heavy items, such as this industrial generator stator.

Above: The An-225's rollout ceremony at Kiev-Svyatoshino on 30th November 1988. Huge numbers of people came to witness the birth of the biggest Antonov aircraft ever – or, for that matter, the world's biggest aircraft.

The An-225, now registered CCCP-82060 and wearing the Le Bourget '89 exhibit code 387, displays its gaping cargo hatch.

Above: The concerted efforts of the Antonov ANTK and its partners saw the Mriya flying again after a seven-year enforced stay on the ground. Here it is seen flying at the Aviasvit-XXI airshow at Kiev-Gostomel' on 14th September 2002.

Aircraft may be strong, but people are stronger if they pull together! These ten Ukrainian athletes proved it by moving the giant airlifter several dozen feet at Kiev-Gostomel' on 14th September 2002, earning a place in the Guinness Book of Records.

Above: Antonovs big and small. The An-32P Firekiller prototype, UR-48004 (note the water tanks flanking the fuselage) looks small compared to the An-225. However, the T-2 microlights parked next to it are also Antonov products!

In 2001 the refurbished An-225 made its first visit to Zhukovskiy in eight years; as on the previous occasion, it flew there to participate in the biennial Moscow airshow.

Above: Another view of the An-225 in the static park at the MAKS-93, with the An-32P beside it. No prizes for guessing which aircraft received the greatest attention.

An artist's impression of how the An-225 would look with the MAKS reusable space system designed by NPO Molniya. Here, the space shuttle really looks puny by comparison with its external fuel tank.

Above: The second prototype An-70 begins its landing gear retraction sequence as it takes off on a demonstration flight at the MAKS-97 airshow.

A KrAZ-255B 6 x 6 lorry tows An-70 UR-NTK to the engine starting point prior to a demonstration flight. The double-hinged multi-section rudder and the many test equipment video cameras are clearly visible here.

Above: The An-70's display routine invariably includes a fairly steep climbout intended to demonstrate its ability to operate from short tactical airstrips. After all, the aircraft was conceived with military uses in mind.

UR-NTK taxies in at Zhukovskiy after the demonstration flight; note the open spoilers. On its first public appearance at the MAKS-97 the An-70 was the undisputed star of the show.

Red Star Volume 11
MYASISHCHEV M-4 and 3M
The First Soviet Strategic Jet Bomber

Yefim Gordon

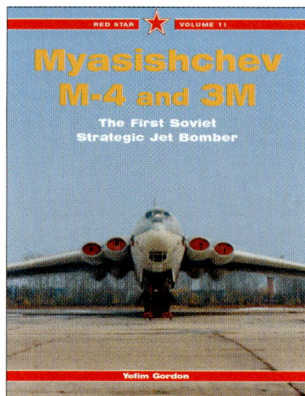

The story of the Soviet Union's first intercontinental jet bomber, the Soviet answer to the Boeing B-52. The new bomber had many innovative features (including a bicycle landing gear) and was created within an unprecedentedly short period of just one year; observers were stunned when the aircraft was formally unveiled at the 1953 May Day parade. The M-4 and the much-improved 3M remained in service for 40 years.

Softback, 280 x 215 mm, 128 pages,
185 b/w, 14pp of colour photographs,
plus line drawings
1 85780 152 0 **£18.99**

Red Star Volume 12
ANTONOV'S TURBOPROP TWINS – AN-24/26/30/32

Yefim Gordon

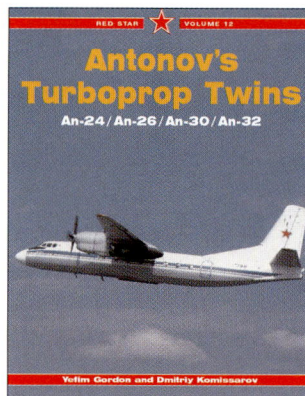

The twin-turboprop An-24 was designed in the late 1950s and was produced by three Soviet aircraft factories; many remain in operation.

The An-24 airliner evolved first into the 'quick fix' An-24T and then into the An-26. This paved the way for the 'hot and high' An-32 and the 'big head' An-30, the latter for aerial photography.

This book lists all known operators of Antonov's twin-turboprop family around the world.

Softback, 280 x 215 mm, 128 pages
175 b/w and 28 colour photographs,
plus line drawings
1 85780 153 9 **£18.99**

Red Star Volume 13
MIKOYAN'S PISTON-ENGINED FIGHTERS

Yefim Gordon and Keith Dexter

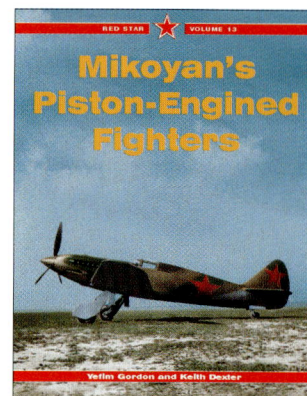

Describes the early history of the famous Mikoyan OKB and the aircraft that were developed. The first was the I-200 of 1940 which entered limited production in 1941 as the MiG-1 and was developed into the MiG-3 high-altitude interceptor. Experimental versions covered include the MiG-9, the I-220/225 series and I-230 series. A separate chapter deals with the I-200 (DIS or MiG-5) long-range heavy escort fighter.

Softback, 280 x 215 mm, 128 pages
195 b/w photos, 6pp of colour artwork,
10pp of line drawings.
1 85780 160 1 **£18.99**

Red Star Volume 14
MIL Mi-8/Mi-17
Rotary-Wing Workhorse and Warhorse

Yefim Gordon and Dmitriy Komissarov

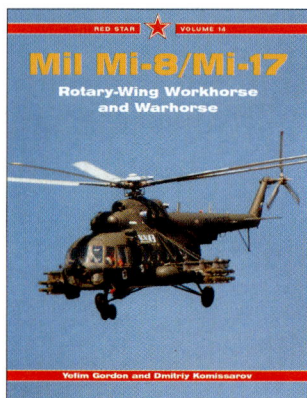

Since 1961, when it first took to the air, the basic design of the Mi-8 has evolved. Every known version, both civil and military, is covered, including electronic warfare, minelaying and minesweeping and SAR. It also served as a basis for the Mi-14 amphibious ASW helicopter.

Over the years the Mi-8 family have become veritable aerial workhorses, participating in countless wars of varying scale. The type is probably best known for its service in the Afghan War.

Softback, 280 x 215 mm, 128 pages
179 b/w and 32 colour photographs,
plus line drawings.
1 85780 161 X **£18.99**

Red Star Volume 15
ANTONOV AN-2
Annushka, Maid of All Work

Yefim Gordon and Dmitriy Komissarov

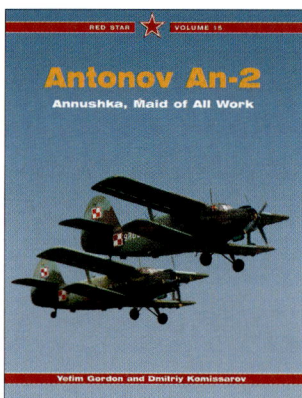

Initially derided as 'obsolete at the moment of birth' due to its biplane layout, this aircraft has put the sceptics to shame. It may lack the glamour of the fast jets, but it has proved itself time and time again as an indispensable and long-serving workhorse. The An-2, which first flew in 1947, has been operated by more than 40 nations.

The An-2 is the only biplane transport which remained in service long enough to pass into the 21st century!

Softback, 280 x 215 mm, 128 pages
c200 b/w and 28 colour photographs,
plus line drawings.
1 85780 162 8 **£18.99**

Red Star Volume 16
SUKHOI INTERCEPTORS
The Su-9/-11/-15 and other types

Yefim Gordon

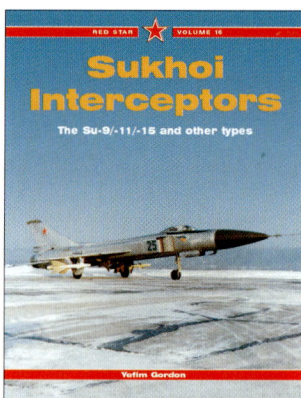

From 1953 Sukhoi produced a line of delta-winged interceptors including the Su-9 in 1958 followed in 1959 by the T-47/Su-11. A new line was started in 1960 with the twinjet T-58 which entered production as the Su-15. This aircraft remained a key element of the Soviet Air Defence Force well into the 1980s. Various versions of the Su-15 are detailed, as are the experimental PT-7/PT-8, T-49 and the unusual two-seat P-1 heavy interceptor.

Softback, 280 x 215 mm, 128 pages
189 b/w photos, 14pp of colour,
plus line drawings.
1 85780 180 6 **£18.99**

Red Star Volume 17
EARLY SOVIET JET BOMBERS
The 1940s and Early 1950s

Yefim Gordon

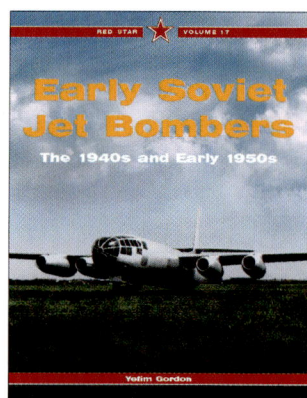

The Soviet Union put German technology to good use when developing its own jet bombers. The first to fly in the USSR was the Junkers EF131. This was followed by the EF140 and the equally unusual T-tailed, Baade 'aircraft 150'. The first wholly indigenous jet bomber was the four-engined IL-22 of 1947. Other experimental Ilyushins – the IL-30, IL-46 and IL-54 are described, as are the Tupolev 'aircraft 77', 'aircraft 82' and the 'aircraft 72/73/78' series.

Softback, 280 x 215 mm, 128 pages
116 b/w photos, 57 b/w illustrations,
14pp of line drawings.
1 85780 181 4 **£18.99**